WEBSTER'S ITALIAN-ENGLISH ENGLISH-ITALIAN DICTIONARY

Galahad Books • New York City

ENGLISH-ITALIAN
DICTIONARY

PRONUNCIATION

a sounds as *a* in father

e   ,,   *e* ,. net

è   ,   ,, *e* ,, where

i   ,,   ,, *i* ,, pin

j   ,,   ,, *y* ,, yes

o   ,,   ,, *o* ,, cot

ò   ,,   ,, *o* ,. mole

u   .,   ,, *u* ,, bull

a, e, i, e, u are always pronounced

h is never sounded.

gli.,., has a liquid sound as in *seraglie*, or he Spanish *ll*.

Days of the Week.		Giorni Della Settimana	
Sunday	.. LaDomenica	Thursday	Il Giovedi
Monday	.. Il Lunedi	Friday ..	Il Venerdi
Tuesday	.. Il Martedi	Saturday	Jl Sabato
Wednesday	Il Mercoledi	Week ..	La settimana

Months of the Year.		Mesi Dell'anno	
January	.. Gennaio	May	.. .. Maggio
February	.. Febbraio	June	.. .. Giugno
March ..	.. Marzo	July	.. .. Luglio
April ..	prile	August	.. Agosto

Ordinal Numbers

First	primo
Second	secondo
Third	terzo
Fourth	quarto
Fifth	quinto
Sixth	sesto
Seventh	settimo
Eighth	ottavo
Ninth	nono
Tenth	decimo
Eleventh	undicesimo
Twelfth	dodicesimo
Thirteenth	decimo terzo
Fourteenth	quattordicesimo
Fifteenth	quindicesimo
Sixteenth	sedicesimo
Seventeenth	diciassettesimo
Eighteenth	diciottesimo
Nineteenth	diciannovesimo
Twentieth	ventesimo
Thirtieth	trentesimo
Fourtieth	quarantesimo
Fiftieth	cinquantesimo
Sixtieth	sessantesimo
Seventieth	settantesimo
Eightieth	ottantesimo
Ninetieth	novantesimo
Hundredth	centesimo
Thousandth	millesimo
Millionth	millionesimo

Dialogues.

Useful Phrases & Idioms.	Frasi Utili e Idiomi
I am very much obliged to you	Le sono molto obbligato
I beg your pardon	Mi scusi, Le domando scusa
I congratulate you	Congratulazioni, mi congratulo con Lei
I pity you	La compiagno
If you please	Per favore
Allow me	Mi permetta
Pray, do not mention it	Prega, non ne parli
Thank you; many thanks	Grazie, tante grazie
No, thank you	No, grazie
With your permission	Con permesso
Good morning, afternoon, day	Buon giorno
Good evening; good night	Buona sera; buona notte
Good-bye	Addio, arrivederci
A pleasant journey	Buon viaggio
How do you do?	Come sta?
I am (not) very well	Molto bene, non molto bene
I am better	Sto meglio
I hope you are better	Spero che stia meglio
And how are you?	E come sta Lei?
Agreed	E'inteso
Are you ready?	E'pronto?
Ask him (her)	Lo domandi a lui (lei). Glielo domandi.
Ask him to come	Gli domandi di venire. Le domandi di venire
I want the bill of fare, please.	Mi favorisca la lista delle vivande.
Put a bottle of wine in ice for me.	Metta una bottiglia di vino in ghiaccio per me.
Bring glasses and some more bread.	Porti dei bicchieri e dell'altro pane.
This wine is corked.	Il vino sa di sughero.
This meat is not fresh.	Questa carne non è fresca.

9

To carry coals to Newcastle	Portar l'acqua al mare
To commit a blunder	Pigliare un granchio
To deceive	Gettar della polvere negli occhi
To dismiss	Congedare
To drink like a fish	Bere come un pesce
To drive	Andare in vettura
To drive very fast	Andare a rompicollo
To fall backwards	Cadere all'indietro
To find it worth one's while	Trovare l'affar suo
To find out a good berth	Far casa ['ira
To fly into a passion	Lasciarsi trasportare dall
To get acquainted	Far la conoscenza di
To give a person permission to speak	Dare la parola a qualcuno
To give it up	Rinunciare
To give largely	Dare a piene mani
To go at full speed	Andare a spron battuto
To go for a sail for a row	Andare in barca
To go from one thing to another	Divagare
To go one's own way	Fare a modo proprio
To grieve	Affliggere, affliggersi
To have a narrow escape	Scamparla bella
To have at one's disposal	Avere sotto mano
To have bad luck	Esser sfortunato
To kick up a row	Fare del baccano
To kill by inches	Far morire a oncia
To laugh in one's sleeve	Ridere sotto i baffi
To lay a bet	Scommettere
To let one go his own way	Lasciargli la briglia su collo

Date. Age.	**Data. Età.**
What day of the week is it?	Che giorno è oggi?
What year is this?	In che anno siamo?
What month is it?	In che mese siamo?
What day of the month is it?	Quanti ne abbiamo oggi?

It is the first of January.	E'il primo di Gennaio.
Do you often come here?	Vien spesso qui?
Once a week.	Una volta la settimana.
Weekly.	Settimanalmente.
I arrived several days ago.	Arrivai alcuni giorni orsono.
I leave to-morrow week (fortnight).	Partirò in una settimana (in quindici giorni) da domani.
He is often late (5 minutes).	Egli è spesso in ritardo (cinque minuti).
To-day is Thursday.	Oggi è Giovedì.
To-morrow is Friday.	Domani è Venerdì.
How old are you?	Che età ha Lei?
I am twenty years old.	Ho venti anni.
How old do you think I am?	Che età crede Lei che io abbia?
I am ten years older (younger) than my brother.	Ho dieci anni di più (di meno) di mio fratello.
Younger brother—Elder brother.	Fratello minore—Fratello maggiore.
She is going on fifty years old.	Si avvicina ai cinquant' anni.
He is over forty.	Ha passato i quarant' anni.

Asking the Time.

Per domandare l'ora

What time is it?	Che ore sono?
Can you tell me what the time is?	Può dirmi che ore sono?
It is nearly six o'clock.	Sono quasi le sei.
It is past four o'clock.	Sono passate le quattro.
Exactly five o'clock	Le cinque precise.
It is exactly half past six.	Sono le sei e mezzo precise
Midday, Midnight.	Mezzogiorno, Mezzanotte
A quarter past two.	Le due e un quarto.
Half past three.	Le tre e mezzo.
A quarter to eight.	Un quarto alle otto.
Twenty minutes to nine.	Venti minuti alle nove.
Ten minutes past one.	La una e dieci
It is about to strike four.	Sono quasi le quattro.
It has just struck five.	Sono le cinque precise.

My watch is stopped.	Il mio orologio è fermato.
My watch is 15 minutes slow (fast).	Il mio orologio ritarda (avanza) di quindici minuti.
My watch is broken.	Il mio orologio è rotto.
I shall take it to the watchmaker.	Lo porterò dall'orologiaio.
It is a keyless watch.	E'un orologio senza chiavetta.
It has been repaired.	E'stato riparato.
I have forgotten to wind it.	Ho dimenticato di caricarlo.
I have lost my watchkey.	Ho perduto la chiavetta del mio orologio.

Health.   Saluti.

How do you do? How are you?	Come sta?
I am very well, and you?	Sto molto bene, e Lei?
Fairly well, thanks.	Abbastanza bene. grazie.
Is your father well?	Sta bene suo padre?
Father and mother are both well.	Papà e Mamma stanno bene.
I am not very well myself.	Io non sto troppo bene.
I have caught a cold.	Ho preso un raffreddore.
I have a cold in my head and toothache.	Ho un raffreddore di testa e mal di denti.
I hope you will soon be better.	Spero che presto stia meglio.
I have sprained my wrist.	Mi sono slogato il polso.
You should see a doctor.	Dovrebbe farsi visitare dal medico.
Where does he live?	Dove abita?
What are his consulting hours?	Quali sono le sue ore di consultazione?
Six to eight o'clock every evening.	Dalle sei alle otto ogni sera.
I shall go to see him this evening.	Andrò da lui questa sera.
I feel very ill.	Mi sento molto male.
I shall get a prescription from the doctor.	Mi farò dare una ricetta dal medico.

12

Visiting.

Is Mr. X., Mrs. X., at home?

What name please?

Please take my card.

Mr. X. is not at home.

Can you tell me when he will be at home?

He will be back to-morrow morning.

My friend, Mr. Z., asked me to call on you.

Please sit down.

I have called on business

What can I do for you?

I called yesterday, but you had just gone out.

I was very sorry to miss seeing you.

I am delighted to make your acquaintance.

It is very kind of you to have called.

La Visita.

Riceve il Signor X., la Signora X.?

Chi posso annunciare?

Questa è la mia carta da visita.

Il Signor X. non è in casa.

Può dirmi quando sarà in casa?

Ritornerà domani mattina.

Il mio amico, Signor Z., mi chiese di venirla a visitare.

Favorisca sedersi.

Sono venuto per affari.

Che cosa posso fare per Lei?

Venni ieri ma Ella era appena uscito.

Mi spiacque molto non aver La incontrata.

Ho molto piacere di conoscer La.

Ella è molto genti di essere venuto

At the Hotel.

Drive me to the Grand Hotel.

Bring in my luggage, porter.

Have you any rooms?

Yes sir, several.

On which floor do you want?

Can I have a single (double) bedded room?

Certainly, either on the first or second floor.

Do you want a front or a back room?

All'Albergo.

Mi conduca al Grand Hotel.

Portiere, porti dentro il mio bagaglio.

Ha una stanza?

Si Signore, varie stanze.

A che piano la desidera?

Posso avere una camera con un letto (doppia)?

Certamente, tanto al primo che al secondo piano.

Desidera una camera sulla parte anteriore o sulla parte posteriore dell'Albergo?

abandon abbandonare
abandoned abbandonato
abandonment abbandono
m; cessione *f*
abate abbattere ; diminuire
abatement diminuzione *f*
abbey badia *f*
abbot abbate *m*
abbreviate abbreviare
abbreviation *n* abbrevia-
zione *f*
abdicate abdicare
abdication abdicazione *f*
abdomen addome; basso
ventre *m*   [*m & f*
abdominal addominale
abduct rimuovere; rapire
abduction abduzione *f*
abductor *n* abduttore *m*
aberration aberrazione *f*
abet incoraggiare
abettor fautore *m*; isti-
gatore *m*
abeyance vacanza *f*;
in – vacante
abhor aborrire; detestare
abhorrence orrore *m*
abhorrent colpito d'orrore
abide dimorare
abiding soggiorno *m*;
stabilità *f*   [*f*
abigail serva *f*; cameriera
ability abilità; capacità *f*
abject abbietto; vile;
– ly bassamente
abjection abbiezione *f*
able capace; abile; to
be – to esser in istato
di; – ness *n* capacità
f; forza *f*
abode dimora *f*; soggiorno *m*   [lare
abolish abolire; annul-

abolition abolizione *f*;
annientamento *m*
abominable abbomina-
bile; detestabile *m & f*
abominate abbominare
abomination abbomina-
zione *f*; orrore *m*
aboriginal primitivo
abortion aborto *m*
abortive abortivo; abor-
abound abbondare [tito
abounding abbondanza;
soverchio *m*
about intorno; circa;
verso; sopra; da; in;
in quanto a; – noon
verso il mezzogiorno;
to be – to essere sul
punto di
above al di sopra; di
sopra; – mentioned,
said suddetto
abrade logorare
abrasion abrasione *f*
abreast di fronte; – of
dirimpetto   [tringere
abridge abbreviare; ris-
abridgment sommario *m*;
diminuzione *f*
abrupt precipitato; brusco; – ly *av* bruscamente;
– ness *n* asprezza *f*;
precipitazione *f*
absence assenza *f*; lontananza *f*; – of mind
distrazione *f*; leave of
congedo *m*
absent assente; to be –
essere distratto *m*
absentee assente dal suo
paese *m*
absolute assoluto; perfetto; – ly assoluta-

mente; affatto

absolution assoluzione *f*

absolve assolvere; slegare

absorb assorbire; inghiottire [*m & f*

absorbent assorbente

abstention astinenza *f*

abstinence astinenza *f*; day of – giorno di digiuno *m*

abstract astratto; compendio *m*; – ly astrattamente

abstract estrarre; involare

abstraction astrazione *f*; sottrazione *f*

absurd assurdo; insensato *m*

absurdity assurdità *f*

abundance abbondanza *f*

abundant abbondante; – ly copiosamente

abuse abuzare; maltrattare [*fp*; errore *m*

abuse abuso *m*; ingiure

abusive abusivo; ingiurioso; – ness *n* abuso

academic, academical accademico *m .* [*m*

academy accademia *f*

accede aderi e; consentire

accelerate accelerare

acceleration acceleramento *m* : prestezza *f*

accent accento *m*; pronuncia *f* [colare

accent accentuare; articolare

accentuate accentuare

accentuation accentuazione *f* [dire

accept accettare; aggradire

acceptable accettabile

acceptance accettazione *f*

accessibility accessibilità *f*

accessible accessibile *m & f*

accessory accessorio

accident accidente *m*;

accidental accidentale; fortuito; – ly accidentalmente; per caso

accommodate accomodare; aggiustare; regolare

accommodation adattazione *f*; aggiustamento *m*; convenienza *f*

accompaniment accompagnamento *m*

accompanist accompagnatore *m*, trice *f*

accompany accompagnare

accomplice complice *m & f*

accomplish effettuare; eseguire [terminato

accomplished compito;

accomplishment *n* compimento *m*; talento *m*

accord accordo *m*; consenso *m*; of one's own – di sua propria volontà *f*; accordare

according, – as secondo che; – to secondo; – ly in conseguenze

account conto *m*; contare; rendere conto di; by all – s secondo il detto generale; on that – per questo motivo; on no – con nessun pretesto; to keep – s tener libri; – book libro *m* de'conti

accountability responsabilità *f* [*m & f*

accountable responsabile

accountant calcolatore *m*; che tiene i libri

accumulation accumulazione *f* [mula

accumulative chi accu-

15

accumulator accumulatore *m*, trice *f*
accuracy esattezza
accurate esatto; corretto; – ly esattamente
accurse maledire
accursed maledeto
accusation accusa *f*
accuse accusare
accustom accostumare; to – one's self avvezzarsi
accustomed abituato
acetate acetato *m*
ache far male; soffrire; my head – s io ho mal alla testa; male *m*; dolore *m*
achieve compiere; finire
achievement compimento *m*; fatto *m*
aching dolore *m*
acid acido *m*
acidity aciddezza *f*
acknowledge riconoscere; confessare
acknowledgment *n* recognizione *f*; confessione
acme apogeo *m*; colmo *m*
acoustic acustico
acquaint avvertire; apprendere
acquaintance conoscenza *f*
acquiesce acconsentire
acquiescence consenso *m*
acquire acquistare; ottenere
acquit pagare; assolvere; –tance *n* pagamento *m*
acre misura di terreno (4046 m. quad)

acrimonious acrimonico; acre; – ly con acrimonia
across per , mezzo; a traverso; per sopra
act fare; operare; atto *m*; in the very – in

flagrante delitto
action azione *f*; fatto *m*; battaglia *f*; processo *m*
active attivo; lesto
activity attività
actor attore *m*; commediante *m*
actress attrice *f*; commediante *f*
actual attuale; reale; – ly attualmente
acute acuto; sottile; – ly sottilmente; – ness perspicacia *f*
adage proverbio *m*
adamant diamante *m*
adapt adattare; aggiustare
adaptable adattabile
adapted adattato; proprio
add aggiugnere; to – up sommare
adder vipera *f*; serpente *m*
addict, to – one's self addarsi; applicarsi
addition *n* somma; addizione *f*
additional addizionale
addle stantio; guastato; – headed, – pated scervellato
address indirizzo *m*
address indirizzare; parlare a
addresser mittente *m*
adduce addurre; allegare
adept adetto; dotto
adequacy sufficienza *f*
adequate uguale; – ness sufficienza *f*
adhere aderire
adherence aderenza *f*
adherent aderente *m*
adjust aggiustare
adjustment aggiustamento *m*
adjutant aiutante *m*
administer amministrare;

fornire [tivo
administerial ammistra-
administrate amminist-
rare [trazione *f*
administration amminis-
administrator amminis-
tratore *m*; direttore *m*
admirable ammirabile
admirably ammirabil-
mente
admiral ammiraglio *m*
admiration ammirazione *f*
admire ammirare
admirer ammiratore *m*
admissible ammissibile
admission ammissione *f*;
entrata *f*; – ticket biglietto *m* d'entrata *f*

admit accordare; am-
mettere
admittance entrata *f*;
concessione *f*; no – here
non si entra qui

admonish avvertire; ri-
prendere
admonition ammoni-
zione *f*; avviso *m*

adolescence adolescenza *f*
adolescent adolescente
m

adopt adottare
adorable adorabile
adoration adorazione *f*
adore adorare
adorn ornare

adrift alla deriva *f*;
abbandono *m*
adroit destro; abile;·
– ness destrezza *f*
adult adulto; adoles-
cente *m*

adulterate adulterare

adulteration adultera-
zione *f*; falsificazione *f*
adulterer adultero *m*

adulteress adultera *f*
adultery adulterio *m*
advance avvicinamento
m; progresso *m*; in -
anticipatamente
advancement promozione
f; progresso *m*
advantage vantaggio *m*;
superiorità *f*; to take –
profittare
advantageous vantag-
gioso; – ly vantaggio-
samente
adventure avventura *f* ;
accidente *m*; avven-
turare
adventurer avventuriere
m
adventuresome arrischi-
ante; ardito
adverb avverbio *m*
adversary avversario *m*
adverse avverso; con-
trario
adversity avversità
advertise annunziare

advertisement avverti-
mento *m*; avviso *m*;
annunzio *m* [siglio *m*
advice avviso *m*; con-
advisable prudente; av-
visato *m* [visare
advise consigliare; av-
advisedly prudentemente
advocate avvocato *m*;
difensore *m*; difendere;
aeronaut aeronauta *m*
aerostat aerostato *m*;
pallone *m* [lontano
afar lungi; – off da
affability affabilità *f*
affable affabile
affair affare *m*
affect affettare
affectation affettazione *f*
affection affezione *f*;

tenerezza f
affectionate affettuoso
affiliate adottare
affiliation filiazione f
affinity affinità f
affirm affermare
affirmation affermazione f
affirmative affermativo;
in the – affermativo-
mente
affix aggiugnere
afflict affliggere
affliction afflizione f
affluence affluenza f
affluent abbondante
afford fornire; dare
afloat a galla
afore innanzi; prima;
avanti; piuttosto; –
mentioned suddetto; –
named sullodato; – said
suddetto; – time già
afraid spaventato
afresh di nuovo
afront di fronte
after dopo; conforme
aftermost ultimo
afternoon vespro m;
dopo mezzodì m
afterwards dopo; più
tardi
again ancora; di nuovo;
di più
against contro; sopra;
verso; – the grain con-
trapelo

age età f; generazione;
of – maggiore m & f;
under – minore m & f
aged vecchio
agency azione f; agenzia f
agenda giornale m; tac-
agent agente m [cuino m
agression agressione f
aggressive ostile
aggressor aggressore m
aggrieve affliggere

aghast spaventato
agile agile
agility agilità f
agitate agitare; discutere
agitation agitazione f
agitator agitatore m
ago passato; long – gran
tempo fa; two days –
due giorni fa; how
long – ? da quanto
tempo?
agonize agonizzare
agonizing straziante;
atroce
agony agonia f
agree accordarsi; convenire; consentire; ac-
cordare
agreeable conforme; gradevole   [accordo
agreed convenuto; d'
agreement accordo m;
contratto; to come to
an – venir d'accordo
agricultural d'agricoltura
agriculture agricoltura f
ahead avanti; innanzi
aid aiuto m; assistenza;
aiutare; soccerrere; in
– of a beneficio di
ail soffrire; what – s you?
ove soffrite, ch'avete?
ailing malatticcio
ailment male m; pena f
aim mira f; punto m;
prender di mira f;
dirigere; mirare
air aria f; vento m;
canto m; ciera f;
aspetto m; – balloon
aerostato m; –blad-
der vescica natatoria;
– gun fucile m a vento
m; – hole spiraglio
m; – pump macchina

f; pneumatica; – **shaft**
ozzo *m*; da far
entrare l'aria *f*; – **tight**
a impermeabile all'aria
f; far prender aria *f*:
espore all'aria *f*; ven-
tilare

airiness leggerezza *f*
airing passeggiata *f*
airless senz'aria *f*
airy aereo; leggiero
aisle parte *f*; laterale·
d'una chiesa *f*
alarm allarme *m*; ris-
veglio *m*; – **clock** oro-
logio-sveglia *f*; allar-
alcohol alcool *m*
alcoholic alcoolico
alcove alcova *m*
alder alno *m* (albero)
alderman consigliere municipale
ale birra *f*; – **brewer**
birraio *m*; – **house**
taverna *f*; – **house-**
keeper tavernaio *m*
alert alerte; vigilante; **on**
the – stante allerta
algebra algebra *f*
alien straniero; strano;
straniero *m*, ra *f*
alienable alienabile *m & f*
alienate alienare
alienation alienazione *f*;
– **of mind** pazzia *f*
alight discendere; cadere
alight accesso
alike somigliante *m & f*
aliment alimento *m*
alimony pensione *f*

all tutto; tutti; **all the**
better tanto meglio;
with – **speed** prestissimo;
by – **means** a qualunque
prezzo; **not at** – punto
punto; **nothing at** –

niente affatto; – **of us**
tutti noi; – **along** lungo
il; **that is all** ecco tutto;
– **at once** di subito;
– **powerful** onnipotente;
allegation allegazione *f*
allege allegare; ad durre;
dichiarare
allegiance fedeltà *f*
allegory allegoria
alleviate alleggiare
alleviation allievamento *m*,
alley andito *m*; vicolo *m*;
blind – angiporto *m*
alliance allenza
alliteration alliterazione *f*
allot ripartire; assegnare
allotment ripartizione ·*f*
nezzo *m* di terra *f*
allow assegnare; per-
mettere
allowance allocazione *f*;
pensione *f*; **to make** –
for tenir conto di
alloy lega *f*; miscuglio *m*;
allegare; alterare
allspice pimento *m*
allude alludere
allure attrarre; sedurre
allurement vezzo *m*;
seduzione *f*
allusion allusione *f*
ally unire; alleato *m*
almighty onnipotente *m*
& f
almond mandoria; **burnt**
– mandoria tostata
almost quasi; presso a
poco

aloft in alto; in aria
alone solo; solamente
along per lungo; di
lungo; alla lunga;
come – venite dunque;
andiamo
alongside accanto; bordo

a bordo
aloof lungi; at largo
aloud alto; *ad* alta voce
alpaca alpaca *m* (stoffa)
alphabet alfabeto *m*
alphabetic alphabetical
  alfabetico
alpine alpino; alpestre
already già [ancora
also anche ugualmente;
altar altare *m*; – piece
  cornice *f*; quadro *m*
  d'altare
alternate alternare; alternativo; alterno
alternation alternativa *f*
alternative alternativo
although sebbene; quan-
  tunque
altogether interamente
alum allume *m*
always sempre
a.m. iniziali di: anno
  mundi l'anno del mondo;
  artium magister maestro
  m d'arti; ante meri-
  diem antimeridiano
amadou esca *f*
amain vigorosamente
amalgam amalgama *f*
amalgamate amalgamare
amanuensis, amanuenses
  secretario *m*; scrivano *m*
amass ammassare
amateur dilettante; vir-
  tuoso *m* [prendere
amaze sbigottire; sor-
amazement stupore *m*
amazon amazzone *f*
ambassador ambasciatore
  m [trice *f*
ambassadress ambascia-
ambition ambizione *f*
ambitious ambizioso
amble ambio *m*; andar
  all' ambio
ambrosia ambrosia *f*

ambulance ambulanza *f*
amenable risponsabile
amend emendare; cor-
  reggere [*f*
amendment emendazione
amends riparazione *f*
amenity amenità *f*
amethyst amatista *m*
amiability amabilità
amiable amabile *m & f*
amicable benevolente
amid, amidst nel mezzo
ammonia ammoniaca *f*
ammunition munizione *f*
amnesty amnistia *f*
among, amongst tra;
  fra; appresso
amount montante *m*;
  totale *m*; montare

amplifier amplificatore *m*
amplify amplificare
amply ampiamente
amputate amputare [*f*
amputation amputazione

amuck furiosamente; to
  run – attaccare con furia
amuse divertire
amusement divertimento
  m; ricreazione *f*
an uno *m*; una *f*
  anachronism anacronis-
  mo *m*
analogous analogo
analogy analogia *f*
analysis analisi *f*
analyst analista *m*
analytic, analytical ana-
analyze analizzare [litico
anarchist anarchista *m*
anarchy anarchia *f*
anatomist anatomista *m*
anatomy anatomia *f*
ancestor antenato *m*
ancestral ereditario

ancestry antenati *m pl*
anchor ancora *f*; to ride

at – esser a l'àncora;
to weigh – levar l'àncora
anchorage ancoraggio *m*
ancient antico; vecchio
and e
angel angelo *m*
angelic angelico
angelus avemaria *m*
anger collera *f*
angle angolo *m*; canto *m*;
pescare colla lenza *f*;
accalappiare
angler pescatore *m*
colla lenza
anglican anglicano; in-
glese *m* & *f*
angling pesca *f* colla
lenza; – ling lenza da
pesca *f*; – rod canna
da pesca
angry in collera
anguish angoscia *f*
angular angolare *m* & *f*
animadvert riprendere
animal animale *m*
animate animare; vivi-
ficare; animato
animation animazione
animosity animosità *f*
annihilate annichilare
annihilation annichila-
mento *m*   [m
anniversary anniversario
annotate annotare
annotation annotazione *f*
announce annunziare;
 – ment annunzio *m*
announcer chi annun-
zia *m*   [estare
annoy incomodare; mol-
annoyance incomodità *f*
annual annuale
annuitant censuario *m*
annuity somma *f* an-
nuale d'una rendita
anoint ungere; fregare
anointed unto

anomalous anomalo
anomaly anomalia *f*
anon subito; or ora
anonymous anomino
another un altro; ancor
un altro

answer rispondere; ris-
posta *f*; soluzione *f*
answerable risponsabile
 m & *f*
ant formica *f*   [m
antagonism antagonismo
antagonist antagonieta *m*
antarctic antartico
antecedent antecedente
 m & *f*   [f
antelope antilopo *m*
anterior anteriore *m* & *f*
anthem antifona *f*
anthology antologia *f*
anthropology *n* antropo-
logia *f*
antic antico *m*
anticipate anticipare
anticipation anticipazione
antidote antidoto *m*   [f
antipathy antipatia *f*
antiquated antico   [f
antique antico; antichità
antiquity antichità *f*
antiseptic antisettico
antithesis antitesi *f*
anus ano *m*
anvil incudine *f*
anxiety ansietà; in-
quietudine
anxious ansioso; ín-
quieto *m*
any qualche; del; della;
degli; alcuno; – body
qualeia; – where dap-
pertutto; (preceduto
d'un negativo) in nes-
suna parte; – more di
più   [to
apart a parte

21

apartment appartamento
apathetic apatico
apathy apatia *f*
ape scimia *f*; imitare
apex sommità *f*; cima *f*
apiece il pezzo; per testa

apologetic, apological
apologetico

apologize far l'apologia
apology apologia *f*
apostrophize apostrofare
apothecary farmacista;
– 's shop farmacia *f*
appal spaventare
appanage appannaggio *m*
apparatus apparecchio *m*
apparel abito *m*; vesti-
mento *m*; vestire
apparent apparente *m & f*
apparition apparizione *f*
appeal appello *m*; ap-
pellare   [parire
appear apparire; com-
appearance apparizione
f; aspetto *m*
appease placare; calmare
appellant appellante *m & f*
appellation appellazione *f*
append appendere
appendage pertinenza *f*;
accessorio *m*
applaud applaudire
applause applauso *m*
apple mela *f*; pupilla *f*
(dell occhio) – tree
melo *m*
appliance applicazione *f*
applicable applicabile *m &*
f   [*m & f*
applicant postulante
application applicazione
f; make – indirizzarsi
apply applicare   [nare
appoint nominare; desig-
appointment nomina *f*
apportion ripartire [& *f*

apposite convenevole *m*
appraise apprezzare
appreciable apprezzabile
appreciate apprezzare
appreciation estimazione
f; valutazione *f*
apprehend pigliare; ar-
restare   [*f*; arresto *m*
apprehension apprensione
apprentice apprendista
apprise apprendere; in-
formare
approach avvicinare; av-
vicinamento *m* [zione *f*
approbation approva-
appropriation appropria-
zione *f*
approval approvazione *f*
approve approvare
approximate ravvicinare:
-ly per approssima-
zione *f*   [*f*
apricot albicocca *f*; -tree
albicocco *m*
apron grembiale *m*
apropos a proposito [& *f*
apt atto; intelligente *m*
aptitude attitudine *f*
aqueduct acquedotto *m*
arbiter arbitro *m*
arbitrary arbitrario
arbitrate arbitrare
arbitration arbitraggio *m*
arbitrator arbitro *m*
arbor albero *m*
arcade valto *f*; arcata *f*
arch arca *f*; volta *f*;
arco *m*; –way volta *f*
archaeological archeolo-
gico
archaeology archeologia *f*
archbishop arcivescovo *m*
archer arciere *m*
archery tiro dell' arco *m*
architect architetto
architecture architettura *f*
archives archivio *m*

arctic artico
ardent ardente m & f – ly
  ardentemente
ardor ardore m
arduous arduo m & f
area area f; superficie
arena arena f
argue argomentare
argument argomento m
argumentative argomen-
aria aria f   [tativo
arise alzarsi; levarsi
aristocracy aristocrazia f
aristocrat aristocratico m
arithmetic aritmetica f
ark arca f; cassa f
arm braccio m; ramo m;
  arma f; – in – a brac-
  cetto; —chair sedia f;
  a   bracciuoli; – hole
  ascella f; armarsi
armistice armistizio m
armless senza bracchi
armourer armaiuolo m
armorial d'armedi stem-
  ma f
armoury arsenale m; sala
  d'armi; armatura f
armour armatura f
arms armi pl; men at –
  gente d'armi m pl
army esercito m; armata
aroma aroma m   [f
aromatic aromatico
around intorno; in giro
arquebus archibugio m
arraign accusare
arrange assettare
arrangement acconcia-
  mento m
arrear prodotto d'una
  rendita f; arretrato m
arrest arresto m; arrestare
arrival venuta f; arrivo m
arrive arrivare
arrogance arroganza f

arrogant arrogante m & f
arrow saetta f; strale m
arse culo m
arsenal arsenale m
arsenic arsenico m
arson incendio m
art arte f; abilità f
arterial arteriale m & f
artery arteria f
artful artistico; astuto
artichoke carciofo m
article articolo m; stipu-
  lazione f; materia f
articulate articolare; ar-
  ticolato   [f
articulation articolazione
artifice artifizio m
artificial artifiziale m & f
artillery artiglieria f
artisan artigiano m;
  operaio m
artist artista m   [to
artless senz'arte f; schiet-
as come; anche; sic-
  come; conforme; –for
  in quanto a; –well cosi
  bene che; —soon –
  tosto chè
ascribe attribuire
ash frassino m; legno
  m; –tree frassino m
ash cenere f; – coloured
  cenerino; – Wednesday
  mercoledi delle ceneri
ashamed vergognoso [f pl
ashes cenceri pl
aside da canto; a parte;
  lay – metter da parte
asinine asinino
ask domandare

asleep in riposo
asparagus asparago m
aspect aspetto m

asphalt asfalto m
aspirant aspirante m & f
aspirate aspirare

aspire aspirare
assailant assalitore
assassin assassino *m*
assassinate assassinare
assassination assassinio *m*
assault assalto *m* [giare
assay saggio *m*; assag-
assayer saggiatore *m*
assemblage complesso *m*
assemble raccogliere
assembly assemblea *f*
assent consentire; assen-
tire; approvazione *f*
assert anermare
assertion asserzione *f*
assess tassare [posta *f*
assessment tassa; im-
assessor assessore *m*
assign assegnare
assignment assegnazione
assimilate assimilare
assimilation assimila-
assist assistere [zione
assistance assistenza *f*
assistant aiutante; assis-
tente *m & f*
assize corte *f*
associate associare; —
with frequentare; as-
sociato *m*; socio *m*
association società; as-
sociazione *f*
assort assortire [*m*
assortment assortimento
assuage placare; calmare
assuagement mitigazione
assume prendere [*f*
assuming presuntuoso
assumption presunzione
f; assunzione *f*
assurance assicurazione *f*;
fiducia *f*
assure assicurare
asterisk asterisco *m*
asthma asma *m*
astonish sorprendere
astonishing stupendo

astonishment stupore *m*
astray fuori del cam-
mino; go — sviarsi
at a; in; dentro; sopra;
dopo; contro; da; —
home in casa; — first
prima; — length final-
mente
atmosphere atmosfera *f*
atmospheric atmospher-
atom atomo *m* [ico *m*
atone espiare; redimere
atonement espia
atop in alto; alla sommità
atrocious atroce *m & f*
atrocity atrocità *f*
atrophy atrofia *f*
attach attaccare; pigliare
attachment affezione *f*;
attaccamento *m*
attack assalire
attacker assalitore *m*
attain pervenire a; otte-
nere [talento *m*
attainment acquisizione *f*;
attaint dichiarare
attempt tentare; assalire;
tentativo *m*; attentato *m*
attend seguire; accom-
pagnare; attendere
attendance servizio *m*;
cura *f* [dipendente *m & f*
attendant domestico *m*;
attention attenzione *f*;
pay — far attenzione;
give — prestar attenzione
attentive attento
attic attico; mansarda *f*
attire veste *f*; ornamento
m [posa *f*
attitude attitudine *f*;
attorney procuratore *m*;
regio; power of — pro-
cura *f*
attract attrarre; attirare
attraction attrazione *f*
attractive attrattivo *m*
attribute attribuire; im-

24

putare

attribute attributo
attune accordare
auction incanto *m*; sub-
asta *f*; – **sale** vendita
all'incanto *m*
auctioneer commissario
m stimatore
audacious audace *m & f*
audacity audacia *f*
audible udibile *m & f*
audience udienza *f*;
uditorio *m*
audit revisione *f* (di
conti); udizione
auditor uditore *m*
augment aumentare
augmentation aumento *m*
aunt zia *f*
auspicious propizio
austere austero; severo
austerity austerità *f*
authenticity autenticità *f*
authenticate autenticare
authentication conferma-
author autore *m* [zione *f*
authoress autrice *f* [*m*
authoritative autorizzato
authority autorità *f*
authorization autorizza-
zione *f*
authorize autorizzare
autocracy autocrazia *f*
autocrat autocrata *m*
autograph autografo *m*
automaton automato *m*
autopsy autopsia *f*
auxiliary ausiliario
avail vantaggio *m*; utilità
f; servire; profittare
available disponibile
avalanche valanga *f*
avenge vendicare; punire
avenger vendicatore *m*
avenue viale *m*
aver affermare

average mezzo termine *m*
averse contrario a
avert distrarre
aviary uccelliera *f*
avidity avidità *f*
avocation occupazione *f*
avoid evitare
await aspettare; attendere
awake vigilante
awaken svegliare
award aggiudicare; sentenza *f*; decisione
aware vigilante; attento
away, go – andarsène;
take – togliere; **send** –
rimandare
awe timore *m*; rispetto
m
awful imponente; solenne,
terrible
awhile per qualche tempo
awkward disadatto; scon-
cio; – **ness** goffaggine
f: incommodità *f*
axe scure *f*
axiom assioma *m*
axis asse *f*
axle asse *f*; –**pin** accia-
rino *m*; –**tree** asse *f*
ay, aye sì; sicuramente;
certamente

aye sempre; per sempre
azote azoto *m*
azure azzurro *m*

B

b. – **flat** bemolle *m*
babble ciarlare; ciarla *f*
babbler chiaccherone *m*
babe bimbo *m*; bam-
bino *m*
baby bambino; bimbo;
— **linen** corredo *m* de

bimbi

back dorso *m*; posteriore *m*; dossiere *m*; fondo *m*; rovescio *m*; indietro; di ritorno; ritornare; appoggiare; **far** – indietreggiare; rinculare

background fondo *m*; **in the** – all'ombra *f*

backward indietro; a ritroreo

bacon lardo *m*; **rasher of** – fetta *f* di lardo

bad cattivo; malo; infermo; **–ly** male

badge marchio *m*

baffle sventare; frustrare

bag sacco *m*; valigia *f*; insaccare

baggage bagaglio *m*; meretrice *f*

bail cauzione *f*; sicurtà; scarecrare sotto cauzione

bailiff bailo *m*; usciere *m*

bait esca *f*; adescare

bake far pane; coucere

baker panattiere *m*

bakery bottega *f* di fornaio *m*

balance bilancia *f*; equilibrio *m*; bilanciere *m*; saldo *m*; bilanciare; aggiustare; dubitare

balcony balcone *m*

bald calvo; **–ness** *n* calvizie *f*

bale balla *f*; imbalare

balk trave *f*; contrariare

ball palla *f*; globo *m*; ballo *m*

ballad ballata *f*

balloon pallone *m*; aerostrato *m*

ballot scrutinio; ballottaggio *m*; per votare; **–box** urna *f*

bamboo bambu

bank banca *f*; **–note** biglietto *m* di banca

banker banchiere *m*

bankrupt fallimento *f*

bankruptcy fallimento *m*

banner bandiera *f*

banquet banchetto *m*

banter scherzo *m*

baptism battesimo *m*

bar barra *f*; stanga *f*

barbarian barbaro

barber barbiere *m*

bard bardo *m*

bare nudo

barefaced a viso *m*

barefooted coi piedi

bareheaded col capo *m*

bargain mercato *m*

barge battello *m*

barley orzo *m*

barn granaio *m*

barnacle morsa *f*

barometer barometro *m*

baron barone *m*

barque barca *f*

barrack baracca *f*

barrel barile *m*

barren sterile

barricade barricata *f*

barrier barriera *f*

basin bacino *m*

basket cesta *f*

bass stuoia *f*

bassoon fagotto *m*

bastard bastardo *m*

bastinade bastonata *f*

bastion bastione

bat nottola *f*

batch fornata *f*

bate sbattere

bath bagno *m*

bathe bagnare

bather bagnaiuolo *m*

battalion battaglione *m*

batten impinguare

batter pasta *f*

battery batteria *f*
battle battaglia *f*
battledore racchetta *f*
battlement merlo *m*
bawl gracchiare
bay alloro *m*; báia *f*;
 − window finestra *f*
bayonet baionetta *f*
bazaar bazar *m*
be essere
beach ripa *f*
beacon fanale *m*
bead grano; di rosario *m*
beak becco *m*
beam trave *f*; raggio *m*
bean fava *f*
bear orso *m*: she − orsa *f*
bear portare
beard barba *f*
bearer portatore *m*
beast bestia *f*
beat vincere; battere
beau elegante *m*
beautiful bello *m*; bella *f*
beautify abbellire
beauty beltà *f*
beaver castore *m*
because chè; perciochè
become divenire; con-
 venire
bed letto *m*; talamo *m*;
 -room, -chamber ca-
 mera *f* da letto; −

 clothes lenzuola *f pl*;
 − stead lettiera *f*
bedlam ospedale *m* dei
 pazzi *m pl*
bedridden a in letto
bee ape *f*; − hive alveare
 m   [faggiuola *f*
beech faggio *m*; − nut
beef bue *m*; boiled −
 lesso *m*; roast − rosbif
 − steak bifteck
beer birra *f*
beet bietola *f*; − root

barbabietola *f*
beetle scarafaggio *m*;
 scarabeo *m*
befall accadere
before prima;
beg domandare; solleci-
 tare; mendicare
beggar mendicante *m*;
 impoverire
begin cominciare

beginner principiante *m*;
 novizio *m*   [origine *f*
beginning principio *m*;
begone vattene!
begrime annerare
beguile ingannare [dursi
behave regolarsi; con-
behaviour condotta *f*
behead decapitare
behest comando *m*
behind dietro; dopo
behold guardare
beholder spettatore *m*
belabour battere
belatedness ritardo *m*
belch rutto *m*; eruttare

believe credere
believer credente *m & f*
bell campana *f*; sonaglio
 m; −clapper batocchio
 m; −rope cordone di
 campanella *f*; −ringer
 campanaio *m*
belligerent belligerante
bellow muggire [*m & f*
bellows soffietto *m*
belly ventre *m*
belong appartenere

beloved diletto; caro
below al di sotto di;
 agiù; laggiù
belt cinturino *m*
bench banco *m*; panca *f*;
 corte *f* [incurvatura *f*
bend bendare; curvare

beneath sotto giù
benediction benedizione *f*
benefactor benefattore *m*
benefice beneficio *m*
beneficial vantaggioso
beneficence beneficenza *f*
beneficiary beneficiario *m*
benefit profitto *m*; vantaggio *m*; profittare
benevolent benefico
benign benigno
bent tendenza *f*; curvato
benumb stupefare
benzine belzuino *m*
bequeath legare

bestow dare; concedere
bet scommessa *f*; scommettere
betray tradire
betrayal tradimento *m*
betroth fidanzare
better migliore; get the – of prevalere
between fra
betwixt fra   [a sbieco
bevel squadra *f*; tagliare
beverage beveraggio *m*
bevy brigata *f*

beware guardarsi

bewitch ammaliare
beyond al di là di; oltre; da lungi; lungi
bias sbieco; linea; tendenza *f*; inclinare
Bible Bibbia *f*

bibliography bibliografia *f*
bibulous spugnoso   [*m*
bicarbonate bicarbonato
bicker arrissarsi
bid   pregare;   offerire; offerta *f*   [*m & f*
bidder maggior offerente
big grosso; grande *m & f*
bigamy bigamia *f*
bigot bacchettone *m*

bile bile *f*
bilge fondo *m*; minore;
bilious bilioso [pancia *f*
bilk frustrare
bill serpe *f*; becco *m*; scritto *m*; annunzio *m*; fattura *f*; nota *f*; – of exchange cambiale *f*; – of fare carta *f* di trattoria; – of lading lettera di carico; stick no – s! proibita l'affissione *f*; –sticker attaccatore *m* di cartelli
billet biglietto *m*
billiards bigliardo *m*
bind   legare;   bendare; obbligare
binder legatore di libri
binding legatura *f*
biographer biografo
biography biografia *f*
bird uccello *m*; – cage uccelliera *f*; – catcher uccelatore *m*; – lime vischio *m*; – 's-eye view a vista d'uccello
birth nascità *f*; – day giorno *m* di nascità; – place luogo *m* nativo; – right primogenitura *f*
biscuit biscotto *m*
bishop vescovo *m*
bishopric vescovado *m*
bit boccone *m*; punta *f*
bitch cagna *f*
bite mordere; morsura *f*
bitter amaro *m & f*
black nero; oscuro; annerare; – amoor negro *m*; – art magia *f* nera; – berry mora *f* di ronco; – bird merlo
blacken annerare
blacking incerato *m*
blackish nericcio
bladder vescica *f*

blade fusto *m*; lama *f*
blameable biasimevole
blame biasimo; torto *m*
blameless irreprensibile
blameworthy degno di biasimo *m*
blanch imbiancare
bland dolce
blank bianco
blanket coperta da letto *m*
blarney adulazione *f*
blaspheme bestemmiare
blast colpo *m* di vento; suono *m*; distruggere; bruciare; − furnace fucina *f*
blaze fiamma *f*; lustro *m*; avvampare; brilliare
bleach imbiancare
bleak pallido; freddo
bleat belare; belamento
bleed salassare [*m*
bleeding salasso *m*
blemish difetto *m*; macchiare
blend mescolare
bless benedire
blessed benedetto
blessing benedizione *f*
blight nebbia *f*; peste *f*
blind cieco; oscuro; stuoia *f*; persiana *f*; accecare; mascherare; − ness cecità *f*
blindfold bendar gli occhi
blink batter gli occhi
bliss felicità *f*
bloated enfiato
block ammasso *m*
blockade blocco *m*; bloccare
blond bionda *f*
blood sangue *m*; -horse cavallo *m* di puro sangue
bloodshed effusione di sangue
bloodshot iniettato di sangue
bloodthirsty sanguinario
bloody sanguinario
bloom fiore *m*; fiorire
blossom fiore *m*
blot scarabocchio *m*
blotch pustola *f*
blotting scarabocchio; − case cartario *m*; − paper carta *f* asciugante
blow colpo *m*; puntura *f*; soffiare; − up saltare; − one's nose soffiare il naso
blowpipe zampogna *f*
blue turchino; azzurro
bluff grosso
blunt grossolano; brusco; rintuzzare *f*
blur macchia
blush rossore *m*; arrossire
boar cinghiale *m*
board tavola *f*; cartone *m*; scrittoio *m*; consiglio *m*· esser in pensione *f*
boarder pensionario *m*
boarding pensione *f*; −house casa di pensione; − school pensionato *m* [tars
boast vanteria *m*; van-
boat battello *m*; barca *f*; steam − battello *m* a vapore;
body corpo *m*; −guard guardia *f* del corpo
bog palude *f*; infangare
boggy paludoso
boil bollire [*m*
boiler caldaia; calderone
boiling bollimento *m*
boisterous impetuoso

bold ardito; coraggioso;
—**ness** arditezza *f*
bole tronco *m*
bolster capezzale *m*
bolt saetta *f*; strale *m*;
scapparsi; schivarsi
bomb bomba *f*
bond legame *m*; obbli-
gazione *f*; buono *m*;
—**man** schiavo *m*
bondage servitù *f*
bone osso *m* disossare
bonfire fuoco *m* di gioia
bonnet cappello; ber-
rettino *m*
bonus benefizio *m*
bony osseo; ossuto
booby goffo *m*
book libro *m*; memoriale
m; registrare; — **binder**
legatore *m*; — **case**
biblioteca *f*; — **keeper**
computista *m*; — **keep-
ing** tenuta *f* dei registri
m pl; —**seller** libraio
m; — **store** magazzino
m di libri
boot stivale *m*; profitto
m; stivalare; profit-
tare; —**hook**, —**jack**
cavastivali *m*; —**maker**
stivalaio *m*; —**tree**
forma *f*
booted stivalato
booth tenda *f* baracca *f*
boots garzone *m*

border bordo *m*; bordare
bore buco *m*; calibro *m*;
scandaglio *m*; persona
f tedio *m*; forare;
bucare; scandagliare
born nato; **be** — nascere
borough borgo *m*
borrow prestare
bosom seno *m*; cuore *m*
botanist botanico *m*
botany botanica *f*

both ambo; l'uno e
l'altro; alla volta
bother imbarazzare; imbarazzo *m*
bottle bottiglia
bottom fondo *m*; fondarsi
bottomless senza fondo
bough ramo *m*   [*m*
bounce saltare; strepito
bound limitare; saltare;
limite; balzo *m*
boundary limite *m*
bounty bontà *f*
bow inchinarsi; saluto *m*
bow arco *m*; archetto *m*;
—**window** finestra *f*
sagliente
bowel intestino *m*; — **s**
viscere *f pl*
bowl bollo *m*; baso *m*;
lanciar una palla
box bosso *m*; scatola *f*;
cassa *f*; palco (di teatro)
schiaffo *m*; sedia (di
cocchiere); camerino;
—**office** uffizio *m* di
locazione *f*
boxing lotta *f* a pugni
boy ragazzo *m*
boyhood fanciullezza *f*
brace paio *m*
bracelet bracialetto *m*
brad punta *f*; — **awl** pun-
brag vantarsi [teruolo *m*
braggart millantatore *m*
braid treccia *f*; intrecciare
brain cervella *m*; intelletto *m*; — **less** scervellato
brake freno *m*
bramble ronco
bran crusca *f*
branch ramo *m*; suc-
cursale *f*
brand torcia *f*; macchia *f*;
marcare

brandish vibrare
brandy acquavite *f*
brassier calderaio *m*
bravery bravura *f*
brawl gridare; zuffa *f*
brawn carne *f* di porco; forza *f*; muscolare
bread pane *m*; **brown** – pane *m* bigio
breadth altezza *f*
break spezzare; rompere; – **open** rompere; – **off** staccare; – **away** staccarsi; – **down** abbattersi; – **in** entrare per forza; –**out** scappare; – **up** rompersi; rottura *f*; interruzione *f*; lacuna *f*; freno *m*
breakage frattura *f*
breaker spezzatore *m*
breakfast far colazione *f*
breast petto *m*; seno *m*; cuore *m*; –**bone** sterno *m*; – **plate** corazza *f* pettorale *m*; – **work** parapetto *m*
breath respiro *m*; fiato *m*; **be out of** – aver perduto il fiato *m*
breed generare; procreare; razza *f*; covata *f*; specie
breeder allevatore *m*
breeding educazione *f*
breeze brezza *f*; vento *m*
brethren fratelli *m pl*
breviary breviario *m*
brevity brevità *f*
brew mescolare; far la birra *f*; mescolarsi; – **er** birraio fabbricante
bribe regalo *m*; corrompere
bribery corruzione *f*

brick mattone *m*; –**layer** muratore *m*
bride sposa *f*; –**groom** sposo *m*; – '**s-maid** damigella d'onore
bridge ponte *m*
bridle briglia *f*
brief breve; breve *m*
bright brillante
brighten brillare
brilliancy lustro *m*
brilliant brillante
brim orlo *m*
brine salamora *f*
bring portare; menare; – **about** compiere; – **forth** far uscire
broad largo; ampio; –**cloth** panno *m* fino; –**side** fianco *m* bordata *f*
broaden allargare
brocade broccato *m*
broil disputa *f*
broker sensale
brokerage sensaria *f*
bronchitis bronchite *f*
bronze bronzo *m*
brook ruscello *m*
broom ginestra *f*
broth brodo *m*
brothel postribolo *m*
brother fratello *m*; –**in-law** cognato *m*
brow ciera *f*; fronte *f*
brown bruno
bruise ammaccare; ammaccatura *f*
brunette brunetta *f*
brush spazzola *f*; pennello *m*; attacco *m*; spazzolare; –**maker** *n* spazzolaio *m*
brutalize imbestiare
brute bruto *m*; bestia *f*
bubble bolla *f*

buck daino *m*; – **skin** pelle *f* di daino
bucket secchia *f*
buckle fibbia *f*; fibbiare

buffoon buffone *m*
bug climice *f*
bugbear spauracchio *m*
buggy carretta *f*
bugle lustrino *m*
build edificare; fabbricare
builder capomastro *m*; costruttore *m*
building edificio *m*;
bulb bulbo *m* [fabbrica *f*
bulge gonfio *m*; curvarsi
bulk grossezza *f*; volume; –**head** tramezzo *m*
bulkiness grossezza *f*
bulky grosso
bull toro *m*
bullet palla *f*
bulletin bollettino *m*
bullion oro *m*; argento *m*
bullock bue *m*
bully bravaccio *m*
bulrush giunco *m*
bulwark bastione *m*
bump bozza *f*
bumper pieno bicchiere *m*
bumpkin villano *m*
burden carica *m*; sopracaricare
burdensome pesante
burgess borghese *m* & *f*
burg borgo *m*
burglar ladro *m*
burglary furto *m*
burgomaster borgomastro *m*
burial sepultura *f*; – **ground** cimeterio *m*
burlesque burlesco
burn brucciare; incendiare; scottatura *f*
burner brucciatore *m*
burnish abbrunire; pulire; – **er** brunitore *m*

burrow tana *f*
bursar economo *m*
burst crepare; rompersi; strepito *m*; esplosione *f*
bury sotterrare
bush cespuglio *m*
bushel staio *m*
bushy cespuglioso

business affare *m*; occupazione *f*
bust busto *m*   [*m*
bustle affrettarsi; tumulto
busy occupato; attivo
but ma; che; che non; senza che; solamente; eccetto
butcher beccaio *m*
butler bottigliere *m*
butt groppa *f*; scopo *m*
butter butirro *m* burro *m*; **bread and** – pane *m* unto col butirro; –**cup** botton *m* d'oro; –**fly** farfalla *f*; – **milk** siero *m*
buttock natica *f*
button bottone *m*; abbottonare; –**hole** occhiello *m*;
buy comprare
buyer compratore *m*
buzz ronzo *m*; ronzare
buzzard babaccione
by da; di; a; in; sopra; presso di; avanti; fra; tra; sotto; –**all means** ad ogni costo

bye dimora *f*; **good** – addio

C

cab biroccio; fiacre *m*; – **man** cocchiere *m*

cabbage cavolo *m*
cabin capanna *f*; cam-

erino m; -boy mozzo m
cabinet gabinetto m
– maker ebanista m
cable gomena f; cavo m
caboose cucina
cackle chiocciare
cactus catto m
cake pasta; tavoletta f;
indurire
calamitous calamitoso
calamity calamità f
calculable calcolabile
calculate calcolare
calculation calcolo m
calendar calendario m
call appello m; visita;
vocazione f; chiamare;
appellare; visitare
callosity callosità f
callous calloso [calma
calm calmo; – ly con
calm calma f; placare
calumniate calunniare
calumniator calunniatore
calumny calunnia f [m
camp campo m;
campare
campaign campagna f
camphor canfora f
can boraccia f; potere;
canal canale m [sapere
canary-bird canarino m
cancel cancellare; annul-
cancer cancro m [lare
candid candido
candidate candidato m
candle candela f
candle-stick candeliere m
canoe canoa; piroga f
canon canone; canonico
canonical canonico [m
canopy baldacchino m;
duomo m [teca f
canvas canavaccio m;
canvass brigare
cap berretto m

capability capacità f
capable capace; abile
capacious vasto; spazioso
capacity capacità f
cape davero; capo m
caper capriola f; far
capriole
capital capitale; eccel-
lente; capitale; lettera.
maiuscola f
capitalist capitalista m
capitulate capitolare
capitulation capitolato m
capricious capriccioso
captain capitano m
captivate cattivare
captive prigionere m
captivity cattività f
captor prenditore m
capture cattura f; cat-
turare
car carro m; carretta f
caravan carovana f
carbon carbonio m
carbonize carbonizzare
card biglietto; m carta f;
cardare
cardinal cardinale m
care cura; sollecitudine
f; curare; stimare
career carriera f [dente
careful attentivo; pru-
carefulness accuratezza
careless negligente
carelessness trascuratezza
[zare
caress caressa f; accarez-
cargo carico m
caricature caricatura f
carnation carnagione f
carnival carnevale m
carol carola f; cantare
carousal orgia f
carpenter carpentiere m
carpet tappeto m; – bag
sacco m

33

carriage trasporto *m*; carrozza; vettura *f*;
carrier portatore *m*
carrot carota *f*
carry portare   [*m*
cart carretta *f*; camione
cartoon cartone *m*

carve indicere; tagliare
carver incisore *m*
carving scultura; trinciatura *f*
cascade cascata *f*
case cassa; scatola *f*
casement finestra *f*
cash denaro; contante *m*; cambiare; scontare
cash-box cassetta *f*
cashier cassiere *m*
cashmere cascimirra *f*
cask botte *f*; barile *m*
casket cassetta *f*
cast getto; tiro *m*; figura; forma *f*; – **iron** ghisa *f*
cast gettare; sbalzare; tirare; cambiare; fon--
castigate castigare [dere
castigation castigo *m*
casting fusione *f*
castle castello *m*
castor oil olio di ricino *m*
casual casuale
casualty casualità *f*
cat gatto *m*   [logare
catalogue catalogo; cata--
catastrophe catastrofe *f*
catch presa *f*; acchiappare; sorprendere
caterpillar bruco *m*
catgut minugia *f*
cathedral cattedrale *f*
catholic cattalico *m*
cattle bestiame *m*
cauliflower cavolfiore *m*
cause causa *f*; motivo *m*; causare
causeless senza causa

cautious cauto
cavalier cavaliere *m*
cavalry cavalleria *f*
cave caverna;

ceaseless incessante
cedar cedro *m*
cede cedere
ceiling soffito *m*
celebrate celebrare
celebrated celebre
celebration celebrazione
celebrity celebrità *f*
celerity celerità *f*
celery sedano *m*
celestial celeste
celibacy celibato *m*
cell cella; casella *f*
cellar cantina *f*
cellular cellulare
cement cemento *m*; cementare
cemetery cimitero *m*
censor censore *m*
censure censura *f*; cen--
census censo *m* [surare
central centrale
centrifugal centrifugo
century secolo *m*
ceremonial ceremoniale *m*
ceremony ceremonia *f*
certain certo; sicuro
certainty certezza; cosa certa *f*
certificate certificato *m*
certify certificare
cessation cessazione *f*
cession cessione *f*
chafe scaldare
chagrin stizza *f*
chain catena; trama *f*; incatenare
chair sedia *f*; seggio *m*; – **man** presidente *m*
chalk creta *f* [vocare
challenge sfida *f*; pro--
chamber camera *f*; gab--

inetto *m*;

champagne sciampagna *f*

champion campione *m*

chance azzardo *m*

chancellor cancelliere *n*

change cambiamento *m*;
variazione *f*; resto *m*;
cambiare; alterare

changeable cambiabile;
incostante

channel canale *m*

chaos caos *m*

chaotic caotico

chapel cappella *f*

chaplain cappellano *m*

chapter capitolo *m*

character carattere *m*;
parte *f*　　　　[tico

characteristic carateris-

characterize caratteriz-

charade sciarada *f* [zare

charcoal carbone di
legno *m*

charge peso; carico *m*;
carica *f*; prezzo; in-
carico *m*; caricare;
affidare; incaricare;
accusare; far pagare

charitable caritatevole

charity carità; elemosina *f*

charm incanto; fascino
m; incantare: invaghire

charter carta *f*; statuto *m*

chase caccia *f*; cacciare

chasm burone *m* fessura *f*

chaste casto

chastise castigare

chastisement castigo *m*

chastity castità *f*

cheap buon mercato

cheat baro; inganno *m*;
imbrogliare

check freno; scacco *m*;
frenare; controllare

checkmate scaccomatto

m; dare scaccomatto

cheek guancia; coscia *f*

cheer festino; applauso *m*

cheer incoraggiare; applaudire; rallegrarsi

cheerful allegro

cheerfulness allegrezza *f*

cheerless tristo

cheese formaggio *m*; −
monger formaggiaio *m*

chemical chimico

chemist chimico *m*

chemistry chimica *f*

cherry ciliegia *f*

chess scacchi *m pl*

chess-board scacchiere *m*

chess-man pedina *f*

chest cassa *f*; petto *m*;
− of drawers armadio *m*

chestnut castagna *f*;
marrone *m*

chew ciccare; masticare

chicken pollastra *f*

child ragazzo; bimbo *m*;
− hood infanzia; fan-
ciullezza *f*; − ish fan-
ciullesco; puerile; −less
senza figlioli; − like da
ragazzo; − ren ragazzi
m pl

chill freddo; ghiaccare

chilly freddoloso

chime cariglione *m*; scampanare

chimney camino *m*;
− sweeper spazzacamino

chin mento　　　　[*m*

china porcellana *f*

chirp cinguettio *m*

chisel cesello; scalpello
m; cesellare

chivalry cavalleria *f*

chloride clorite *m*

chloroform cloroformio *m*

chocolate cioccolata *f*

choice scelta; elezione *f*

choir coro *m*

choose scegliere; eleggere

chop costoletta *f*; spaccare

chord corda *f*

chorus coro *m*

Christ Cristo *m*

Christian cristiano *m*

Christianity cristianità *f*

Christmas Natale *m*

chronic cronico

chronicle cronaca *f*

chronology cronologia *f*

chrysanthemum crisan-

chubby paffuto [temo *m*

chuckle sogghignare

church chiesa *f*

churchyard cimitero *m*

churn zangola *f*; follare

cider sidro *m*

cigar sigaro *m*; —holder
fumasigari *m*

cinder cenere *f*

cipher cifra *f*; zero *m*

circle cerchio; circolo *m*

circuit circuito; giro *m*

circular circulare

circulate circolare

circulation circolazione *f*

circumcision circoncisi-
one *f*   [enza *f*

circumference circonfer-

circumstance circostan-
za *f*

circus circo *m*

citation citazione *f*

cite citare

citizen cittadino;

city città *f*

civic civico

civil civile; cortese

civilian borghese *m*

civility civilità; cortesia *f*

civilization civilizzazione*f*

civilize civilizzare

clack battolare

claim reclamo *m*; riven-
dicazione *f*; reclamare;
pretendere

clang clangore *m*

clank tintinnire

clap scoppio *m*; battere
le mani

class classe *f*; classate

classic(al) classico

classify classificare

clatter chiasso *m*; far
rimbombare

clause clausola *f*

claw artiglio *m*

clay argilla *f*

clean netto;   pulito;
nettare;   pulire

cleanliness pulitezza

cleanly pulitamente

cleanse purificare; pulire

clear chiaro;   limpido;
manifesto;   chiarire;
nettare;   dissodare

clearance disimpegno *m*;
quitanza *f*

clearing dissodamento *m*

cleave fendere

cleaver fenditoio *m*

cleft fessura *f*

clemency clemenza *f*

clement clemente

clergy clero *m*

clergyman ecclesiastico *m*

clerical clericale

clerk commesso *m*

clever abile; capace

cleverness abilità *f*

client cliente *m*

cliff balza *f*

climate clima *f*

climax cima *f*

climb arrampicare

clime clima *f*

clinch ribadire

cling attaccarsi

36

clip tosare; tondere
cloak mantello *m*
clock pendola *f*; orologio
m; -maker oriuolaio *m*
close chiuso; serrato,
pesante; chiudere
closet camerino; gabin-
etto *m*
clot grumo *m*; coagulare
cloth panno; tessuto *m*;
clothe vestire [drappo *m*
clothes abiti *m pl*
clothing abbigliamento *m*:
vestiti *m pl*
cloud nube *f*; nuvolo *m*
cloudy nuvoloso
clove garofano *m*
clover trifoglio *m*
clown mascalzone *m*
club circolo: casino *m*;
mazza *f*; fiore (carte) *m*;
contribuire
clump blocco; gruppo *m*
clumsy rozzo; malaccorto
cluster grappolo; capan-
nello *m*
clutch afferrare; artiglio *f*
coach carrozza *f*; ripe-
titore *m*;
coagulate coagulare [*f*
coagulation coagulazione
coal carbone *m*; -cellar
buca del carbone *f*
coalition coalizione *f*
coarse grossolano
coarseness ruvidezza *f*
coast costa *f*; costeggiare
coat veste *f*; abito *m*;
intonacare;
coax accaressare
cobweb ragnatelo *m*
cock gallo *m*; chiave *f*:
- fight combattimento
di galli; - sure certis-
simo
cocoa cacao *m*

cocoa-nut cocco *m*
cod merluzzo *m*
code codice *m*
coffin bara *f*; feretro *m*
cog dente *m*
cogitate meditare
cogitation escogitazione *f*
cognizance conoscenza *f*
cogwheel ruota dentata*f*
cohabit coabitare
coherent coerente
coil rotolo (corda) *m*;
spira *f*; ravvolgere
coin moneta *f*; denaro
m; coniare
coinage monetaggio *m*
coincide coincidere
coke coke *m*
cold freddo
collar collare; colletto *m*
collar-bone clavicola *f*
collate collazionare
collateral collaterale
colleague collega; socio *m*
collect raccogliere; riu-
nire; colletta *f* [colta *f*
collection collezione; rac-
collective collettivo
collector collezionista *m*[*f*
college collegio *m*; facoltà
colloquial di conversa-
zione
colon due punti *m pl*
colonist colono *m*
colonize colonizzare
colony colonia *f*
colossal colossale
colour colore; colorito
m; colorare; pingere
colt puledro *m*
column colonna *f*
comb pettine; favo *m*;
pettinare; cardare
combat combattimento
m; combattere *m*
combatant combattente

combination combinazione; coalizione *f*
combine unire
combustible combustibile
combustion combustione *f* [provenire
come venire; avvenire;
comedian comico *m*
comedy commedia *f*
comet cometa *f*
comfort conforto; benessere *m*; comodità *f*; confortare; racconsolare
comfortable confortevole
comforter consolatore *m*
comma virgola *f*
command comando *m*; comandare [*m*
commander comandante
commandment comandamento *m* [orare
commemorate commem-
commemoration commemorazione *f*
commence comiciare
commencement cominciamento *m*
commend commendare; raccomandare
commendable commendabile
commendation commendazione: lode *f*
commensurate commensurato [commentare
comment commento *m*;
commentary commentario *m*
commerce commercio *m*
commercial commerciale
commission commissione *f*; dar commissione; incaricare [sionario *m*
commissioner commisscommit commettere
committee comitato *m*
commodity comodità *f*

common comune; ordinario; terre comunali *f pl*; —ly comunemente; law giustizia *m*; comune;
– place luogo *m* comune;
– sense buon senso;
– wealth repubblica *f*
commotion commozione *f*
commune comune *m*; comerire
communicable comunicabile
communicate comunicare
communication comunicazione *f* [cativo
communicative comunicommunion comunione *f*
community comunità *f*
commutable commutabile
commute commutare
compact patto *m*
compact compatto; – ly compattamente
companion compagno; camerata *m*
company compagnia; società *f*
comparable comparabile
comparative comparativo
compare comparare
comparison comparazione *f* [mento *m*
compartment compartimento compass bussola *f*
compasses compasso *m*
compassion compassione *f*
compassionate compassionare
compel costringere
complainant querelante *m & f* [male *m*
complaint lagnanza *f*;
complaisant compiacente
complement complemento *m*

38

complete completo; completare; finire [m
completion compimento
complex complesso
complexion colorito m; complessione f
compliance compiacenza f
complicate complicare
complication complicazione f
compliment complimento m; complimentare
complimentary complimentoso
compose comporre; calcomposed calmo [mare
composer compositore m
composition composizione f [m
composure calma; posatezza f
compound composto m; comporre; combinare
comprehend comprendere
comprehension comprensione f [sivo
comprehensive comprencompress compressa f; comprimere
comprise comprendere
compromise compromesso m; compromettere
compulsion compulsione f
compulsory compulsivo
computation computo
compute computare
comrade camerata m
conceal nascondere
concede concedere
conceit vanità f; concetto m
conceive concepire
concentrate concentrare
conception concezione f; concetto m

concern affare; interesse m; inquietudine; casa f; concernere; riguardare; importare a
concerned interessato; inquieto
concert concerto m; concertare
concession concessione f
concise conciso
conclude conchiudere; terminarsi
conclusion conclusione f
conclusive conclusivo
concrete concreto m
concur concorrere
concussion concussione
condemn condannare
condemnation condanna f
condensation condensazione f
condense condensare
condescend condiscendere;
conduce condurre; contribuire
conducive conducevole
conduct condotta f; condurre; dirigere
conductor conduttore m
confectionery confettureria f [zione f
confederacy confederaconfederate confederato
confer conferire; donare
conference conferenza f
confess confessare
confession confessione
confessional confessionale
confessor confessore m [m
confide confidare
confidence confidenza f
confident certo; sicuro
confidential confidenziale
confine confine m; confinare; imprigionare

confinement confinamento *m*; detenzione *f*
confirm confermare
confirmation confermazione *f*
confiscate confiscare
conflagration incendio *m*; conflagrazione *f*
conflict conflitto *m*; lottare
conform conformare
conformable conforme
conformity conformità *f*
confound confondere
confront confrontare
confuse confondere
confusion confusione *f*
confute confutare
congeal congelare; gelare
congenial congeniale
congratulation congratulazione *f*
congregate congregare
congregation congregazione *f*
congress congresso *m*
conjecture congettura *f*; congetturare
conjugate congiugare
conjunction congiunzione *f*
connect connettere; riunire [clientela *f*
connection connessione ;
conquer conquistare; vincere [vincitore *m*
conqueror conquistatore;
conquest conquista *f*

conscience coscienza *f*
consecration consacrazione *f*
consecutive consecutivo
consent consenso; consentimento *m*; consentire [*f*

consequence conseguenza
consequential d'importanza
conservative conservativo
conservatory serra *f*
conserve conservare
consider considerare
considerable considerevole
considerate considerato
consideration considerazione *f*; motivo *m*
consign consegnare; affidare [*m*
consignee consegnatario
consignment consegna *f*
consist consistere
consistency consistenza *f*
consistent consistente
consolable consolabile
consolation consolazione *f*
console consolare
consolidate consolidare
consonant conforme; consonante *f*
conspicuous cospicuo
conspiracy cospirazione *f*
conspirator conspiratore
conspire cospirare [*m*
constancy costanza *f*
constant costante
constellation costellazione *f* [zione *f*
consternation costernazione
constipation stitichezza *f*
constituent costituente; elettore *m*
constitute costituire
constitution costituzione *f*
constrain costringere
constraint costringimento
construct costruire [*m*
construction costrutto *m* struttura *f*
consumption consumo *m*; consunzione *f* [tisico
consumptive consuntivo;
contact contatto *m*

40

contagion contagio *m*
contagious contagioso;
morboso
contain contenere
contaminate contaminare
contamination contam-
inazione *f*
contemn sprezzare
contemplate contemplare
contemplation contem-
plazione *f* [poraneo *m*
contemporary contem-
contempt sprezzo *m*
contemptible sprezzabile
contemptuous sprezzante

contiguous contiguo
continence continenza *f*
continent continente *m*
continental continentale
contingency contingenza *f*
contingent contingente *m*
continual continuo
continuance continuanza*f*
continuation continuazi-
one *f*
continue continuare; pro-
lungare; dimorare
continuity continuità *f*
contortion contorsione *f*
contour contorno *m*
contraband di contrab-
bando; contrabbando *m*
contract contratto *m*;
contrarre
contraction contrazione *f*
contractor contraente *m*
contradict contraddire
contradiction contraddi-
zione *f*
contrary contrario; op-
posito [contrastare
contrast contrasto *m*;
contribute contribuire
contribution contribuzi-
one *f*
contrite contrito

contrivance invenzione *f*
contrive inventare

control controllo *m*;
autorità *f*; controllare;
dirigere [arbitro *m*
controller controllore;
controversial di contro-
versia
controversy controversia*f*

convalescence convales-
cenza *f* [cente *m & f*
convalescent convales-
convene convocare [*f*
convenience convenienza
convenient conveniente;
comodo
convent convento *m*,
convention convenienza *f*
conventional convenzion-
converge convergere [ale
conversation conversa-
zione *f*
converse intrattenersi
conversion conversione *f*;
convertimento *m*
convert convertito *m*;
convertire
converter convertitore *m*

convey trasportare
convict condannato *m*;
condannare
conviction convinzione *f*
cook cuoco *m*; cucinare
cookery cucina *f*
cook-shop rosticceria *f*
cool fresco; freddo
rinfrescare
cope contendere
copious copioso
copper rame; cupro *m*;
caldaia *f* [*m*
coppice, copse bosco ceduo
copy copia *f*; esemplare
m; copiare; imitare;
—book quaderno *m*

41

copying-press copialettere *m*

copyist copiatore *m*

copyright proprietà letteraria *f*

coquet civettare

coquette civetta *f*

coquettish da civetta

coral corallo *m*

cord corda *f*; incordare

cordial cordiale; cordiale *m*

cordiality cordialità *f*

core torso *m*

cork sughero; turacciolo *m*; turare; – **screw** cavaturacciolo *m*

corn grano; callo *m*; – **flower** fioraliso *m*

cornelian cornalina *f*

corner cantone; angolo *m*

coronation incoronazione

coroner procuratore del re *m* [orale *m*

corporal corporale; cap-

corps corpo *m*

corpse cadavere *m*

corpulence corpulenza

corpulent corpulento

correct corretto; giusto; correggere

correction correzione *f*

correspond corrispondere; – **ence** corrispondenza *f*; – **ent** corrispondente *m* & *f*

corridor corridoio *m*

corroborate corroborare

corrode corrodere

corrosion corrosione *f*

corrupt corrotto; corrompere

corruption corruziore *f*

corset busto *m*; fascetta *f*

cosmetic cosmetico *m*

cosmopolitan cosmopolita *m* & *f* [costare

cost costo; prezzo *m*;

cosy ad agio [villico *m*

cottage casetta *f*; – r

cotton di cotone; cotone *m*; bambagia *f*

couch letto; canapè

cough tosse *f*; tossire

council consiglio *m*

councillor councellor consigliere *m*

counsel consiglio; avvocato *m*; consigliare

count, – ess conte *m*; contessa *f*

count contare; calcolare

countenance cera; faccia *f*; approvare

counter contra; banco *m*; – **act** contraporre; – **feit** contrafatto; contrafazione *f*; contraffare; – **mand** contrordine *m*; contromandare; – **part** controparte *f*; – **sign** controfirmare

countless innumerevole

country paese *m*; – **man** contadino; villico *m* [accoppiare

couple coppia *f*; paio *m*;

courage coraggio *m*

courageous coraggioso

course corsa *f*; corso *m*; correre; **of** – ben inteso

court corte *f*; tribunale *m*; —**martial** corte marziale *f*;

courteous cortese [enza *f*

courtesy cortesia; river-

cousin cugino *m*; cugina

cove baia *f* [contrattare

covenant contratto *m*;

cover coperta *f*; coperto *m*; coprire

covey covata *f*

cow vacca *f*; intimidire

42

coward(ly) codardo *m*
cowardice codardia *f*
cower tremare
cowl cappucio *m*
cowslip tasso barbasso *m*
coy schifiltoso
crab granchio di mare *m*
crack crepatura; spac-
 catura *f*; crepare;
 spaccare; fendere
crackle scoppiettare
cradle culla *f*; cullare
craft mestiere *m*; astuzia
crafty astuto
crag rupe; balza *f*
cram impinzare
cramp granchio *m*
cranberry mortella palus-
crane grù; grua *f* [tre *f*
crank manovella; leva *f*
cranny screpolatura *f*
crape crespo *m*
crash scroscio *m*; catastrofe *f*; scrosciare
crate gabbia *f*
crazy matto
creak scricchiolare
cream crema *f*
crease piega *f*; spiegazzare
create creare
creation creazione *f*
creator creatore *m*
creature creatura *f*
credence credenza *f* [*pl*
credentials credenziali *m*
credible credibile
credit credenza *f*; credito *m*; credere
creditable onorevole;
 digno di fede
creditor creditore *m*
credulous credulo
creed credenza *f*; credo *m*
creek seno *m*; cala *f*
creep tracinarsi; — er

piantra rampante *m*
crescent crescente; luna
 nuova *f*
crime delitto; reato *m*
criminal criminale; reo
 m; delinquente *m* & *f*
cringe abbassarsi
cripple storpio; zoppo
 m; storpiare
crisis crisi *f* [increspare
crisp croccante; friabile;
critic critico *m*
critical critico
criticise criticare
criticism criticismo *m*
croak gracchiare
crocodile coccodrillo *m*
crook pastorale; uncino *m*.
crooked tortuoso
crop messe; raccolta *f*;
 seminare; tosare
cross obliquo; contrario;
 croce *f*; incrociare;
 attraversare; — **bow**
 balestra *f*; – **examination**
 interpellazione *f*
crossing traversata *f*
crotchet ghiribizzo *m*
crow corvo *m*; cantare;
 vantarsi
crowd folla; ressa *f*
crown corona *f*; cima *f*;
 (in)coronare
crucial severo; rigoroso
crucible crogiuolo *m*
crucifix crocifisso *m*
crucifixion crocifissione *f*
crucify crocifiggere
crude crudo
cruel crudele
cruelty crudeltà *f*
cruise crociera *f*; incrociare
crumb mollica *f*
crumble sbriciolarsi
crumple spiegazzare

43

crusade crociata *f*

crush folla *f*; urtare
crust crosta *f*; incrostare
crutch gruccia *f*
cry grido; pianto *m*; gridare; piangere

cue stecca *f*; motivo *m*
cuff paramano; polsino *m*; schiaffeggiare
cuirass corazza *f*
cuirassier corazziere *m*
culinary culinario
cull cogliere
culminate culminare
culpable colpevole
culprit prevenuto *m*
cultivate coltivare
cultivation, culture coltivazione; cultura *f*
cumbersome pesante
cunning astuzia *f*; astuto
cup coppa; tazza *f*
cupboard credenza *f*; armadio *m*
cupidity cupidità *f*
cupping-glass ventosa *f*
cur mastino *m*
curable curabile
curacy cura *f*
curate curato; vicario *m*
curator curatore *m*
curb freno *m*; frenare
curd giuncata *f*
curdle quagliare
cure cura *f*; rimedio *m*; curare; guarire
curiosity curiosità *f*

currency corso *m*; circolazione *f*
current corrente
cursory superficiale; – ily rapidamente
curt corto
curtail restringere
curtain cortina *f*
curtsey riverenza *f*

curve curva *f*; curvare
cushion cuscino *m*
custard crema *f* [ione *f*
custody custodia; prigcustom** costume; uso *m*; – ary abituale; ordinario; –er cliente *m & f*; – -house dogana *f*
cut taglio *m*; ferita; stampa *f*; tagliare; fendere
cutlass scimitara *f*
cycle ciclo; biciclo *m*
cymbal cembalo *m*
cylinder cilindro *m*
cynic cinico *m*
czar(ina) czar(ina) *m & f*

D

dab colpetto *m*; percuoter leggiermente
dabble imbrattare
daffodil asfodillo *m*
dagger pugnale *m*
daily quotidiano; giornaliero; ogni giorno
daintiness delicatezza *f*
dainty delicato

dairy latteria *f*; – maid venditrice di latte *f*
daisy margherita *f*

dam diga *f*; arginare
damage danno; male *m* danneggiare |
dame dama; signora *f*
damn dannare; condannare

damnation dannazione *f*
damp umido; umidità *f*
dance danza *f*; ballo *m*; danzare [ballerina *f*
dancer ballerino *m*;
dandelion smirnio *m*
dandy elegante *m*

danger pericolo *m*
dangerous pericoloso
dangle dondolare
dare osare
daring audace
dark oscuro; tenebroso
darken oscurrare
darkness oscurità *f*
darling caro; diletto *m*
darn rammendare
dart dardo *m*; dardeggiare
data dati; questio
date data *f*; dattero *m*;
daughter figlia; figliola *f*;
– -in-law nuora *f*
dawn alba; aurora *f*;
spuntare
day giorno; di *m*
dazzle abbagliare
deacon diacono *m*
dead morto; inanimato;
– **letter office** officio
lettere rifiutate
deaden indurire
deadly mortale; funesto
deaf sordo
deafen assordare
deafness sordità *f*
deal abete *m*; quantità;
a great – molto
dealer negoziante *m*
dean decano *m*
dear caro; costoso
dearness carezza *f*; caro
m
dearth scarsezza *f*
death morte *f*; –-**bed**
letto di morte; – **like**
di morte

debit debito *m*; addebi
debtor debitore *m*
decamp levar il campo
decant decantare
decanter caraffa *f*

decapitate decapitare
decay decadenza ; de-
cadere   [*f*; morire
decease decesso *m*; morte
deceased defunto *m*
deceit inganno *m*
deceitful perfido
deceitfulness falsità
deceive ingannare
deceiver ingannatore *m*
decency decenza *f*
decent decente; modesto
deception inganno *m*;
illusione *f*
decide decidere
decision decisione *f*
decisive decisivo
deck ponte *m*; ornare
declaration dichiarazione
declare dichiarare   [*f*
decline declino *m*; decadenza *f*;   declinare
decompose decomporre
decorate decorare: ornare
decoration decorazione *f*;
ornamento *m*
decoy allettamento *m*;
allettare [*m*; diminuire
decrease decrescimento
decree decreto *m*; decretare
decrepit decrepito
dedicate dedicare
dedication dedica; consacrazione *f*
deduce, deduct dedurre
deduction deduzione *f*
deed fatto; atto *m*;
azione *f*; gesta *f pl*
deem stimare; pensare
deep profondo; alto;
deepen affondare [oscuro
deer daino *m*; daina *f*
default difetto *m*; defal-
care; – **er** contumace *m*
defeat sconfitta; rotta *f*;

sconfiggere
defect difetto *m*

defence difesa; fortificazione *f*
defend difendere
defendant difendente
defensive difensivo
defer deferire
deference deferenza *f*
defiance sfida *f*; sprezzo
deficiency deficienza *f*
deficient deficiente
deficit deficit *m*
define definire
definite definito
definition definizione

deformed deforme
deformity deformità
defraud defraudare

defy sfidare
degenerate degenerato; degenerare

degradation degradazione
degrade degradare   [*f*
degree grado; stato *m*
deity divinità ; deità
deliberate deliberato; deliberare
delicacy delicatezza *f*
delicate delicato
delicious delizioso
delight delizia *f*; dilettare
delightful delizioso; piacevole
delineate delineare
delinquency delinquenza *f*
delinquent delinquente *m*
delirious delirante   [& *f*
delirium delirio *m*   [are
deliver consegnare; liber-
deliverance, delivery liberazione; consegna *f*;
dell valletta *f*   [parto *m*
delude deludere   [dare
deluge diluvio *m*; inon-

delusion delusione *f*
delusive illusorio
demand domanda *f*;
reclamo *m*; domandare;
chiedere
democracy democrazia *f*
democratic democratico
demolish demolire
demolition demolizione *f*
demon demone; demonio
m   [diabolico
demoniac(al) demoniaco;
demonstrate dimostrare
demonstration dimostrazione *f*

den tana *f*; antro *m*
denial diniego; negamento *m*
denominate denominare
denote denotare
denounce denunciare
dense denso; fitto
density densità *f*
dentist dentista *m*
denunciation denunzia *f*
deny negare; rifiutare
depart partire; ritirarsi
department dipartimento
m
departure partenza *f*
depend dipendere
dependence, – cy dipendenza
dependent dipendente *m*
& *f*
depict dipingere
depilatory depilatorio *m*
deplorable deplorevole
deplore deplorare
deportment contegno *m*
depose deporre [positare
deposit deposito *m*; de-
deposition deposizione *f*
depraved depravato
depravity depravazione *f*
deprecate deprecare   [*f*
deprecation deprecazione

depreciate deprezzare [*f*
depredation depredazione
depredator depredatore
depress deprimere
depression depressione *f*
deprivation privazione *f*
deprive privare   [*f*
depth profondità; altezza
derange scompigliare
derangement sconcerto *m*
derelict abbandonato
derivation derivazione *f*
derive derivare
derogatory derogatorio
descend discendere
descendant discendente
m & f   [pendio *m*
descent scesa; origine *f*:
describe descrivere; dipingere   [genere *m*
description descrizione *f*;
desecrate profanare
desert deserto; merito
m; disertare
deserter disertore *m*
deserve meritare
design disegno; scopo *m*;
disegnare
designate designato
designation designazione *f*
designing intrigante
desirable desiderabile
desire desiderio *m*; desiderare
desk leggio *m*; cattedra *f*
desolate desolato; devastare
desolation desolazione *f*
despair disperazione *f*;
disperare
despatch dispaccio; invio
m; prontezza *f*; spedire
desperate disperato
desperation disperazione *f*
despicable sprezzabile

despise sdegnare
dessert frutta *f*
destination destinazione *f*
destine destinare
destiny destino; fato *m*
destitute destituto
destitution destituzione *f*
destroy distruggere
destruction distruzione *f*
desultory sconnesso
detach staccare; distaccare
detached isolato
detachment staccamento
detail dettaglio *m*; detta-
gliare
detain ditenere; ritardare
detect scoprire
detection scoperta *f* [*m*
detective agente segreto
deteriorate deteriorare
determinate, determinato
determination determinazione *f*   [risolvere
determine determinare;
detest detestare
detestable detestabile
dethrone detronizzare
detract detrarre
detraction detrazione *f*
detractor calunniatore *m*
detriment detrimento *m*
detrimental pregiudizie-
vole
deuce due; diavolo!
devastate devastare
develop sviluppare
development sviluppo *m*
deviate deviare [divisa *f*
device spediente *m*;
devil diavolo; demone *m*
devilish diabolico
devious sviato
devise inventare

dexterity destrezza *f*
diabetes diabete *f*

47

diabolical diabolico
diagonal diagonale *f*
diagram diagramma *m*
dial meridiana *f*
dialect dialetto; idioma *m*
dialogue dialogo *m*
diameter diametro *m*
diamond diamante; quadro (carte) *m*   [cata *f*
diaper biancheria damas-
diarrhœa diarrea *f*
diary diario; giornale *m*
dice dadi *m pl*   [tare
dictate dettame *m*; det-
dictation dettatura *f*
dictatorial dittatorio
diction dizione *f*
dictionary dizionario *m*
die dado; punzone *m*;
diet dieta *f*   [morire
differ differire
difference differenza
different differente
difficult difficile
difficulty difficoltà *f*
diffidence diffidenza, ti-
midità *f*
diffusion diffusione *f*
dig scavare
digest digerire
digestion digestione *f*
dignify esaltare; onorare
dignity dignità *f*
digress digredire
dilate dilatare
dilemma dilemma *m*
diligence diligenza *f*
dim oscuro; vago;
offuscare
dimension dimensione *f*
diminish diminuire
diminutive diminutivo
dimple fossetta *f*
din baccano *m*
dine pranzare
dining-room sala da pran-

zo *f*
dinner pranzo *m*
diocese diocesi *f*
direct diretto; dirigere
direction direzione *f*;
consiglio; indirizzo *m*
dirt fango *m*
dirty sporco; sporcare
disability incapacità *f*
disable invalidare   [*m*
disadvantage svantaggio
disadvantageous svantag-
gioso
disaffected disaffezionato
disagree discordare
disagreeable sgradevole[*m*
disagreement disaccordo
disallow disapprovare
disappear scomparire   [*f*
disappearance scomparsa
disappoint far mancare
disappointment disap-
punto *m*   [zione *f*
disapproval disapprova-
disaster disastro *m*
disastrous disastroso
disavow sconfessare
disband disperdere
disbelief incredulità *f*
disbelieve non credere
disburse sborsare
disc disco *m*
discard rigettare; scar-
tare
discernible discernibile
discernment discerni-
mento *m*
discharge scarico *m*;
suppurazione *f*; con-
gedo *m*; scaricare;
suppurare; pagare;
congedare
disciple discepolo *m*
discipline disciplina *f*
disclaim sconfessare
disclose rivelare
disclosure scoperta *f*

discolour scolorire
discomfit sconfiggere
discomfort disagio *m*
discompose turbare
disconcert sconcertare
disconsolate desolato
discontent malcontento *m*
discontented scontento
discontinue discontinuare
discount sconto *m*; scontare
discourage scoraggiare
discourse discorso *m*; discutere
discover scoprire
discovery scoperta *f*
discredit scredito *m*; non
discreet discreto [credere
discrepancy discrepanza *f*
discretion discrezione *f*
discriminate distinguere
discuss discutere
discussion discussione *f*
disdain sdegno *m*; sdegnare
disease malattia *f*; male *m*
diseased ammalato
disembark sbarcare
disfigure sfigurare
disgrace disgrazia; onta *f*; svergognare
disgraceful disonorevole
disguise travestimento *m*; camuffare [gustare
disgust disgusto *m*; disdish piatto *m*; piatti *m pl*; servire
dishonest disonesto
dishonesty disonestà *f*
dishonourable disonorevole [*f*
disinherit diserdare
disinterested disinteres-
disjoin disunire [sato
dislike avversione *f*
dislocate dislogare

disloyal sleale; perfido
dismal lugubre
dismay spavento *m*; spaventare
dismiss licenziare
dismissal licenziamento; congedo *m*
disobedience disobbedienza *f*
disobedient disobbediente
disobey disobbedire
disoblige disobbligare
disorder disordine; male *m*
disorderly in disordine
disorganize disorganiz-
disown ripudiare [zare
disparage screditare
disparity disparità *f*
dispassionate spassionato
dispel dissipare
dispensary dispensario *m*
dispensation dispensa *f*
dispense dispensare
disperse disperdere
disposal disposizione *f*
dispose disporre; vendere
disposition disposizione *f*
dispossess spossessare
disproportionate sproporzionato
disputant disputante *m*
dispute disputa *f*; disputare [incapacità *f*
disqualification inabilità;
disqualify rendere incapace; disabilitare
disregard noncuranza *f*; sprezzare
disreputable screditabile
disrespectful irriverente
dissatisfaction scontento
dissect dissecare [*m*
dissection dissezione *f*
dissemble dissimulare

49

disseminate disseminare
dissension dissensione f
dissent dissenso m; dis-
  sentire [f
dissertation dissertazione
dissimilar dissimile
dissipate dissipare
dissipated dissipato
dissolute dissoluto
distort storcere
distortion storsione f
distract distrarre
disracted distratto
distrain sequestrare
distress stretta f; affliggere
distribute distribuire

district distretto m
distrust diffidenza f;
  sospetto m
disturb disturbare
disturbance disturbo m;
  agitazione f

dive immergersi
diver palombaro m
diverge divergere
diverse diverso
diversity diversificare
diversion diversione f;
  divertimento m
divert sviare; divertire
divide dividere; disunire
dividend dividendo m
divine divino; prete m;
  indovinare

divinity divintà f

division divisione; vota-
  zione f

divorce divorzio m;
  divorziare
divulge divolgare
dizziness vertigine f
dizzy vertiginoso
do fare ; effettuare
docile docile
dock bacino; banco m;

dauco m

doctor dottore; medico m
doctrine dottrina f
document documento m
dodge rigiro m; rigirare
dog cane m
dogged ostinato
dogma domma m
doll bambola; fantoccia f
dollar dollaro m
dome duomo m; cupola f
domestic domestico m;
  domestica f [care
domesticate addomesti-
dominant dominante
dominate dominare
dominion dominio
donation donazione f
donkey asino; asinello m
donor donatore m
doom destino m
door porta f
dose pressa; dose f;
  dosare [giare
dot punto m; punteg-
dotage rimbambimento m
double doppio m; dop-
  piare
doubt dubbio m; dubitare
doubtful dubbio; incerto
doubtless indubitabile
dough pasta f
dove colomba f
dowager vedova f
dower dote f
down giù; in basso; a
  terra; piumino m;
  duna f; – cast abbas-
  sato; – fall caduta f;
  – ward, – wards giù; in
  giù; a basso [nechiare
doze sonnetto m; son-
dozen dozzina f
drachm dramma f
draft tratta f; disegnare
drag tramaglio m; tirare
dragon, dragoon dragone

50

drain canale; fossa *f*; prosciugare [*m*

drainage prosciugamento

drake anitra *m*

draw tirare; trascinare; disegnare; infondere; cavare; — **back** svantaggio *m*; — **ee** trattario *m*;

drawing-room salotto *m*

drawl strascicare (parole)

dread timore *m*; temere

dreadful terribile

dress abito; costume *m*; veste *f*; vestire; abbigliare; guarnire;

drift tendenza *f*; mucchio *m*; galleggiare

drill trivella *f*; esercizio *m*; forare; esercitare

drink beveraggio *m*; bere

drip gocciolare

dripping sugo dell'arrosto

drive scarrozzata *f*; spingere; cacciare

driver cocchiere; conduttore *m*

drizzle pioviggina *f*

droll comico

droop languire

drop goccia; scesa *f*; lasciar cadere; cessare

drought siccità; sete *f*

drover mandriano *m*

drown annegare; innondare

drowning annegamento *m*

drowsy sonnolente

drudgery lavoro faticoso *m*

drug droga *f*

druggist droghiere *m*

drum tamburo *m*

drummer tamburino *m*

drunk(en) ubbriaco; ebbro

drunkenness ebbrezza *f*

dry secco; seccare; —

goods merceria *f*; — **nurse** aia *f*

dubious dubioso

duchess duchessa *f*

duck anitra *f*; immergere

duel duello *m*

duet duetto *m*

duke duca *m*

dull tupido; pesante; scuro; stupidire; offuscare; stancare

dullness stupidità; oscurità *f*

duly debitamente

dumb muto; — **found** rendere muto; — **ness** mutezza *f*

dungeon prigione (sotterranea) *f*

duplicate duplicato; duplicare

duplicity duplicità *f*

durable durevole

duration durata *f*

during durante

dusk crepuscolo *m*

dust polvere *m*; spolverare; —**er** strofinaccio *m*; — **hole** mondezzaio *m*; — **man** spazzino *m*; — **y** polveroso

dutiful obbediente

duty dovere; servizio;

dwell dimorare; abitare; — **ing** abitazione *f*

dwindle diminuire

dye tingere; tinta *f*

dyer tintore *m*

dying morente; spento

dynamite dinamite *f*

E

each ciascuno; ognuno; — **other** l'un l'altro

eager ardente; vivo;

51

– ly ardentemente; **– ness** ardore *m*

eagle aquila *f*; **–t** aquilino *m*

ear orecchio *m*; spica *f*:

early primaticcio; precoce; matiniero; per tempo; di buon ora

earn guadagnare; meritare

earnest serio; premuroso; sincero; caparra *f*

earnestness serietà; premura; sincerità

earth terra; argilla *f*; **– en** di terra cotta; **– enware** terraglia *f*; **– ly** terrestre; **– quake** terremoto *m*

earwig forfecchia *f*

ease facilità *f*; sollevare

easel cavalletto *m*

easiness facilità *f*

east d'est; orientale; est; oriente *m*; **– erly** all'est; dell'est

Easter Pasqua *f*

easy facile; agevole

easily facilemente

eat manigare

eatable commestibile

eatables commestibili *m*

eccentric eccentrico [*m*

ecclesiastic ecclesiastico

echo eco *m*; echeggiare

eclipse ecclisse *f*

economical economico

economist economista *m* & *f*

economize economizzare

economy, economics eco-

ecstacy estasi *f* [nomia *f*

eddy vortice ; *m*

edge taglio; filo; orlo *m*; affilare; orlare

edible mangiabile

edict editto *m*

edification edificazione *f*

edifice edificio *m*

edit compilare

edition edizione *f* [*m*

editor editore; redattore

educate educare

education educazione *f*

eel anguilla *f*

efface cancellare

effect effetto *m*; effet-

effective effettivo [tuare

effects effetti; beni *m pl*

effectual efficace

effeminate effemminato

efficient efficiente

effort sforzo; tentativo *m*

effrontery sfrontatezza *f*

egg ovo *m*; **– -cup** ovaiolo *m*; **– shell** guscio d'uovo

egoism, egotism egoismo; egotismo *m*

egotist egoista *m* & *f*

eight otto *m*

eighteen diciotto *m*

eighteenth diciotesimo; decimottavo *m*

eighth ottavo *m*

eighty ottanta *m*

either l'uno o l'altro; qualunque; ciascuno

ejaculation giaculazione *f*

eject gettare (fuori); spossessare; espellere

elastic elastico *m*

elasticity elasticità *f*

elate esaltare

elation esaltazione *f*

elbow gomito *m*

elder maggiore; seniore; sambuco *m*

elderly attempato

eldest primogenito

elect eletto; eleggere

election elezione *f*

elector elettore *m*

electrical elettrico
electrician elettricista *m*
electricity elettricità *f*
electrify elettrizzare
electrotype elettrotipia *f*
elegance eleganza *f*
elegant elegante
elegy elegia *f*
element elemento; – **ary** elementare
elephant elefante *m*
elevate elevare
elevation elevazione *f*
elevator elevatore *m*
eleven undici *m*
eleventh undecimo *m*
elicit elicere
eligible eleggibile
eliminate eliminare
elope fuggire con un' amante
eloquence eloquenza
eloquent eloquente
else altro; altrimenti
elsewhere altrove
elucidate dilucidare
emancipate emancipare
embalm imbalsamare
embankment arginamento *m*
embargo embargo *m*
embark imbarcare
embarrass imbarazzare
embarrassment imbarazzo *m*
embassy ambasciata *f*
embellish abellire
embers ceneri *f pl*
embezzle appropriarsi
embroidery ricamo *m*
embroil imbrogliare; confondere
emerald smeraldo *m*
emerge emergere
emergency emergenza *f*
emetic emetico *m*

emigrant emigrante *m & f*
emigrate emigrare
emigration emigrazione *f*
eminence eminenza; cele- brità *f* [bre
eminent eminente; cele-
emissary emissario *m*
emission emissone *f*
emit emettere
emollient emolliente
emotion, emozione *f* [*m*
emperor imperatore *m*
emphasis enfasi *f*
emphatic enfatico
empire impero *m*
employ impiegare
employee impiegato *m*
employer padrone *m*
employment impiego *m*
empress imperatrice *f*
empty vuoto; vuotare
emulate emulare
enable metter in grado
enact decretare [tare
enamel smalto *m*; smal-
enclose inchiudere
enclosure chiusa; cinta *f*
encompass circondare
encore bis! bissare
encounter incontro *m*; incontrare
encourage incoraggiare
encouragement incoraggiamento *m*
encyclopaedia enciclopedia *f*
end fine; estremita *f*; finire; terminare
endanger metter in pericolo [tentare
endeavour sforzo *m*;
endless senza fine; eterno
endorse girare
endorsement girata *f*
endow dotare; donare

endowment dote *f*; dono
endurable sopportabile [*m*
endurance tolleranza *f*
endure tollerare
enemy nemico *m*
energetic energico
energy energia *f*
engage ingaggiare; impegnare; prendere a servizio
engagement impegno ; invito; combattimento
engender generare [*m*
engine macchine; locomotiva *f*
engineer ingegnere *m*
engrave intagliare
engraver incisore *m*
engraving intaglio *m*
engross ingrossare
enhance far risaltare
enigma ennima *f*
enigmatical enimmatico
enjoin commandare
enjoy godere
enlarge allargare
enlargement ingrandimento *m*
enough abbastanza;
enrage esasperare [basta
enrich arrichire
ensign bandiera *f*; portabandiera *m*; — **bearer** porta bandiera *m*
enslave far schiavo
ensue seguire [sostituire
entail bene sostituto;
entangle intralciare
enter entrare; inscrivere
enterprize impresa. *f*
enterprising intraprendente [tire
entertain trattenere; ver-
entertainment trattemimento; divertimento *m*
enthusiasm entusiasmo *m*
enthusiast entusiasta *m*

enthusiastic entusiatico
entice sedurre; indurre
entire intiero
entitle intitolare
entrance entrata *f*
entreat supplicare
entry entrata *f*; registratura *f*
enumerate enumerare
enunciate enunciare
envelope busta *f*
enviable invidiabile
envious invidioso
envoy inviato *m*
envy invidia *f*; invidiare
epicure epicureo *m*
epidemic epidemico; epidemia *f*
epilepsy epilessia *f*
episcopal episcopale
episode episodio *m*
epitaph epitaffo *m*
epoch epoca; era *f*
equal eguale; eguagliare
equality egualità *f*
equalize egualizzare
equanimity equanimità *f*
equator equatore *m*
equilibrium equilibrio *m*
equinox equinozio *m*
equip equipaggiare
equipment equipaggio *m*
equitable equo
equity equità *f*
equivalent equivalente *m*
equivocate equivocare
era era; epoca *f*
eradicate sradicare; estir-
erase raschiare [pare
erasure raschitura *f*
erect diritto; erigere
erection erezione *f*
ermine ermellino *m*
err errare; ingannarsi
errand messagio *m*
erratic errante; erratico

54

erroneous erroneo
error errore; sbaglio *m*
eruption eruzione *f*
escape fuga *f*; sfuggire
escort scorta *f*; scortare
essay saggio *m*; tentare
essence essenza *f*
essential essenziale
establish stabilire
establishment stabili-
  mento *f*
estate stato *m*; terra;
  fortuna *f*
esteem stima *f*; stimare
estimate stima *f*; stimare
estrange alienare
estuary estuario *m*
eternal eterno
eternity eternità *f*
ether etere *m*
ethereal etereo
ethical etico
ethics etica *f*
evacuate evacuare
evade evitare; eludere
evaporate svaporare
evasion evasione *f*; sot-
  terfuggio *m*
evasive evasivo
even eguale; pari;
  giusto; anche; persino
evening sera *f*
event evento; caso *m*
eventual eventuale
ever sempre
evergreen sempre verdi *m*
everlasting eterno
every ogni; ognuno;
  tutti i; tutte le
eviction evizione *f*
evidence evidenza; tes-
  timonianza *f*
evident evidente
evil cattivo; male
exalt elevare
examination esame; in

terrogatorio *m*; in
  spezione *f* [pezionare
examine esaminare; is
example esempio *m*
exasperate esasperare
excavate scavare
excavation escavazione
exceed eccedere
exceedingly eccessiva-
excel eccellere [mente
excellence — cy eccel-
  lenza *f*
excellent eccellente
except eccetto; fuorchè;
  eccettuare [eccetto *m*
exception eccezione *f*;
exceptional eccezionale
excess eccesso *m*
excessive eccessivo
exchange cambio; aggio
  m; borsa *f*; cambiare;
  permutare
excite eccitare
excitement eccitamento *m*
exclaim esclamare [*f*
exclamation esclamazione
exclude escludere
exclusive esclusivo
excommunicate scom-
  municare
excruciating crucciante
excursion escursione *f*

excuse scusa *f*; scusare
execute eseguire
execution esecuzione *f*
executioner giustiziere *m*
executive potestà esecu-
  tiva *f*
executor esecutore *m*
exemplify esemplificare
exempt esentare
exercise esercizio; dovere
  m; esercitare
exert impiegare
exertion sforzo *m*

exhale esalare
exhaust esaurire [m,
exhaustion esaurimento
exhibit mostrare; − er mostratore
exhibition esposizione f
exhilarate esilarare
exhilaration esilaramento m
exhort esortare
exile esilio; esule m; esiliare.
exist esistere; essere
existence esistenza f
exit esito m; uscita f
exonerate esonerare
exorbitant esorbitante
expand espandere
expanse estensione f
expansion espanzione f
expect aspettare; attendere; − ancy aspettativa
expectation aspettazione; speranza; pretesa f
expectorate espettorare
expediency espediente m
expedient spediente m
expedite spedire
expedition spedizione f
expel espellere
expend spendere
expenditure spesa f
expense spesa f
expensive dispendioso; costoso   [provare
experience esperienza f;
experiment prova f; sperimentare
expert esperto
expiration termine m
expire spirare; morire
explain explicare
explanation explicazione f
explanatory spiegativo
explicit esplicito
explode esplodere
exploit gesta f
exploration esplorazione f

explore esplorare
explosion esplosione f
explosive esplosivo
export esportare
exportation esportazione f
export duty dazio d'uscita
expostulate rimostrare [f
expostulation rimostranza
exposure esposizione f
expound esplicare
express espresso m; esprimere
expression espressione f
expressive espressivo
extension estensione f
extensive estensivo
extent estensione f
extenuate estenuare [f
extenuation estenuazione
exterior esteriore m
exterminate estirpare [m
extermination sterminio
external esterno
extinct estinto
extinction estinzione f
extinguish estinguere
extinguisher spegnitoio m
extraordinary straordinario
extravagance stravaganza f
extravagant stravagante
extreme estremo m
extremity estremità f
exultation esultazione f
eye occhio m; cruna (d'ago) f; guardare; osservare; −−ball pupilla f; −brow ciglio m; − -lash ciglio m; − -lid palpebra f; − sight vista f; − -witness testimonio oculare m

56

F

fable favola *f*; – d favoloso

fabric fabbrica *f*; edificio *m*; tessuto *m*

fabricate fabbricare

fabrication fabbricazione; costruzione *f*

fabulous favoloso

face faccia *f*; volto *m*; faccetta *f*; affrontare

facilitate facilitare

facility facilità *f*

fact fatto; atto *m*; in – infatti

faction fazione *f*

factor fattore; agente *m*

factory fabbrica; manifattura *f*

faculty facoltà *f*; talento *m*

fade languire

fail mancare

failure mancanza *f*; fallimento *m*

faint svenuto; svenire

fair bello; biondo;

fairly bene   [fiera *f*

fairy fata *f*

faith fede; credenza *f*

faithful fedele

fall caduta *f*; cadere; diminuire; – **asleep** addormentarse; – **back** indietreggiarsi; – **in love** innamorarsi;

falsehood menzogna *f*

falsification falsificazione *f*

falsify falsificare

falter esitare

fame fama *f*; –d famoso

familiar familiare; intimo

familiarity familiarità *f*

familiarise familiarizzare

family famiglia; spezie *f*

famine fame *f*

famish affamare

famous famoso   [tilare

fan ventaglio *m*; ventanatic(al)** fanatico *m*

fanciful capriccioso

fancy fantasia; idea *f*; immaginare

fang dente *m*

fantastical fantastico

far lontano; distante; – **fetched** ricercato

farce farsa *f*

farm masseria *f*; coltivare

farmer affitaiuolo *m*

farming coltivazione *f*

fashion moda; voga *f*

fashionable alla moda

fast fermo; rapido; dissoluto; subito; digiuno

fasten attaccare   [*m*

fastidious fastidioso

fat grasso *m*

fatal fatale

fatality fatalità *f*

fate fato *m*

fated fatato

father padre *m*; – -**in-law** suocero *m*; – **land** patria *f*; – **less** orfano; . – **ly** paterno

fathom braccio *m*; penetrare; – **less** senza fondo

fatigue fatica *f*; affaticare

fatness grassezza *f*   [care

fatten ingrassare

fault fallo; errore *m*; pecca *f*; – **less** senza colpa; – **y** imperfetto

favour favore *m*; – **able** favorevole   [favorita *f*

favourite favorito *m*;

fear timore *m*; temere;

– ful timido; terribile;
– fully terribilmente;
– less senza paura
feasible fattibile
feast festa *f*; festeggiare
feat fatto; atto *m*
feather penna; piuma
feature lineamento *f*
federal federale
federation federazione *f*
fee emolumento
feeble debole
feed cibo *m*; cibare
feel tasto; – er antenna *f*
feeling sensazione; sensibilità *f*
feeling sensibile; vivo
feline felino
fell pelle *f*; abbattere
fellow socio; compagno; simile *m* [associazione
fellowship compagnia;
felon fellone *m*
felony fellonia *f*
felt feltro *m* [f
female femminile; donna
feminine femminile
fence palificata; cinta; *f*: palificare; cingere
fender parafuoco *m*
fern felce *f*
ferocious feroce
ferry batello *m*; – man tragittatore *m*
fertile fertile
fertility fertilità *f*
fertilize fertilizzare
fervent, fervid fervido
fester corrompere
festival festa *f*
festive festivo; gaio
festivity festività *f*
feud guerra intestina *f*
feudal feudale
fever febbre *f*
feverish febbroso

flow corrente *f*; colare
flower fiore *m*; florire; – -girl floraia *f*; – y fiorito
fluctuate fluttuare
fluctuation fluttuazione *f*
flue gola di camino *f*
fluent fluente
fluid fluido *m* [agitare
flurry trambusto *m*;
flush rossore *m*; arrossire [agitare
fluster agitazione *f*;
flute flauto *m*; – d scanalato [giare
flutter battito *m*; aleg-
fly mosca *f*; volare; fuggire
foal puledro *m*; figliare
foam schiuma *f*; spumare
foaming spumante
fob borsellino *m*
focus foco *m*
fodder foraggio *m*
foe nemico *m*
fog nebbia *f*
foggy nebbioso
foil fioretto *m*; frustrare
fold piega *f*
foliage fogliame *m*
folk gente
follow seguire
follower seguace *m*
folly follia *f*
food cibo; vitto *m*
fool(ish) stupido *m*
fool gabbare
foot piede *m*; zampa *f*;
for perchè; perocchè; per; quanto a; come
forage foraggio *m*
forbearance pazienza *f*
forbid proibire; interdire
force forza *f*
forcible energico; forte
ford guado *m*; guadare
fore anteriore; antece-

58

dente; prima; – **arm**
cubito; – **bode** presagire; – **fathers** antenati
m pl; – **finger** indice *m*;

field campo *m*
fiend demonio *m*
fierce feroce; ardente
fiery di fuoco; ardente
fife piffero *m*
fifteen quindici *m*
fifteenth quindicesimo *m*
fifth quinto *m*
fiftieth quinquagesimo;
cinquantesimo
fifty cinquanta *m*
fig fico [combattere
fight combattimento *m*;
figurative figurativo
figure figura *f*; forma *f*;
figurare
filbert nocciola; avellana
filch birbanteggiare
file fila; lima *f*; filare;
filial filiale [limare
filigree filigrano *m*
film membrana *f*; velo *m*
filter filtro *m*; filtrare
filth fango *m*
find trovare
fine bello; fine
fine ammenda *f*; multare
finery ornamento *m*
finger dito *m*
finish finitezza *f*; finire
finite limitato
fire fuoco; incendio *m*;
incendiare; – **-arms**
armi da fuoco *m pl*;
– **brick** mattone ritroso;
– **-brigade** corpo dei
pompieri; – **damp** fuoco
di mina; – **-engine**
pompa per incendio *f*;
– **-escape** apparecchio
di salvataggio *f*; –**grate**
grata del camino; – **man**

pompiere *m*; – **-proof**
a prova di fuoco; –
works fuoco artificiale *m*
firm fermo; stabile
firmament firmamento *m*
first primo; principio;
– **born** primogenito; –
-rate eccelente
fish pesce *f*; pescare
–**bone** resta *f*; – **erman**
pescatore *m*;
fist pugno *m*
fit atto; idoneo; degno
di; accesso; parossismo
m; adattare; aggiustare; assettare
five cinque *m*
fix dilemma *m*; fissare;
– **ture** rattenuta
flabby floscio
flag bandiera *f*;

flake fiocco *m* [me giare
flame fuoco *m* fiam-
flank fianco *m*; fiancare
flannel flanella *f*
flap lembo *m*; falda *f*;
battere leggermente
flare fiamma *f* brillare
flash sprazza di luce *m*;
far splendere
flask fiasca; boccetta *f*
flat piatto; piano; stup-
flatten appianare [ido *m*
flatter adulare; – **er**
adulatore *m*; – **y** adulazione *f*
flavour sapore; gusto *m*;
far gustoso
flaw difetto *m*
flea pulce *m*
flee fuggire
fleece vello *m*
fleet rapido; flotta *f*
flesh carne *f*
flexible flessibile
flicker tremolare

flight volo *m*; – **y** leggiero
flinch tergiversare
fling lanciare
flirt civetta *f*; civettare
flock fiocco *m*; affollare
flood diluvio *m*; inondare
floor piano; palco *m*
florid florido
florist florista *m*
flounder impantanarsi;
flour farina *f* [dimenarsi
flourish fanfara *f*; fiorire;
  prosperare

four quattro *m*
fourteen quattordici *m*
fourteenth quattordicesi-
  mo; decimoquarto
fourth quarto *m*
fox volpe *f*; – **-glove**
  digitale *f*; – **y** volpino;
  astuto
fraction frazione *f*
fracture frattura *f*; rom-
fragile fragile   [pere
fragment frammento *m*
fragrant fragrante
frail frale; debole
frailty fralezza *f*
frame forma; armatura;
  struttura; inteleiatura
  f; corpo *m*; formare;
  disporre; corniciare
franchise franchigia *f*
frank franco; affrancare
fraternity fraternità *f*

free libero; franco;
  gratuito; liberare
freedom libertà
freemason frammassone
freeze gelare   [*m*
freight nolo; carico *m*
frenzy frenesia *f*
frequent frequente; numeroso; frequentare
fresh fresco; recente;
  – **en** rinfrescare; – **ness**

60

  frescura; – **water** acqua
fret rodere   [dolce
fretful afflitto
friar monaco *m*
friction frizione *f*
friend amico *m*; amica *f*
friendship amicizia *f*
fright paura *f*; – **en**
  spaventare; – **ful** spav-
frigid frigido   [entevole
fringe frangia *f*; bordo *m*
frisk saltellare
frivolity frivolezza *f*
frivolous frivolo
frock vestina; veste *f*
frog rana; granocchia *f*
frolic scherzo *m*; – **some**
  scherzoso   [sino da
from da; con; per;
foreign(er) straniero *m*
forest foresta *f*; bosco *m*
forfeit confisca *f*
forge ferriera *f*; fucinare
  f
forgery contraffazione *f*
forget obliare; – **ful** immemore; – **fulness** di-
  menticanza *f*; – **me-not**
  miosotide *f*
forgive perdonare
forgiveness perdono *m*
fork forchetta *f*; biforcarsi; – **ed** forcuto
forlorn abbandonato
form forma; guisa *f*;
  banco *m*; formare
formal formale
formality formalità *f*
former primo; prece-
  dente; – **ly** altre volte
  già; prima
formidable formidabile
formula formola *f*
fornication fornicazione
fort forte *m*
forth avanti; **and so** –

e così di seguito; -
coming a presso ad ap-
parire; - with subito
fortieth quarantesimo *m*
fortification fortificazione
fortify fortificare   [*f*
fortnight quindicina *f*;
- ly quindicinale
fortunate fortunato
fortune fortuna *f*
forty quaranta *m*
forward avanzato; pre-
suntuoso; avanti; spe-
fossil fossile *m*   [dire
foster nutrire; - -brother
fratello di latte *m*;
- -father balio *m*; -
-mother balia *f*
foul sporco; impuro;
found fondare [sporcare
foundation base *f*; fon-
damento *m*
founder fondatore *m*
frost gelo *m*; - bitten
a gelato; - y glaciale
froth spuma; schiuma *f*;
spumare; - y spumante
froward perverso
frown cipiglio *m*
frozen gelato
frugal frugale
frugality frugalità *f*
fruit frutto *m*;
fruitless sterile
frustrate frustrare
fry frittura *f*; friggere
fudge sciocchezza!
fuel combustibile *m*
fugitive fuggitivo *m*
fugue fuga *f*
fulfil adempire
fulfilment realizzazione *f*
full pieno; intero
fuller follone *m*
fume fumo *m*; fumare
fumigate far suffumigi

fumigation suffumigio *m*
fun scherzo *m*
function funzione *f* [*m*
fund fondo *m*
fundamental fondamen-
funeral funerale *m* [tale
fungus fungo *m*
funnel imbuto *m*
funny comico
fur pelliccia *f*
furious furioso
furl serrare
furnace fornace *f*
furnish fornire; mobiliare
furniture mobilia *f*
fury furia *f*
futile futile
futility futilità; inanità
future futuro   [*m*
futurity futuro; avvenire

G

gabardine gabbano *m*
gabble ciaramellare
gag sbarra *f*; imbavag-
gage pegno *m*   [liare
gaff rampone *m*
gaiety gaiezza *f*
gaily gaiamente
gain guagagno *m*; guad-
agnare; lucrare; otten-
gainsay contraddire [ere
gait andatura *f*
gaiter ghetta *f*
gala gala *f*
galaxy costellazione
gale tempesta *f*
gall noce di galla; bile
f; irritare
gallant galante
gallantry eroismo *m*;
galanteria *f*
gallery galleria *f*
galleon gallion *m*
galley galera *f*

61

gallic francise
gallon hallone *m* [litr.
 1.54) [pare
gallop galoppo *m*; galop-
gallows patibolo *m*
galosh galoscia *f*
galvanize galvanizzare
gamble giuocare
gambler giuocatore *m*
gang banda *f*
gangway passavanti *m*
gap breccia; apertura *f*
gape sbadigliare
garb vestito; abito *m*
garbage rifiuto *m*
garble troncare; alterare
garden giardino *m*; -er
 giardiniere *m*; - ing
 giardinaggio *m*
gargle gargarismo *m*;
 gargarizzare
garland ghirlanda *f*
garlic aglio *m*
garment abito; vestito *m*
garmer ammassare
garnet granato *m*
garnish guarnire
garret soffitta *f*
garrison guarnigione *f*
gas gas *m*; - burner-lamp
 becco di gas; - light
 illuminazione a gas;
gash ferita larga *f*;
 sfregiare
gasp anelito *m*; anelare
gate porta *f*; portone *m*
gather raccogliere; ac-
 cumularsi; - er racco-
 glitore *m*; - ing riunione *f*; ascesso *m*
gaudy ostentato
gaunt magro
gauze garza *f*
gay vivace   [templare
gaze sguardo *m*; con-
gear ingranaggio; ap-

parecchio *m*
gelatine gelatina *f*
gem gemma ; gioia *f*
gender genere *m*
general generale *m*
generalize generalizzare
generate generare
generation generazione
 f
generic generico
generosity generosità *f*
generous generoso
genial geniale
genius genio *m*
gentle gentile; grazioso;
 - man gentiluomo *m*; -
 - ness gentilezza
genuine genuino
geography geografia *f*
geology geologia *f*
geometry geometria *f*
geranium geranio *m*
germ germe *m*
gesture gesto *m*
get ottenere; acquistare;
 - away andarsene; -
 - off togliere; - over
 sormontare; - the better
 of vincere; - up levarsi
ghastly orrido
ghost spettro *m*
giant gigante *m*
gift dono *m*
gifted dotato
gigantic gigantesco
gills branchie *f pl*
gin gin *m*; trappola *f*
ginger zenzero *m*; -
 bread pan pepato *m*
girl ragazza; fanciulla *f*
girlish di ragazza
girth giro *m*
give dare; donare; - in,
 - up, - way cedere
glacial glaciale
glad felice; - den ralle-

grare; allietare; − **ness**
gaiezza *f*; − **some** gaio
glade radura *f*; viale *m*
glance piglio *m*
gland glandula *f*
glare luce smagliante *f*;
guardo feroce *m*
glass vetro; specchio *m*;
− **blower** soffiatore; −
house vetreria; − **shade**
globe di vetro; − **works**
vetrerie

glaze inverniciare
glazier vetraio *m*
gleam scintilla *f*; scintillare   [olatore *m*
glean spigolare; −**er** spig-
glee gioia *f*
glen gola; valle *f*
glide scorrere

glimpse occhiata *f*
glisten, glitter brillare;
lustro *m*
gloat guardar fisso
globe globo *m*
gloom oscurità
gloomy oscuro; tristo
glorify glorificare
glorious glorioso
glory gloria; fama *f*
gloss lustro *m*; lustrare
glossary glossario *m*
glove guanto *m*; − **r**
guantaio *m*
glow calore; ardere;
− **ing** ardente; − **-worm**
lucciola *f*
glue colla *f*; incollare
glutton ghiotto *m*; − **ous**
goloso; − **y** ghiotteria
f
go andare; partire;
− **abroad** andar all'estero; − **after** seguire;
− **ahead** inoltrarsi; −
mediatore *m*; − **by** passar

davanti; − **forth** uscire;
− **forward** avanzare; −
in entrare; − **off** andar-
sena; esplodere; − **on**
continuare; − **out** andar
fuori; − **over** attraversare; verificare; − **up**
salire; − **with** accom-
pagnare; − **without** far
senza
goal termine *f*
goat capro *m*
God Dio; Iddio *m*;
− **child** figlioccio *m*;
− **dess** dea *f*; − **father**
padrino; − **like** divino;
− **liness** pietà *f*; − **ly**
pio; devoto; − **mother**
matrina *f*
gold d'oro; oro *m*;
gonorrhœa gonorrea *f*
good buono; bene; −
bye! addio *m*; − **Friday**
Venerdì santo *m*; − **ly**
bello; − **-natured** di
buon cuore; − **ness**
bontà *f*; − **s** merci *f pl*;
beni *m pl*
goose oca *f*
gorgeous magnifico
gory insanguinato
gospel vangelo *m*
gossip comare *f*; ciarlare
govern governare; − **able**
governabile; − **ness** governante *f*; − **ment** amministrazione *f*; − **or**
governatore *m*
gown veste; toga *f*
grace grazia *f*; favore *m*;
− **ful** grazioso;
gracious grazioso; clemente; − **ly** graziosa-
mente
grade grado *m*

gradual graduale
graduate laureato m;
graduation graduazione f
graft innestare [venare
grain grano m; vena f;
grammar grammatica f
granary granaio m
grand grande; grandioso;
 – child nipotino m; –
 eur grandezza f; –
 father nonno; avo m;
 – mother nonna; ava; f
granite granito m
grant concessione f; dare
granulated granato
grape uva f
grass erba f
grasshopper grillo m
grassy erboso
grate grata; graticola f
 grattugiare
grateful riconoscente
grater grattugia f
gratify gratificare
gravity gravità f
gravy sugo (di carne) m
gray grigio
graze pascere pascolare
grease grasso m ungere
greasy grasso
great grande; –coat soprabito m; – ness grand-
 ezza f
greediness avidità f
greedy avido
green verde; fresco;
 verdume m; – gage
 regina claudia f; –
 grocer fruttivendolo m;
 – horn sbarbatello m;
 – house serra f; – ish
 verdognolo; – s legumi
 m pl; – sward erbuccia
greet salutare; – ing
 saluto m
gridiron graticola f

grief dolore m
grievance querela f
grieve affliggere
grievous gravoso
grill arrostire sulla grati-
grim torvo; feroce; [cola
grimace smorfia f
grin sogghigno
grind macinare; stone
 macina f
grip presa f; stringere
groan gemito m; gemere
grocer droghiere m
grocery drogherie f pl
groin inguine; angolo m
groom palafreniere m
groove scanalatura f;
 scanalare
grope brancolare
gross grosso; grossa f
grotesque grottesco
ground terreno; fondo
 m; stabilire; toccare;
grove boschetto m
grovel strisciar per terra
grow crescere; coltivare
growl grugnito m; grug-
 nire [aumento m
growth crescimento
grudge rancore m
gruff rauco
grumble brontolare
grunt grugnito m
guarantee garanzia f;
 garantire
guard guardia f; con-
 duttore m; guardare
guardian guardiano m
guess congettura f;
 indovinare
guest convitato m
guidance condotta f
guide guida f; condut-
 tore m; guidare; – book
 guida f
guild corporazione f

guile astuzia *f*
guilt delitto *m*
guiltless innocente
guilty colpevole
guitar chitarra *f*

gull gabbiano *m*; gabbare
gulp sorso *m*; ingozzare
gum gomma *f*; ingommare
gun fucile; cannone *m*; − -boat cannoniera *f*; − cotton cotone fulminante;

gurgle gorgoglio *m*
gush sgorgo *m*; sgorgare
gusset borsellino *m*
gust colpo di vento *m*
gusty burrascoso [trare
gut intestino *m*; sventguttapercha guttaperca *f*
gutter gronda *f*; scolare

H

haberdasher merciaio *m*
haberdashery merceria *f*
habit uso; abito *m*
habitable abitabile
habitation abitazione *f*
haggard macilente
haggle stiracchiare
hail grandine; gragnola *f*; grandinare; salutare
hair capello *m*; pelo *m*; − brained scervellato; − -brush spazzola per capelli *f*; − -dresser barbiere *m*; − -dye tintura per capelli *f*; − less senza capelli; − -pin forcella *f*; − -wash lavatura cosmetica *f*; − y peloso
halcyon di alcione; calmo

hale robusto; sano
half metà *f*; mezzo *m*
halfpenny soldo *m*

hall entrata; sala *f*
hallow consacrare
hallucination illusione *f*
halo aureola *f*
halt zoppo; sosta; alto *m*; fare alto
halter capestro *m*
ham garetto *m*
hamlet casale *m*
hammer martello *m*
hammock amaca *f* [pare
hamper corba *f*; incephand mano *f*; ago; operaio *m*; − barrow barella *f*; − bill annuncio *m*; − book manuale *m*; − cuffs manette *f pl*; − ful manata *f*; − icraft mestiere *m*; − kerchief fazzoletto *m*; − − le manico *m*; maneggiare; − maid serva *f*
handsome bello
ᵗndwriting scrittura *f*

handy destro
hang sospendere
hank matassa *f*

happen avvenire
happiness felicità *f*
happy felice; beato

harass affaticare

harbour porto; rifugio *m*; albergare
hard duro; difficile; − en indurire; − -hearted inumano; − iness arditezza *f*; − ly duramente; − ness durezza *f*; − of hearing duro d'orecchi; − ship privazione *f*; − ware chincaglieria *f*; − y robusto

65

hare lepre *m & f*
harm male *m*; far male;
– **ful** dannoso; – **less**
innocuo
harmonize armonizzare
harmony armonia *f*
harness finimenti *m pl*;
harp arpa *f*
harrow erpicare; erpice
m   [cordante
harsh aspro; duro; dis-
harshness asprezza *f*
harvest messe *f*; raccolto
hassock cuscino *m*
haste fretta *f*
hasten accelerare
hasty frettoloso
hat cappello *m*; – -**box**
cappelliera *f*; – -**rack**
cappellinaio *m*;
hatch covare; nascere
hatchet accetta *f* [(ucelli)
hate odio *m*; detestare;
– **ful** odioso
hatred odio *m*
haunt soggiorno *m*; baz-
zicare; visitare
have avere; tenere
haven porto *m*; rada *f*
havoc guasto *m*
hawk falco; sparviere *m*
hawker merciaiolo *m*
hawser ansiera *f*
hawthorn biancospino *m*
hay fieno *m*
haystack maragnuola *f*
hazard azzardo
hazardous azzardoso
haze nebbia *f*
hazel nocciola *f*; di
hazy nebbioso [nocciola
he egli; lui; quegli;
colui
head testa *f*; capo *m*;
– **ache** mal di testa *m*;
health salute; sanità *f*

healthy sano   [amassare
heap mucchio *m*;
hear sentire; intendere;
ascoltare; – **er** uditore
m; – **ing** udito *m*; – **ken**
ascoltare; –**say** inteso-
dire
hearse carro funebre *m*
heart cuore; centro *m*
hearth focolare *m*
heartily cordialmente
heartless senza cuore;
hearty cordiale [vigliacco
heat calore *m*; scaldare
heater scaldatore *m*
heath erica; brughiera *f*
heathen pagano *m*
heather erica *f*
heave elevare   [*m*
heaven cielo; firmamento
heavenly celeste
heavy grave; pesante
heckle diliscare
hectic etico; tisico
hedge siepe *f*; assiepare
hedgehog spinoso *m*
heed cura; guardia *f*;
heir, heiress erede *m & f*
heirloom mobile; inalien-
hell inferno *m* [abile *m*
helm timone *m*
helmet elmo; casco *m*
help aiuto *m*; assistere;
– **ful** utile; – **less** senza
soccorso; – **lessness** abbandono *m*;
hem orlo *m*; orlare
hemisphere emisfero *m*
hemorrhage emorragia *f*
hemp canapa *f*
hen gallina *f*
hence quindi; di quà
henceforth ormai
henpecked governato dalla moglie   [suoi; sue
her la; lei; suo; sua;

66

herb erba *f*

herd gregge *m*; mandria *f*
here quà; qui; di quà;
– **about(s)** di quà; quà
vicino; – **after** d'ora
innanzi; vita futura *f*;
by con questo mezzo;
cosi; – **in** in ciò; in
codesto ; – **of** di codesto;
– **on** su codesto ; su ciò ;
– **tofore** finora ; un
hereditary ereditario
heresy eresia *f*
heritage eredità *f*
hermit eremita *m*
hero eroe *m* ; – **ic** eroico ;
– **ically** eroicamente ; –
ine eroina *f*; – **ism**
eroismo *m*
herring aringua *f*
hers suo; sua; d'essa;
il di lei; la di lei
herself essa; se stessa; si
hesitate esitare
hesitation esitazione *f*
heterogeneous eterogeneo
hew tagliare
hibernate invernare
hide cuoio *m*; pelle *f*;
nascondere; celare
hideous orrendo
high alto; elevato; –
land paese montagnoso;
– **lander** montanaro; –
ly grandemente; – **ness**
hind cerva *f*; villico *m*
hinder impedire
hinge cardine *m*
hint avviso *m*; insinuare
hip anca *f*
hire nolo *m*; pigione *f*
his suo; sua; suoi; sue
hiss sibilo *m*; zittire
historian, historical stori-
history storia *f*   [co *m*

hit colpo *m*; botta *f*;
colpire; battere
hitch intoppo *m*; attaccare
hither quà; di quà
hive arnia *f*
hoar bianco; canuto
hoard gruzzolo *m*; cumu-
[lare
hold presa; stiva *f*;
contenere;   arrestare
holder possessore *m*
holdfast rampone *m*
hole buco *m*; apertura *f*
holiday festa; vacanza *f*
holiness santità *f*
hollow cavo; scavare
holly agrifoglio *m*
holster fonda da pistola *f*
holy santo; benedetto
homage omaggio *m*
home dimora; casa;
patria *f*; – **less** sezza
dimora; – **liness** sem-
plicità *f*; – **ly** semplice;
– **sickness** nostalgia *f*;
– **wards** verso casa
homicide omicida *m & f*
honest onesto
honesty onestà; probità *f*
honey miele *m*; – **moon**
luna di miele *f*; – **suckle**
caprifoglio *m*
honorary onorario
honour onore *m*; onorare
honourable onorevole
hood cuffia *f*; cappucio *m*
hoof unghia *f*
hook gancio *m*; uncinare
hop salterello; luppolo
m; saltare
hope speranza *f*; sperare;
– **ful** pieno di speranza;
– **less** senza speranza
horizon orizzonte *m*
horizontal orizzontale

horn corno *m*
hornet calabrone *m*
horrible orribile; orrendo
horror orrore *m*
horse cavallo *m*; caval-
leria *f*; on − -back, a
cavallo; —dealer mar-
cante di cavalli *m*; − -fly
tafano *m*; − -hair crine
(di cavallo) *m*; − manship
equitazione *f*; − -power
forza d'un cavallo *f*;
horticulture orticoltura *f*
horticulturist orticoltore
hose calza *f*; tubo *m*
hosiery calzatura *f*
hospitable ospitale   [*m*
hospital ospedale; ospizio
hospitality ospitalità *f*
host ospite; oste *m*
hostage ostaggio *m*
hostess ostessa *f*
hotel albergo *m*; osteria *f*
hound bracco *m*
hour ora *f*; − glass
oriuolo a sabbia
hourly di ora in ora
house casa; dimora *f*;
alloggiare; − breaker
ladro per frattura;
− hold casalingo; casa *f*;
m; − keeper, − wife
massaia *f*; − less senza
casa; − maid serva di
casa *f*
how come; quanto;
− ever pero; pure;
− much quanto
howl grido; urlo *m*;
gridare; urlare
hug abbracciare
huge enorme
hull baccello; scafo *m*
hum ronzio *m*; mor-
human umano [morare
humane umano
humanity umanità *f*

humble umile; umiliare
humbug ciarlatano *m*
humidity umidità *f*
humiliate umiliare
humility umiltà *f*
humming-bird colibri *m*
humorous umoristico
humour umore

hundred cento; centina
f; − fold centupio; − th
centesimo *m*; − weight
mezzo quintale *m*
hunger fame *f*; aver fame
hungry affamato
hunt caccia *f*; cacciare
hunter, huntsman caccia-
tore *m*
hurdle cannicio *m*;
− race corsa delli siea
f *pl*
hurl lanciare
hurricane uragano *m*
hurry fretta; precipita-
zione *f*; affrettare
hurt male; danno *m*;
− ful dannoso
husband marito; sposo
m; risparmiare;

hutch madia *f*

hyacinth giacinto *m*
hydraulic idraulico
hydrogen idrogeno *m*
hydrophobia idrofobia *f*
hyena iena *f*
hygiene igiene *f*
hymen imene *m*
hymn inno *m*
hyperbole iperbole *f*
hyphen lineetta d'unione
f
hypnotism ipnotismo *m*
hypocrisy ipocrisia *f*
hypocrite, hypocritical
ipocritico *m*
hypothesis ipotesi *f*

68

I

I io
iambic iambico
ice ghiaccio *m*; ghiacciare; – cream sorbetto
icicle ghiacciuolo *m*
icy glaciale
idea idea *f*; – l ideale
identical identico
identify identificare
idiom idioma *m*
idle(r) ozioso *m*; – ness pigrizia *f*
idol idolo *m*;
if se
ignite accendere
ignorance ignoranza *f*
ignoramus ignorante *m*
ignorant ignorante
ignore ignorare
ill indisposto; cattivo;
illegal illegale [male
illegible illeggibile
illegitimate illegittimo

illiterate illetterato
illness malattia *f*
illogical illogico
illuminate illuminare
illusion illusione *f*
illusive, illusory illusorio
illustrate illustrare
illustration illustrazione *f*
illustrious illustre
image immagine *f*
imaginable immaginabile
imaginary immaginario
imagination immaginazione *f*
imagine immaginare
imbecile imbecille *m*
imitate imitare

imitation imitazione *f*
immaculate immacolato
immaterial immateriale
immature immaturo
immediate immediato
immemorial immemorabile
immense immenso [bile
immerge, immerse immergere [*m & f*
immigrant immigrante
immigrate immigrare
imminent imminente
immobility immobilità *f*
immoderate smoderato
immodest immodesto
immolate immolare
immoral immorale
immortal immortale
immortality immortalità *f*
immoveable immobile
immunity immunità *f*
immure murare
imp folletto *m*
impair deteriorare
impale impalare
impart impartire
impartial imparziale
impassable impassabile
impassioned appassionato
impassive impassibile
impatience impazienza *f*
impatient impaziente
impeach denunciare
impeachment imputazione *f*
impede impedire [*m*
impediment impedimento
impel impellere
impend essere sospeso
impersonate rappresentare [enza *f*
impertinence impertinimpervious impervio
impetuosity impetuosità *f*
impetuous impetuoso
implacable implacabile

implant impiantare
implement arnese *m*
implicate implicare
implicit implicito
implore implorare
imply implicare
impolite inurbano
import importare
importance importanza *f*
important importante [*f*
imposition imposizione;
 impostura *f* [*f*
impossibility impossibilità
impossible impossibile

impostor impostore *m*
impotent impotente
impoverish impoverire
impracticable impratica-
 bile [*f*
impregnable imprendibile
impregnate impregnare
impress impronta *f* im-
 prontare
impression impressione *f*
impressive espressivo
imprint imprimere
improbable improbabile
improper sconvenevole

improve migliorare
improvement migliora-
 mento; progresso *m*
imprudence imprudenza *f*
imprudent imprudente
impudence impudenza *f*
impudent impudente
impulse impulso *m*
impunity impunità *f*
impure impuro
in in; tra, fra; per; su;
inability inabilità *f*
inaccessible inaccessibile
inaccuracy inesattezza *f*
inaccurate inesatto
inactive inattivo
inadequate inadequato
inadmissible inammissi-

70

bile
inadvertent inavvertente
inalienable inalienabile
inanimate inanimato
inanity inanità; vanità *f*
inapplicable inapplicabile
inappropriate disadatto
inattentive disattento
inaudible inaudibile
inaugurate inaugurare
inborn innato

incandescent incandes-
 cente [*m*
incantation incantesimo
incapable incapace
inch pollice *m*
incident incidente *m*
incise incidere
incision incision *f*
incite incitare
incivility inciviltà *f*
inclemency inclemenza *f*
inclination inclinazione
incline pendenza *f*; in-
 clinare [prendere
include inchiudere; com-
inclusive inclusivo
incoherent incoerente
income rendita
incomparable incompar-
 abile [bile
incompatible incompati-
incompetent incapace
incomplete incompleto
incomprehensible incom-
 prensibile [bile
inconceivable inconcepi-
inconclusive inconclu-
 dente
incongruous ncongruo
inconsistent inconsistente
inconsolable inconsolabile
inconstant incostante
incontestable incontesta-
 bile
incontinent incontinente

inconvenience inconvenienza
inconvenient incomodo
incorporate incorporare
incorporation incorporazione
incorrect scorretto
incorrigible incorreggibile
increase aumento *m*; accrescere
incredible incredibile
incredulity incredulità
increment incremento *m*
incrust incrostare
inculcate inculcare
incumbent incombente; benefiziario *m*
incur contrarre
incurable incurabile
indebted indebitato; obbligato
indecisive inconcludente
indeed in verità

indefinite indefinito
indelible indelebile
indelicate indelicato
indemnify indennizzare
indemnity indenni ità *f*
indent intaccare: indentatura
independence indipendenza
independent indipendente
index indice *m*; lista *f*

indicate indicare
indication indicazione *f*
indict accusare
indifference indifferenza *f*
indigenous indigeno
indigent povero
indigestion indigestione *f*
indignant indignato [*f*
indignation indignazione
indignity indegnità *f*

indisposition indisposi-

71

zione *f*
individual individuale; individuo *m*

indomitable indomabile
indubitable indubitabile
induce indurre
inducement ragione *f*; motivo *m*
indulge concedere
indulgence indulgenza *f*
industrial industriale
industrious industrioso
industry lavoro *m*; industria *f*

ineffectual inutile

ineligible ineleggibile
inequality inegualità *f*
inert inerte; pigro
inertia inerzia *f*

inevitable inevitabile

inexcusable inescusabile
inexhaustible inesauribile
inexorable inesorabile
inexperienced, inexpert inesperto
inexplicable inesplicabile
inexpressible inesprimibile

infancy infanzia *f* [*m*
infant bambino; infante
infantry fanteria *f*

infatuate infatuare
infect infettare
infectious contagioso

infer inferire
inferior inferiore *m*
inferiority inferiorità *f*
infernal infernale
infest infestare

infidel infedele *m*
infinite infinito
infirm infermo
infirmary infermeria *f*

inflame infiammare
inflammation infiamma-
  zione f
inflate gonfiare; enflare
inflation gonfiamento m
inflexible inflessibile
inflict infliggere [influire
influence influenza f;
influential influente
inform informare
informal senza ceerimoni
informant informatore m
information avviso m
infringe infrangere
infuriate render furioso
infuse infondere
infusion infusione; in-
  troduzione f
ingenious ingegnoso
ingenuity ingegnosità f
inhale inspirare
inherent inerente; innato
inherit ereditare
inheritance eredità f
inhuman inumano
inimical ostile
inimitable inimitabile
iniquitous iniquo
initial primo; iniziale m
initiate iniziare
initiation iniziazione f
inject iniettare
injection iniezione f
injunction ingiunzione f
injure ingiuriare
injury ingiuria f
injustice ingiustizia f
ink inchiostro m
inland interno; interiore
inlet entrata f
inmate convivente m & f
inn albergo m;
innate innato
inner interiore; interno
innocence innocenza f
innocent innocente
innovation innovazione f

innumerable innumere-
  vole
inopportune inopportuno
inquest inchiesta f
inquire chiedere
inquisitive curioso
insane insano
insanity demenza f
inscribe nscrivere
insect insetto m
insecure non sicuro
insecurity mancanza di
  sicurezza f; pericolo m
insert inserire
inside del didentro
insight conoscenza in
  tima f   [cante
insignificant insignifi-
insincere poco sincero
insinuate insinuare
insist insistere; esigere
insolence insolenza f
insolent insolente
insoluble insolubile
insolvency fallimento m
insolvent insolvibile
  fallito
inspect esaminare
inspection ispezione f
inspector ispettore m
inspire ispirare
install installare   [m
installation installamento
instalment pagamento a
  termine   [esempio m
instance istanza f
instant istante; urgente
instantaneous istantaneo
istantly all'istante ;
  subito
instead invece; in luogo
instep collo del piede m
instigate instigare; inci-
instil istillare   [tare
instinct istinto m
instinctive istintivo
institute istituire

72

institution istituo *m*
instruct istruire
instruction istruzione *f*
instructive istruttivo
instrument instrumento
insufferable insopportabile

insurance assicurazione *f*
insure assicurare
insurer assicuratore *m*
insurgent insorto *m*
insurmountable insuperabile

integrity probità *f*
intellect intelletto *m*
intelligence intelligenza
intelligent intelligente
intelligible intelligibile
intemperate intemperante
intend intendere
intense intenso
intensity intensità *f*
intent intento *m*; — ion
intenzione *f*; — ional
intenzionale
inter seppellire; interrare
intercede intercedere
intercept intercettare
intercession intercessione
interchange cambiare [*f*
intercourse relazione *f*
interdict interdire
interest interesse *m*; interessare
interfere intervenire
interim interim *m*
interior interiore *m*
interlace intrecciare
interloper intruso *m*
interlude intermezzo *m*
interment sepoltura *f*
international internazionale

interpret interpretare
interpreter interprete *m*

interrogate interrogare
interrupt interrompere
interruption interruzione
interval intervallo *m*
intervene intervenire
interview abboccamento
m; intervistare
intestine intestino *m*
intimacy intimità *f*
intimate intimo *m*; intimare
intimidate intimorire
into in; ne ; tra
intolerable intollerabile
intolerant intollerante
intone intonare; cantare
intoxicate ubbriacare

intrepid intrepido
intricate intricato
intrigue intrigo *m*
intrinsic intrinseco
introduce introdurre [*f*
introduction introduzione
introductory introduttivo
intrude intrudersi
intruder intruso *m*
intrust affidare
intuition intuizione *f*
inundate inondare
invade invadere
invader invasore *m*
invalid invalido; infermo;
invalido *m*
invalidate invalidare
invaluable inestimabile
invasion invasione *f*
invent inventare; — ion
invenzione *f*; — ive inventivo; — or inventore
m; — ory inventario *m*
inverse inverso
invert invertire
invest investire
investigate investigare
investiture investitura *f*
investment investimento

invigorate rinvigorire
invincible invincibile
inviolable inviolabile
inviolate inviolato
invisible invisibile
invitation invito *m*
invite invitare
invocation invocazione *f*
invoice fattura *f*; fattur-
invoke invocare   [are
involuntary involontario
involve involgere; compromettere;   implicare
invulnerable invulnera-
inward interno   [bile
inwards all'indentro
iodine iodio *m*
iron ferreo; ferro *m*;
  stirare; –**ical** ironico;
irony ironia *f*
irradiate irradiare
irrational irrazionale
irreconcilable irreconcili-
  abile   [abile
irrecoverable irrecuper-
irredeemable irredimi-
irregular irregolare [bile
irregularity irregolarità *f*
irresolute irresoluto
irrespective indipendente
irresponsible irresponsa-
  bile
irretrievable irreparabile
irreverent irreverente
irrevocable irrevocabile
irrigate irrigare
irrigation irrigazione *f*
irritable irritabile
irritate irritare
irruption irruzione *f*
isinglass colla di pesce *f*
island, isle isola *f*
islander isolano *m*
isolate isolare
isolated isolato; solitario
isolation isolamento *m*
issue uscita;   distribu-

zione; prole *f*; risultato
m; uscire; distribuire;
emettere
isthmus istmo *m*
it il, lo, la; egli; esso
italics corsivo *m*
itch rogna *f*; prurito *m*;
prudere
item articolo *m*; nota *f*
itinerary itinerario *m*
its suo, sua suoi, sue
itself sè; sè stesso
ivory avorio *m*
ivy edera *f*

J

jabber ciarlare;
jack girarrosto; cavastivali; cricco *m*; – **al**
sciacallo *m*; – **ass** som-
aro *m*; – **daw** cornacchia; taccola *f*; – **et**
giacchetta; camiciola *f*
jade rozza cavallaccio;
affaticarsi
jail prigione *f*
jam conserva; serrare
jar giara; vibrazione
vibrare
jaundice itterizia *f*
jaw mascella *f*
jay ghiandaia *f*
jealous geloso
jealousy gelosia *f*
jeer beffare
jelly gelatina *f*
jeopardy rischio *m*
jerk scossa *f*
jessamine gelsomino *m*
Jesus Gesù *m*   [pillare
jet getto; gè *m*; zam-
jewel gioiello *m*; gemma
f; – **ler** gioielliere *m*;

- lery gioielleria *f*
job bisogna *f*
jockey fantino *m*
jocose giocoso
join unire
joint giuntura; articolazione *f*; arrosto *m*; congiunto; in comune
joke scherzo *m*; burlare
jolly allegro; gaio
jolt trabalzamento *m*
jostle spingere
journal giornale *m*
journalism giornalismo *m*
journalist giornalista *m* & *f*
journey viaggio *m*; viaggiare; esser in viaggio
journeyman giornaliere *m*
joust giostra *f*
joy gioia *f*; – ful, – ous gioioso; – less tristo
judge giudice *m*; giudicare
judgment giudizio; decretò *m*
judicial giudiziale
judicious giudizioso
jug brocca; mezzina *f*
juggler giocoliere *m*
juice succo (frutti); sugo (carne) *m*
juicy soccoso; sugoso
jumble guazzabuglio *m*
jump salto *m*; saltare
junction unione *f*
junior juniore *m*
juniper ginepro *m*
just giusto; equo; ap-
justice giustizia *f* [punto
justifiable giustificabile
justification giustificazione *f*
justify giustificare
justness giustizia *f*

jut aggettare
juvenile giovanile

K

kangaroo canguro *m*
keel chiglia; carena *f*
keen aguzzo; penetrante; acuto; vivo
keenness acutezza *f*
keep tenere, mantenere; – back ritenere: – er guardiano; – ing guardia *f*; – -off respingere;
key chiave *f*; –board tastiera *f*; – hole bucco della serratura *m*; –
kick calcio *m*
kid capretto *m*; – gloves guanti bianchi *m pl*
kidnap rapire
kidney rognone *m*
kill uccidere; ammazzare
kiln fornace *f*
kin(dred) parentela ; famiglia *f*; consanguineo
kind benevolo ; buono ; bene ; genere *m*
kindle accendere ; ecci-
kindness bontà [tare
king re *m*; – dom regno *m*; – ly reale ; da re
kinsman parente *m*
kiss bacio *m*; baciare
kitchen cucina *f*; –
kite poiana *f*; cervovolante *m*
kitten gattino *m*
knack destrezza ; arte *f*
knapsack zaino *m*
knead impastare
knee ginocchio *m*
kneel inginocchiarsi
knicknack crepunde *f pl*

knife coltello *m*;
knight cavaliere *m*
knighthood cavalierato *m*
knit far maglie; riunirsi
knob bernoccolo *m*;
 maniglia *f* [urtare
knock colpo *m*; bussare;
knot nodo; gruppo *m*;
 annodare
knotty nodoso; difficile
know sapere; conoscere
knowing intelligente
knowledge conoscenza;
 sapienza *f* [under cedere
knuckle falange *f*; −

L

label etichetta *f*; cartello
labial labiale *f* [*m*
laboratory laboratorio *m*
laborious laborioso
labour laborare; lavoro
lace gallone; passamano
 m; stringa *f*; stringare
lacerate lacerare
lack bisogno *m*; mancare
lackey lacchè *m*
laconic laconico
lacquer lacca *f* [*m*
lad giovanetto; ragazzo
lady signora; dama *f*;
 − like di signora; − ship
 signoria *f* [mente
lag camminare lenta-
laggard tentennone *m*
lair tana *f*; covo *m*
lake lago *m*
lamb agnello *m*; figliare
lame zoppo; storpiare
lameness zoppicamento *m*
lament lamento *m*;
 lamentare
lamp lampada; lucerna
 f; − -post lampada *f*;
 − shade ventola *f*; para-

lume *m*
land terra *f*; regione
 f; sbarcare; − au lando
 m; − ed fondiario;
 − -holder proprietario di
 fondi *m*; − ing-place
 approdo *m*; − lady pro-
 prietaria *f*; − -lord proprietario *m*; − -lubber
 marinaio d'acqua dolce;
 − mark caposaldo *m*;
 − scape paesaggio *m*;
 − slip frana *f*; − -tax
 imposta fondiaria
lane sentiero *m*
language lingua *f*
languid languido; fiacco;
 − ly languidamente
languish languire
languor languore *m*
lank magro; sparuto
lantern lanterna *f*
lap grembo *m*; falda *f*;
 lambire
lappel rovescio *m*
lapse lasso; errore *m*;
larceny latrocinio *m*
lard lardo *m*
large largo; grosso
lark allodola; burla *f*
larynx laringe *f*
last ultimo; scorso;
 forma *f*; durare
lasting permanente
latch saliscendo *m*; alla-
 ciare
late tardo; recente
lately ultimamente
latent latente
lateral laterale
lather saponata *f*; insap
 onare
latin latino
latitude latitudine *f*
latter ultimo
laugh riso; ridere;
 -able ridevole; −ing

76

ridente; **-ing stock** risata; **-ter** risata *f*

launch scialuppa *f* lanciare

laundress lavandaia *f*

laundry lavanderia *f*

laurel lauro *m*

lava lava *f*

lavatory lavatoio *m*

lavender lavanda *f*

lavish prodigo; prodigare

law legge *f*; decreto *m*

lawful legale

lawn erbaio *m*; rensa *f*

lawsuit lite *f*; processo *m*

lawyer avvocato *m*

lax molle; fiacco

laxative lassativo *m*

lay laico; porre; mettere

layman laico *m*

laziness pigrizia

lazy pigro

lead piombo *m*; **-pencil** matita *f*

lead condurre; guidarre

leaden di piombo

leader capo; conduttore;

leak apertura; falla *f*; trapelare; **- age** trapelamento *m*; infiltrazione

lean magro; scarno; appoggiare; inclinare

leanness magrezza *f*

leap salto *m*; saltare; **- frog** cavallo da canciullo; **- -year** anno bisestile *m*

learn imparare; studiare

learned instruito; erudito

learning erudizione

lease contratto d'affitto; appigionare

leash guinzaglio *m*

least minimo; più piccolo; meno; **at -** almeno

leather cuoio *m*; pelle *f*

leathern di cuoio

leave permissione *f*; congedo *m*; lasciare; abbandonare

left sinistro; sinistra *f*

leg gamba *f*

legacy legato *m*

legal legale; **- ity** legalità *f* **- ize** legalizzare

legate legato *m*

legatee legatario *m*

legend leggenda *f*

legendary legendario

legibility leggibilità *f*

legible leggibile

legion legione *f*

legislation legislazione *f*

legislator legislatore *m*

legitimate legittimo

leisure agio; ozio *m*

lemon limone *m*; **- ade** limonata *f*; **- squeezer** strizzalimoni *m*

lend prestare

length lunghezza *f*; **- en** allungare

lenient leniente

lens lente *f*

lent quaresima *f*

lessen diminuire

lesson lezione *f*

let lasciare; permettere a

lethargy letargo *m*

letter lettera; epistola *f* **- -box** buca delle lettere

lettuce lattuga *f*

level livellato; livello; piano *m*; mira; livellare;

lever leva *f* [spianare

levity levità *f*

levy leva *f*

lewd dissoluto

liabilities passivo *m*

liability responsabilità *f*

liable responsabile

liar mentitore *m*

libel libello *m* diffamare
liberal liberale
liberate liberare
liberty libertà *f*
librarian bibliotecario *m*
library biblioteca *f*
license autorizzare
lick leccata *f*; leccare
lid coperchio *m*
lie menzogna *f*; giacere;
mentire
lieu in – of in luogo di
lieutenant luogotenente *m*
life vita *f*; – boat battello
di salvimento *m*; – less
senza vita; – time tempo
della vita *m*
lift ascensore *m*; mano *f*;
alzare; sollevare
ligament ligamento *m*
light chiaro; luminoso;
biondo; lume *m*; illum-
inare; incontrare; – en
alleggerire; illuminare;
– house faro *m*; – ing
illuminazione *f*; – ly
leggermente; – ning ful-
mine *m*;

like simile; uguale;
tale; come; da simile *m*;
amare; volere che; tro-
vare buono; – en com-
parare; –ly probabile;
– wise parimente
liking gusto *m*
lilac lilla
lily giglio *m*; – of the
valley mughetto *m*
limb membro; ramo *m*
lime calce *f*; – kiln
fornace da calce *f*; – tree
tiglio *m*
limit limite *m*; limitare
limp fiacco; molle; zoppicamento *m*
limpid limpido

line linea; corda *f*
lineage lignaggio *m*
lineament tratto *m*
linen tela *f*; di tela
lion, lioness leone *m*;
leonessa *f*
lip labbro *m*; orlo *m*
liquefy liquefare
liquid liquido *m*
liquidate liquidare
liquor liquore *m*
lisp scilinguare
list lista *f*; catalogo;
listen ascoltare

literary letterario
literature letteratura *f*
lithographer litografo
lithography litografia *f*
little piccolo; poco
liturgy liturgia *f*
live vivo; vivere; – li-
hood sussistenza *f*;
– liness vivacità *f*; – ly
liver fegato *m*   [vivace
livery levrea; pensione
livid livido   [(cavalli) *f*
lizard lucerta *f*
load carico *m*; caricare
loam terra grassa *f*
loan prestito *m*
loath avverso
loathe detestare
loathsome odioso
lobby vestibolo *m*
lobster astaco *m*
local locale
locality località *f*
lock serratura; chiusa;
ciocca *f*; serrare a
chiave; – et medag-
lioncino *m*; – out spiaggia *f*; – smith serruriere
lodge loggia *f*; alloggiare;
– r pigionale *m & f*
lodging alloggio *m*
loft soffita *f*
lofty alto; sublime

log ceppo; loche *m*
logarithm logaritmo *m*
logic logica *f*; — al logico;
lone(ly) solo; isolato *f*;
— liness solitudine *f*; —
some solitario; desolato
long lungo; bramare;
evity longevità *f*
longing brama *f*
longitude longitudine *f*
look sguardo *m*; aspetto
m; guardare; parere
— for cercare
loose sciolto; rilassato;
— n sciogliere; rilassare
lord signore; padrone *m*;
lose perdere; mancare
loser perditore *m*
loss perdita *f*
lot sorte; fortuna
lotion lozione *f*
lottery lotteria *f*
loud forte; — ly ad alta
voce [girandolare
lounge giro; sofà *m*;
louse pidocchio *m*
love amore *m*; amare;
— liness amorevolezza;
vaghezza *f*; — ly gra-
zioso; — r amante *m & f*
loving amoroso; amante;
affettuoso
low basso; triste; vol-
gare
low muggire
lower abbassare
lower offuscarsi
lowly basso; umile
loyal leale; fedele
loyalty lealtà *f*
lozenge pasticca *f*
lubricate lubricare
lucid lucido
luck fortuna *f*; azzardo
lucrative lucrativo
luggage bagaglio *m*;

— ticket ricevuta del
bagaglio; — van carro
del bagagli
lukewarm tiepido
lull momento di calma
m; calmare
lullaby canto *m*
lumbago lombaggine *f*
lumber scarti *m pl*
luminary luminare *m*
luminous luminoso
lump massa *f*; grumo *m*
lunacy demenza *f*
lunar lunare
lunatic lunatico; pazzo
m; — asylum manicomio
m [dare
lunch merenda *f*; meren-
lung polmone *m*
lure esca *f*; allettare
lurch barcollare
lurid lurido
lurk nascondersi
luscious sdolcinato
lust lussuria; sensualità
f; — ful lascivo; — iness
vigore *m*; — y vigoroso
luxuriate crescere rigog-
liosamente; vivere nel
lusso
luxurious sontuoso
luxury lusso *m*
lye ranno *m*

M

macaroni maccherone *m*
macaroon biscotino *m*
mace mazza; mace *f*
macerate macerare
machination macchina-
zione *f* [meccanismo *m*
machine macchina *f*; — ry
mad pazzo; matto;

– den render furioso;
– ness demenza f
madam signora f
magazine magazzino
 gironale m
maggot vermicciolo m
magic magia f; – al
 magico; – ian mago m
magistrate magistrato m
magnanimous magnani-
magnate magnate m [mo
magnesia magnesia f
magnet magnete m; – ic
 magnetico; – ism mag-
 netismo m; – ize mag-
 netizzare
magnificent magnifico
magnify magnificare
magnitude grandezza f
mahogany acaiu m [m
maid vergine; serva f;
 – en verginale;
mail maglia; valigia f;
 corriere m;
maim mutilare
main principale; essen-
 ziale; grosso; oceano
 m; – land terra ferma;
 – ly principalmente; –
 tain mantenere; – ten-
 ance mantenimento m
maize maia m
majestic maestoso
majesty maestà f
major maggiore m
majority maggiorità f
make struttura; natura
 f; fare; creare; obbli-
 gare; – believe far cre-
 dere; maniera f; – r
 fabbricante m; – shift
 peggio m
malady malattia f
malaria malaria f
male maschio m
malevolence malevolenza
malice malizia f   [f

malicious malevolo
malign malignare
malignant maligno
malt malto m
mammoth mammut m
man uomo; marito m;
 pedina (dama) f; equi-
 paggiare
manacles manette f pl
manage dirigere
manageable maneggiabile
management direzione f
manhood virilità; natura
 humana; bravura f
maniac, maniacal man-
 iaco; pazzo m
manifest manifesto; evi-
 dente; manifestare;
 mostrare; – ly manifes-
 tamente   [zione f
manifestation manifesta-
manikin umetto; busto
mankind il genere umano
manly maschile   [m
manner maniera f
mannerly cortese
manœuvre manovra f
mansion casa grande f
manslaughter omicidio m
mantelpiece cappa di
 camino m
mantle mantello m
manual manuale m
manufactory fabbrica f
manufacture fabbricare
manufacturer fabbricante
 m   [tilizzare
manure letame m; fer-
manuscript manoscritto
many molti   [m
map carta geografica;
maple acero m [mappa f
mar guastare   [mo m
marble marmoreo; mar-
March Marzo m; marcia
 f; progresso m; mar-
 ciare

marchioness marchesa *f*
mare giumenta *f*
margarine margarina *f*
margin margina *f*; orlo *m*
mark segno *m*; segnare;
 marcare
marker segnatore (giuoco)
 segno (libro) *m*
market mercato *m*
marl marga *f*
marmalade marmellata
marmoset scimiotto *m*
marmot marmotta *f*
marquee tendone *m*
marquis marchese *m*
marriage martrimonio *m*
married maritata
marrow midollo *m*
marry sposare
marsh palude *f*
marshal maresciallo *m*;
 ordinare
mart mercato *m*
martial marziale
martyr martire *m* & *f*
marvel maraviglia *f*;
 ammirare
marvellous maraviglioso
masculine mascolino
mask maschera *f*; mas-
 cherare
mason muratore *m*
masonry muratura *f*
masquerade mascherata *f*
mass massa *f*
massacre massacro *m*;
 massacrare
massive massiccio
master maestro; pad-
 rone; direttore *m*;
 superare; dominare;
mat stuoia *f*; intrecciarsi
match zolfanello; partito:
 uguale *m*; accordarsi:
 maritarsi; – box scatola

da zolfanelli; – maker
fabbricante di zolfanelle
 m & *f*
mate consorte *m* & *f*;
 compagno *m* [portante
material materiale; im-
material materiale *m*
maternal materno
maternity maternità *f*
mathematical matematico
mathematician matema-
 tico [*f*
mathematics matematica
matrimony matrimonio *m*
matron matrona *f*
matter materia; cosa *f*;
 marcia (med); soggetto
 m; importare; premere
mattress materasso *m*
mature maturo; mat-
 urare
maturity maturità *f*
mayor sindaco *m*
maze laberinto *m*; per
me me; mi [plessità *f*
meadow prato *m*
meagre magro
meal pasto *m*; farina *f*
mean basso; medio;
 mezzo *m*; media *f*;
 intendere; voler dire;
 – ing significativo;
 disegno *m*; ness
 sordidezza *f*; – time nel
 intervallo
meander serpeggiare
measles rosolia *f*
measure misura; dimen-
 sione *f*; misurare
meat carne *f*; cibo *m*
mechanic meccanico;
 operaio *m*
mechanical meccanico
mechanism meccanismo
medal medaglia *f* [*m*

meddle impacciarsi
mediate esser mediatore
mediator mediatore m
medical medico
medicine medicina f
meed ricompensa f; premio m
meek sommesso
meet incontrare; trovare
meeting incontro m; riunione f

membrane membrana f
memento memento m
memoir memoria f
memorable memorabile
memorandum nota f
memorial memoriale m; petizione f
memory memoria f
menace minaccia f; minacciare
mend raccomodare; emmenial servile [endarsi
mental mentale
mention menzione f; menzionare
mercantile mercantile
mercenary mercenario m
merchandize mercanzia
merchant negoziante
merciful clemente
mercury mercurio m
mercy misericordia f
merge immergere
meridian meridiano m
merit merito m; meritare
meritorious meritorio
merry gioviale
mesh maglia f
mess mensa f; guazzabuglio; pasticcio m
message messaggio m
messenger messaggiero m
Messiah Messia m
metal metallo m; - lic metallino; - lurgy metallurgia f

metaphor metafora f
meteor meteora f
meter contatore m
method metodo m

microscope microscopio m
midday mezzogiorno m
middle mezzo; centro m
midnight mezzanotte f
midshipman guardia marina f
midst mezzo; centro m
midwife levatrice f
might potenza f
migrate emigrare
mild dolce
mildew golpe f
mile miglio m
military militare m
militia milizia f
milk latte m; mungere; - man lattaio m; - y latteo; di latte; - y way via lattea f
mill mulino m; fabbrica f; macinare; follare;
milliner modista f
million milione m
mimic mimico; mimo m; imitare
mince sminuzzare
mind mente f; intelletto; m; osservare; fare attenzione a
mine mina f; minare; il mio la mia
miner minatore m
mineral minerale m
mineralogy mineralogia f
mingle mischiare
minister ministro; prete m; ministrare
ministry ministerio m
minor minore; minorenne m & f
minority minorità f
minstrel menestrello m

mint menta *f*; moneLare
minute minuto *m*; nota *f*
minute minuto
miracle miracolo *m*
miraculous miracoloso
mirage miraggio *m*
mire fango *m*
mirror specchio *m*
miscalculation errore di
  calcolo *m*   [aborto *m*
miscarriage insuccesso;
miscarry fallire; abortire
miscellaneous miscellaneo
mischance disavventura *f*
mischief male; danno *m*
mischievous malizioso
miserable miserabile
misery miseria *f*
misfortune sventura *f*
misgiving apprensione *f*
mishap disavventura *f*
mislead sviare
mismanage dirigere male
misprint errore di stampa
  m
miss signorina; svista *f*;
  difetto *m*; mancare;
  fallire; ommettere
missile proiettile *m*
mission missione *f*
missionary missionario *m*
mist nebbia *f*
mistake sbaglio; errore;
  m sbagliare; ingannarsi
mister signore *m*
mistletoe vischio *m*
mistress padrona; am-
  ante *f*   [diffidare di
mistrust diffidenza *f*

misty nebbioso
misunderstand capir male
misunderstanding con-
  cetto erroneo *m*
mob folla *f*; maltrattare
mobilize mobilizzare
mock falso; contraffare;

mode modo *m*; maniera *f*
model modello; model-
  lare   [erare
moderate moderato; mod-
modern moderno
modest modesto; pudico
  – y modestia *f*
modify modificare
modulate modulare
mohair pelo di capra
moist umido; – en um-
  ettare; – ure umidità *f*
mole talpa *f*; neo; molo
molest molestare
mollify mollificare
moment momento; – ary
  momentaneo; – ous di
  momento
monarch monarca *m* & *f*
monarchy monarchia *f*
monastery monastero *m*
money moneta *f*;
mongrel misto; meticcio
monk monaco *m*   [*m*
monkey scimmia *f* [*m*
monogram manogramma
monopoly monopolio *m*
monotonous monotono [*m*
monster mostro *m*
month mese *f*
monument monumento *m*
mood umore *m*
moody mesto
moon luna *f*; – light,
moor landa; brughiera
  f; moro *m*; amarrare;
mop spazzatoio *m*
mope annoiarsi
morality morale *m*
morbid morboso
more più; maggiore
morning mattina *f*
morsel boccone *m*
mortal mortale; umano
mortality mortalità *f*
mortar calcina *f*; mor-

taio *m*
morgage ipoteca *f*
mosquito zanzara *f*
moss(y) musco(so) *m*
most più; molto; il più
moth falena *f*   [*m*
mother madre *f*; − -**in
law** suocera *f*; − -**of-
pearl** madreperla; nac-
chera *f*; − **less** senza
madre; − **ly** materno
motion movimento *m*;
mozione *f*; − **less** senza
motive motivo *m* [moto
motley variopinto
motor motore *m*
motto motto *m*
mould forma; matrice;
muffa *f*; terriccio *m*;
formare; modellare; − **er**
formatore *m*; −**y** muffato
mount(ain) monte; montagna *f*; montare; − **eer**
montanaro *m*; − **ous**
montagnoso
mourn lamentare; − **er**
piangitore *m*; − **ful**
lugubre; − **ing** dolore *m*
mouse sorcio *m*   [*pl*

moustache mustacchi *m*
mouth bocca; gola *f*;
− **ful** boccone *m*; − **piece**
imboccatura *f*
movable mobile
move movimento; muo-
vere
movement movimento *m*
mow falciare; − **er** fal-
ciatore *m*; − **ing-mach −
ine** falciatrice *f*
much molto; grande
mud fango *m*; − **dy**
fangoso
multiple molteplice
multiplication moltiplica-
zione *f*

84

multiply moltiplicare
multitude moltitudine *f*
multitudinous numeroзo
mummery mascherata
mummy mummia *f*
mumps stranguglion[i] *m pl*
munch masticare
mundane mondano
municipal municipale
munition munizione *f*
murder omicidio *m*;
assassinare; uccidere ;
− **er** assassino *m*
murky tenebroso
murmur mormorio *m*;
mormorare
muscle muscolo *m*
muscular muscolare
muse musa *f*; meditare
mushroom fungo *m*
music(al) music(ale)
musician musico *m*
musk muschio *m*
musketry moschetteria *f*
muslin mussolina *f*
mussel gongola; arsella
f; muscolo *m*   [dovere
must mosto *m*; muffa *f*;
mustard mostarda *f*
musty muffato
mute muto *m*
mutilate mutilare
mutilation mutilazione
mutiny rivolta *f*
mutter mormorare
mutton montone *m*;
mutual mutuo; reciproco;
− **ly** mutuamente
muzzle muso *m f*
my mio; mia; miei· mie
myself io stesso;   me
stesso
mysterious misterioso
mystery mistero *m*
mystify mistificare
myth mito *m*; − **ology**
mitologia *f*

N

nag cavallino *m*; importunare [inchiodare
nail unghia *f*; chiodo *m*;
naked nudo
nakedness nudità
name nome *m*; riputazione *f*; nominare ; chiamare; – d chiamato; – less senza nome; – ly cioè; vale a dire; – sake omonimo *m*
nap sonnellino; pelo *m*
narcotic narcotico *m*
narrate narrare
narrative narrazione *f*
narrow stretto; limitato;
nasal nasale [restringere
national nazionale; – ity nazionalità *f* [*m*
native nativo; indigeno
natural naturale [& *f*
naturalist naturalista *m*
nature natura; indole *f*
naught nullo; niente· zero *m*
naughty cattivo
nausea nausea *f*
nauseous nauseabondo
navel umbilico *m*
navigable navigabile
navigate navigare
navigation navigazione *f*
navigator navigatore *m*
navy marina; flotta *f*
navvy lavoratore *m*
nay no; anzi
neap basso; morto; – tides acque morte
near vicino; intimo; prossimo; accosto ; – ·ly vicino; quasi; circa; – ness prossi-

mità *f*
neat netto; lindo; – ness nettezza *f* [mente
necessarily necessaria-
necessary necessario; –ies cose necessarie *f pl*
necessitate necessitare
necessity necessità *f*
neck collo *m*; gola *f*; – lace collana *f*; – tie cravatta
need bisogno *m*; necessità *f*; aver bisogno di
needful necessario
neediness indigenza
needle ago *m*
neglect negligenza *f* negligere
negligence negligenza
negotiate negoziare
negotiation negoziazione *f*
neighbour vicino; prossimo *m*; – nood vicinità
nephew nipote *m*.
nerve nervo *m*; invigorire
nervous nervoso
nest nido *m*; – ling uccel-
nestle cacciarsi [lino *m*
net netto; rete *f*
neuter, neutral neutro; neutrale
neutrality neutralità *f*
neutralize neutralizzare
never mai; giammai; – theless nullameno; tuttavia
new nuovo; novello
news notizia *f*; – vendor venditore di giornale; – paper giornale *m*
New-Year's day capo d'anno *m* [dopo
next prossimo; seguente
nice gustoso; bello
nickel nichel *m*

niece nipote *f*

night notte *f*; – ingale usignuolo *m*; – ly notturno; ogni notte; – –nurse nottante *m* & *f*

nimble agile

nine nove *m*; – teen dicianove *m*; – teenth decimonono *m*; – tieth novantesimo *m*; – ty novanta *m*

ninth nono *m*

nip pizzicare

nipple capezzolo *m*; tetta *f*

no nessuno; niuno; no

nobility nobiltà *f*

noble nobile

nobleman nobile *m*

nobody nessuno; veruno

nocturnal notturno

nod segno di testa *m*

noise rumore *m*

noisy strepitoso

nominal nominale

nominate nominare

nomination nomina *f*

nominee persona nominata *f*   [veruno

nonsense assurdità *f*

nonsensical assurdo

nook angolo *m*

noon mezzogiorno *m*

noose laccio; nodo scornor nè   [solo *m*

normal normale

North nord *m*

nose naso; muso *m*

nostril narice *f*

not non; no; niente

notable notevole

notary notaio *m*

notch tacca *f*; intaccare

note nota *f*; biglietto; notare; osservare

noted noto; eminente

nothing nulla; niente *m*

notice notizia *f*; avviso *m*; menzionare

noticeable percettibile

notify notificare

notion nozione *f*

nourish nutrire   [*m*

nourishment nutrimento

novel novello *m*

novelist novellista *m* & *f*

novelty novità *f*

novice novizio *m*

now ora; al presente; – –a-days oggi; – and then di tempo in tempo

nude nudo

nudity nudità *f*

nugget pepita *f*

nuisance noia *f*

null nullo

numerical numerico   [*f*

numerous numeroso

nun monaca; religiosa *f*

nunnery convento di monache *m*

nurse nutrice; bambinaia *f*; allattare; cullare

nursery camera dei fanciulli *f*; semenzaio *m*; pepiniera *f*; – –man pepinierista *m*

nut noce; chiocciola *f*; – –cracker rompi noci *m*; –meg noce moscata *f*

nutrition nutrizione *f*

nutritious nutritivo

nutshell guscio di noce *m*

O

O! oh!
oaf scempio *m*
oak quercia *f*;
oar remo *m*
oasis oasi *f*
oath giuramento *m*
oatmeal farina di avena *f*
oats avena *f*
obedience obbedienza *f*
obedient obbediente
obese grasso
obey obbediare
obituary funeraio
object oggetto; scopo *m*;
obiettare
objection obiezione *f*
objective oggettivo
obligatory obbligatorio
oblige obbligare
obliging obbligante
obliterate obliterare
oblivion oblio *m*
oblong oblungo *m*
obnoxious odioso
obscene osceno
obscure oscuro
obscurity oscurità *f*
observance osservanza *f*
observant osservante
observation osservazione
observatory osservatorio
observe osservare [*m*
observer osservatore *m*.
obsolete disusato
obstacle ostacolo *m*
obstinacy ostinatezza *f*
obstinate ostinato
obstruct ostruire
obstruction ostruzione *f*
obtain ottenere
obtainable ottenibile

obtrusive intruso
obtuse ottuso
obviate ovviare a
obvious ovvio; chiaro
occasion occasione *f*;
cagionare
occasional occasionale
occult occulto
occupant occupante *m & f*
occupation occupazione *f*
occupy occupare
occur occorrere
occurrence occorrenza *f*
ocean oceano *m*
ochre ocra *f*
octagon ottagono *m*
octagonal ottangolare
octave ottava *f*
of di; del; sopra; per;
off via; lontano [da
offence offesa; delitto *m*
offend offendere
offender offensore *m*
offensive offensivo
offer offerta *f*; offerire
offering oblazione *f*
office uffizio; servizio *m*
officer official ufficiale *m*
officiate ufficiare
old vecchio; antico
olive oliva *f*
omelet frittata *f*
omen pronostico *m*
ominous sinistro
omission omissione *f*
omit omettere
omnipotent onnipotente
on sopra; su; disopra;
a; di; sotto; in; avanti
once una volta; un
tempo; at – alla volte
one uno; solo; si; uno;
alcuno
onion cipolla *f*
only solo; unico; sola-

mente
onward progressivo ;
opal opale *f*
opaque opaco; oscuro
open aperto; franco
open aprire; schiudere;
- **er** apritore *m*; - **ing**
apertura *f*
opera opera *f*; —**glass**
cannochiale *m*; —**house**
teatro dell'opera *m*
operate operare
operation operazione *f*;
effetto *m*;
operator operatore *m*

opinion opinione *f*
opium oppio *m*
opossum sariga *f*
opponent avversario *m*
opportune opportuno; a
proposito
opportunity occasione *f*
oppose opporre
opposite opposto; dirimpetto
opposition opposizione *f*
oppress opprimere
oppression oppressione *f*
oppressor oppressore *m*
optical, optician ottico *m*
optimist ottimista *m* &
option scelta *f*
optional facoltativo
opulence opulenza *f*
or od; oppure
oral orale
orange arancio; arancia *f*
orchard brolo; frutteto *m*
orchestra orchestra *f*
orchid orchide *f*
ordain ordinare
ordeal prova *f*
order ordine; metodo;
mandato *m*; ordinare;
comandare; **postal** -

vaglia postale *f*; - **ly**
regolato [decreto *m*
ordinance ordinanza *f*;
ordinary ordinario
ordnance artiglieria *f*
ore minerale *m*
organ organo *m*; - **ic**
organico; - **ist** organista *m* & *f* ; - **ization**
organizzazione *f*; - **ize**
organizzare
orient oriente *m*
oriental orientale
orifice apertura *f*
origin origine *f*
original originale
originality originalità *f*
originate creare
ornament ornamento *m*;
ornamentare
ornithology ornitologia *f*
orphan orfano *m*
orthodox ortodosso
orthography ortographia *f*
oscillate oscillare
osier vimine *m*
ostensible ostensibile
ostentatious pomposo
ostler mozzo di stalla *m*
ostrich struzzo *m*
other altro; - **s** altri

our nostro; nostra; - **s**
il nostro [noi
ourselves noi medesimi;
out fuori; senza; - **bid**
rincarare su; - **break**
eruzione; insurrezione *f*;
- **cast** espulso *m*; - **do**
soprastare; - **er** esteriore; - **fit** corredo *m*;
- **going** uscita *f*; - **grow**
sorpassare; - **law** pros-
critto *m*; proscrivere;
oven forno *m*
over su; sopra; troppo;
di più; in; per

88

overbalance pesare più di
overcast offuscare [cadere
overcoat soprabito *m*
overcome vincere
overflow inondare
overgrown immenso
overhang piegare sopra
overhead in alto
overhear udire
overlay affogare
overlook sorvegliare
overpower sopraffare
oversight negligenza *f*
overtake raggiungere
overthrow rovina *f*;
  rovesciare
overturn versare
overweight soprappeso *m*
overwhelm sommergere
owe dovere a
owl gufo *m*
own proprio; avere
owner proprietario *m*
ox bue; bove *m*
oxide ossido *m*
oxygen ossigeno *m*
oyster ostrica *f*
ozone ozono *m*

P

pace passo; mandar
  adagio
pacify pacificare
pack pacco; mazzo
  (carte) *m*; imballare;
  – age balla *f*; – et
  pacchetto *m*;
pad cuscinetto; des-
  chetto; ovattare;
paddle pagaia *f*; remare
paddock prato *m*; pas-
  tura *f*
padlock lucchetto *m*

page pagina *f*; paggio *m*
pail secchia *f*
pain pena *f*
painful doloroso
paint colore *m*; dipingere
painter pittore *m*
painting pittura *f*
pair paio *m*; coppia *f*;
  appaiare
palace palazzo *m*
palate palato; gusto *m*
pale pallido; steccone;
  territorio *m*
paleness pallore *m*
palette tavolozza *f*
palisade palizzata *f*
pall drappo mortuario
  m; rintuzzarsi
palliate palliare
palliation palliamento *m*
palliative palliativo *m*
pallid pallido
palm palma *f*
palmistry chiromanzia *f*
pancake frittella *f*
pander piaggiare; mez-
pane vetro *m* [zano *m*
panel quadrello *m*
pang dolore acuto *m*
panic panico *m*
pannier paniere *m*
pansy viola *f*
pant palpitazione *f*;
  palpitare
panther pantera *f*
pantile tegola *f*
pantomime pantomima *f*
pantry dispensa *f*
papal papale
paper carta *f*; giornale *m*
papist papista *m & f*
par pari *m*
parade parata; piazza
  f; sfoggiare
paradise paradiso *m*
paradox paradosso *m*

parallel parallelo *m*;
eguagliare
paralysis paralisia *f*
paralytic paralitico
paralyze paralizzare
parch seccare
parchment pergamena *f*
pardon perdono *m*; *f*
perdonare
pare sbucciare; tondere
paregoric paregorico *m*
parent padre· *m*; madre
f; – s genitori *m pl*
parentage parentado *m*
parenthesis parentesi *f*
parish parrocchia *f*
park parco *m*
parliament parlamento *m*
Parmesan parmigiano *m*
parody parodia *f*
parrot pappagallo *m*
parsley prezzemolo *m*
parsnip pastinaca *f*
parson parroco; curato *m*
part parte; porzione *f*;
dividere
partial parziale
partiality parzialità *f*
participate partecipare
particle particella *f*
particular particolare;
speciale; fastidioso;
particolare *m*
particulars informazioni
f pl
partition partizione *f*
partly in parte; parte
partner compagno; socio
party parte *f*; serata
pass passo *m*; stretta *f*;
permesso *m*; passare;
approvare
passable passabile
passage passaggio *m*
passenger viaggiatore *m*
passion passione *f*

passive passivo *m*
Passover Pasqua *f*
passport passaporto *m*
past passato; scorso
patrol sentinella *f*; pat-
tugliare   [*m*
patron padrone; patrono
patronize patrocinare
pattern modello *m*
pauper povero *m*
pause pausa *f*; riflettere
pave pavimentare
pavement pavimento;
marciapiedi *m*
pavilion padiglione *m*
paw zampa *f*; zampare
pay paga *f*; soldo; stipen-
dio *m*; pagare; saldare
payable pagabile
payment pagamento *m*
pea pisello *m*
peace pace; calma *f*;
– able, – ful pacifico
peach pesca *f*
peacock pavone *m*
peak picco *m*; cima *f*
peal scampanio; scoppio
m; scampanare
pear pera *f*
pearl perla *f*
peasant contadino *m*
peat torba *f*
pebble selce; ciottolo *m*
peck beccare
peculiar peculiare
pecuniary pecuniario
pedestrian pedestre *m*
pedigree genealogia *f*
pedler merciaiolo ambu-
lante *m*   [scorzare
peel scorza; buccia *f*;
peep sguardo furtivo *m*
peer pari *m*
pen penna *f*; pecorne *m*;
stabbiare; scrivere
penal penale

penalty penalità *f*

penance penitenza

pencil matita *f*; pennello *m*; disegnare [ante

pending pendente; dur-

penetrate penetrare

penetration acutezza *f*

peninsula penisola *f*

penniless senza denari

pension pensione *f*; pensionare

pensive pensieroso

people popolo *m*; nazione; gente *f*; popolare

pepper pepe *m*; impepare

per per; al; allo

perceive vedere; percepire

percentage percentuale *f*

perception percezione *f*

perch pertica *f*; appollaiarsi

perennial perenne; perpetuo [zionare

perfect perfetto; perfe-

perfection perfezione *f*

perforate perforare

perform fare; operare

performance esecuzione; rappresentazione *f*

performer esecutore *m*

perfume profumo *m*; profumare

peril pericolo *m*

period periodo *m*; epoca *f*

perish perire

perishable caduco; avariabile (merce)

peritonitis peritonite

perjure spergiurare

perjury spergiuro *m*

permanent permanente

permeate permeare

permissible permissibile

permission permesso *m*

permit permesso *m*;

permettere

perpendicular perpendicolare

perpetrate perpetrare [*m*

perpetrator perpetratore

perpetual perpetuo

perpetuate perpetuare

perplex confondere

perplexity perplessità *f*

persecute perseguitare

persecution persecuzione *f*

persecutor persecutore *m*

perseverance perseveranza *f*

persevere perseverare

persist persistere

persistent persistente

person persona *f*; individuo *m* [prio

personal personale; pro-

personate contraffare

personify personificare

perspective di prospettiva; prospettiva; vista *f* [*f*; sudore *m*

perspiration traspirazione

perspire sudare

persuade persuadere

persuasion persuasione *f*

persuasive persuasivo

pert impertinente

pertinacious pertinace

pertinent a proposito

pet favorita *m & f*

petal petalo *m*

petition petizione *f* supplicare

petrify petrificare

petroleum petrolio *m*

petticoat gonella *f*

pettifogger avvocataccio

petty piccolo [*m*.

petulance petulanza *f*

pew stallo; banco *m*

pewter peltro *m*

phaeton faeton *m*

phantom spettro *m*
pharisee fariseo *m*
pharmaceutical farma-
phase fase *f*   [ceutico
pheasant fagiano *m*
phenomenon fenomeno *m*
phonograph fonografo *m*
phosphate fosfato *m*
phosphorus fosforo *m*
photograph — y foto-
   grafia *f*; — er fotografo
phrase frase *f*
phrenology frenologia *f*
phthisic(al) tisico
phthisis tisichezza *f*
physical fisico
physician medico *m*
physiology fisiologia *f*
pianist pianista *m & f*
piano pianoforte *m*;
   grand — piano a coda

pick piccone *m*; cogliere;
pickle salamoia *f*; sala-
   moiare; salare
picklock grimaldello;
   ladro *m*
pickpocket borsaiolo *m*
picture pittura *f*; quadro
   m: dipingere;
picturesque pittoresco
pie pasticcio *m*; torta *f*
piece pezzo; frammento
pier pila *f*; molo *m*
pierce forare; penetrare
piety pietà *f*
pig porco; verro *m*;
pigeon piccione *m*
pike picca *f*; luccio *m*
pile mucchio *m*; pila *f*;
   palo *m*; ammucchiare
piles emoroide *f pl*
pilgrim pellegrino *m*

pilgrimage pellegrinaggio
pill pillola *f*
pillar pilastro *m*; colonna
pillow guanciale *m*
pillow-case federa *f*

pilot pilota *m*; governare
pimple pustola *f*
pin spillo *m*; caviglia *f*;
   rinserrare
pinch pizzico *m*; pizzi-
   care
pine pino; abete *m*;
   languire; — -apple an-
   anasso *m*
pink rosa; garofano *m*;
   tagliare
pinnacle pinnacolo *m*;
   cima *f*
pioneer pioniere *m*
pious pio; devoto
pipe pipa *f*; tubo; zam-
   pognare
pirate pirata *m*
pitch pece *f*; grado;
   tono *m*; gettare; precipitare; immergere;
   cadere; — er brocca *f*:
pivot perno *m*   [*m*
placard cartellone; affisso
place luogo; posto *m*;
   piazza *f*; collocare;
   mettere
placid placido   [tare
plague peste *f*; tormen-
plaid plaid *m*; stoffa
   scozzese *f*
plain piano; brutto;
   campagna *f*; piano *m*
plaint lamento *m*
plaintiff querelante;
   attore *m*
plaintive lamentevole
plait piegatura; piega *f*;
   pieghettare   [nare
plan disegno *m*; diseg-
plane pialla *f*; platano *m*;
planet pianeta *f* [piallare
plank tavola *f*
plant pianta *f*; materiale
   m piantare; — ation
   piantagione *f*; — er

piantatore *m*
plaster gesso; impiastro *m*; impiastrare; ingessare
plastic plastico
plate piatto *m*; piastra argenteria *f*; placcare; inargentare
platform piattaforma *f*
play giuoco *m*; ricreazione *f*; teatro *m*; giuocare (a); sonare; divertirsi; – **er** giocatore; attore *m*; – **ful** giocoso; scherzevole; – **fully** scherzavolmente; – -**house** teatro *m*; – **thing** trastullo *m*
plea difesa; scusa *f*
plead litigare; scusarsi su; allegare
pleasant piacevole; grato
pleasantry facezia *f*
please piacere (a); soddisfare   [volontà *f*
pleasure piacere *m*;
pledge pegno *m*; impegnare; garantire
plentiful abbondante
plenty abbondanza *f*
pleurisy pleurisia *f*
pliable pieghevole
pliers mollette *f pl*
plight stato; pegno *m*; impegnare
plot trama *f*; intrigo; pezzo di terra *m*; cospirare
plough aratro *m*; arare;
pluck tiramento; coraggio *m*; cogliere
plug turacciolo *m*; turare
plum prugna *f*
plumber piombaiolo *m*
plump grassotto
plumpness grassezza *f*

plunder bottino *m*; spogliare   [gere
plunge tuffo *m*; immer-
plural plurale *m*
plush felpa *f*   [mente
ply lavorare assiduamente; affogare (uova);
poach cacciare furtiva-
pocket tasca *f*; buco (biliardo) *m*; intascare; – -**book** portafogli *m*;
poem poema *m*
poet poeta *m & f*
poetry poesia *f*
point punta *f*; punto *m*; puntare; indicare
pointed appuntato
poise pesare
poison veleno *m*; avvelenare
poisonous velenoso
poke spinta *f*; spingere; attizzare;
pole polo *m*; pertica *f*; timone *m*
police polizia *f*; – **man** sbirro; questurino *m*
policy politica *f*
polish lustro *m*; pulire
polite cortese; – **ness** cortesia *f*
political politico
politician politico *m*
politics politica *f*
poll elezione; lista elettorale *f*; votare
pollute contaminare
polyglot polyglotta
pomade pomata *f*   [*f*
pomegranate melangrana
pommel pomo *m*; battere
pomp pompa *f*
pompous pomposo
pond stagno *m*
ponder meditare

ponderous pesante
poniard pugnale
pontiff pontefice *m*
pony cavallino *m*
poodle barbone *m*
pool pozzanghera; posta (giuoco) *f*
poor povero
poorly indisposto
pop scoppietto *m*; scop-
pope papa *m*   [piarc
popery papismo *m*
poplar pioppo *m*
poppy papavero *m*
populace popolaccio *m*
popular popolare
porch portico; vestibolo
pore poro *m*   [*m*
pork carne di porco *f*;
porridge minestra *f*
port porto *m*; – wine vino di Oporto *m*
portable portabile
portrait ritratto *m*
portray dipingere
position posizione
positive positivo
possess possedere; – ion possessione *f*; – or pos-sessore *m*
possibility possibilità *f*
possible possibile
posporre; – ponement posposizione *f*;
pot vaso *m*; pentola;
potato patata *f*
potent potente
pottery terraglia *f*
pouch saccoccia *f*
post posta *f*; posto; palo *m*; postare; im-postare; andare in posta; – age porto *m*;
– –card cartolina postale
– man porta-lettere *m*;
– –office posta *f*;   pone

poultry pollame *m*
pound libbra (peso); lira sterlina *f*; pestare
pour versare
pout fare il broncio
poverty povertà *f*
powder polvere *f*; pol-verizzare
power potere *m*; facoltà *f*
– ful potente; – less impotente
practical pratico
practice pratica *f*
practise praticare
practitioner esercente *m*
praise lode *f*; elogio *m*; lodare;
prank scappata *f*
pray pregare; supplicare;
– er preghiera *f*; – er-book libro di preghiere *m*
preach predicare
preacher predicatore *m*
preamble preambolo *m*
precarious precario
precaution precauzione *f*
precede precedere
precedent precedente *m*
precept precetto *m*
precinct precinto
precious prezioso
precipitate precipitato; precipitare
precise preciso
precision precisione *f*
preclude precludere
precocious precoce   [*m*
predecessor predecessore
predict predire; presagire
prediction predizione *f*
predispose predisporre
predominate predominare
prefix prefisso *m*; pre-figgere
pregnancy pregnazza *f*
pregnant incinta; pregno (di)   [pregiudicare

94

prejudice pregiudizio *m*;
prelate prelato *m*   [*m*
preliminary preliminare
prelude preludio *m*
premature prematuro
premeditate premeditare
premier primiero; primo
  ministro *m*
premises locali *m* *pl*;
  premesse *f* *pl*
premium premio *m*
preparation preparazione *f*
preparatory preparatorio
prepare preparare
prepay pagare anticipatamente   [are
preponderate preponder-
preposition preposizione *f*
prepossession preoccupa-
  zione *f*
preposterous prepostero
prerogative prerogativa *f*
prescribe prescrivere
prescription ricetta; prescrizione *f*
presence presenza *f*
present presente; corrente; dono; regalo *m*
present presentare
presentation presentazione *f*   . [mento *m*
presentiment presenti-
presently quanto prima
preservation preserva-
  zione *f*   [serva-
preserve preservare; con-
preserves (game) bandita
preside presedere   [*f*
president presidente *m*
press torchio; armadio
  m; stampa *f*; premere;
  stringere; – **ing** urgente
  – **ure** pressione *f*
presume presumere
presumption presunzione *f*
presumptuous presuntuoso
pretence finta *f*

prey preda *f*; predare;
  rodere
price prezzo; valore *m*;
  – **less** inestimabile
prick puntura *f*; pungere
pride orgoglio *m*
priest prete; sacerdote *m*
prim affettato
primary primiero; primitivo
primitive primitivo
prince principe *m*; – **ly**
  principesco; – **ss** prin-
  cipessa *f*
principal principale ;
  mastro;   principale;
  padrone; capitale *m*
principle principio *m*
print stampa; impres-
  sione *f*; stampare;
  imprimere; – **er** tipo-
  grafo *m*; –**ing** stampa *f*
prior precedente; priore
prison prigione *f*
prisoner prigioniere *m*
privacy retiratezza *f*
private privato; particolare; segreto
privilege privilegio *m*
prize premio *m*; preda *f*;
  apprezzare
probable probabile
probation noviziato *m*
probe tenta *f*; tentare
problem problema *m*
procedure procedura *f*
proceed procedere
proceeding procedimento
process processo *m*
procession processione
proclaim proclamare
proclamation proclama
procrastinate procrastinare

procreate procreare
prodigal prodigo *m*
prodigy prodigio *m*
produce prodotto *m*;
produrre; − **r** pro-
duttore *m*
product produtto *m*;
− **ion** produzione *f*; − **ive**
produttivo [fanare
profane profano; pro-
profanity profanità *f*
profess professare
profession professione *f*
professional professionale
professor professore *m*
proffer proporre
proficiency talento *m*
profile profilo *m*
profit profitto *m*; profittare (a); − **able** pro-
fittevole
profligate libertino *m*
profound profondo
profuse profuso
profusion profusione *f*
progeny progenie *f pl*
programme programma
prognostic pronostico [*m*
progress progresso *m*;
progredire
prohibit proibire
prohibition proibizione *f*
project progetto *m*; progettare
projectile proiettile *m*
promenade passeggio *m*;
passeggiare in
prominent prominente
promiscuous promiscuo
promote promuovere
promotion promozione *f*
prompt pronto; lesto;
prong rebbio *m*; punta *f*
pronoun pronome *m*
pronounce pronunziare
pronunciation pronunzia *f*
proof prova; bozza *f*;

saggio
prop puntello; palo *m*;
puntellare; sostenere
propagate propagare
propel propulsare
propensity tendenza *f*
proper proprio
property proprietà
prophecy profezia *f*
prophesy predire
proportion proporzione *f*
proposal proposta *f*
propose proporre
proposition proposizione *f*
proprietor proprietario *m*
propriety convenevolezza
prorogue prorogare [*f*
prosaic prosaico
prose prosa *f*
prosecute proseguire [*f*
prosecution prosecuzione
prosecutor accusatore *m*
prospect prospetto *m*;
ispezionare

prosper prosperare
prosperity prosperità *f*
prosperous prospero
prostitute prostituta *f*
prostrate prostrato;
prostrare
protect proteggere
protection protezione *f*
protector protettore *m*
protest protesta *f*; protestare; − **ation** pro-
testazione *f*
protract protrarre
protrude avanzare
proud fiero
prove provare
proverb proverbio *m*
proverbial proverbiale
provide provvedere
provision provvisione *f*
provisional provvisorio
provocation provocazione
provoke provocare [*f*

prow prua *f*
prowess valore *m*
prowl cercar la preda;
  girar intorno
proximity prossimità *f*
proxy deputato *m*
prudence prudenza *f*
prudent prudente
prune prugna *f*; potare
prussic acid acido prus-
  sico *m*
pruriency pizzicore *m*
prurient pizzicante
psalm salmo *m*
psalter saltero *m*
psychology psicologia *f*
public pubblico; pub-
  blico *m*
publican vinaio; oste;
  pubblicano *m*   [*f*
publication pubblicazione
public-house taverna *f*
publicity pubblicità *f*
publish pubblicare
publisher editore *m*
pudding torta *f*
puddle guazzo *m*
puff soffio *m*; ciarla-
  tanata *f*; soffiare;
  sbuffare
pull tirata; lotta *f*;
  tirare:
pulse polso; legume *m*
pulverize polverizzare
pumice pomice *f*
pump pompa; tromba *f*;
  pompare
pumpkin zucca *f*
pun bisticcio *m*; giuochi
  di parole
punch pulcinella; pun-
  zone; ponce *m*
punctilious puntiglioso
punctual puntuale   [*f*
punctuation puntuazione
punish punire; - able

punibile; - ment puni-
  zione
punt earchetta *f*
puny piccino; sparuto;
  meschino   [pupilla *f*
pupil alunno; scolare *m*;
purchase acquisto *m*;
  comprare; - r compra-
  tore *m*
pure puro; chiaro; mero
purgative purgativo; pur-
  gante *m*
purgatory purgatorio *m*
purge purgare; purificare
purification purificazione *f*
purify purificare
purity purità *f*   [morio
purl smerlatura; mor-
purloin involare [pora *f*
purple porporino; por-
purport senso; tenore *m*
purpose intenzione *f*;
  disesno *m*; utilita *f*;
  on - a posta; to no -
  in vano *f*
purse borsa *f*; - r com-
  putista; - y bolso
purslain porcellana *f*
pursuant conforme a
pursue proseguire
pursuit inseguimento *m*;
  occupazione *f*
purvey provvedere; - or
  provveditore; forni-
  tore *m*
pus pus *m*; puzza *f*
push colpo; impulso *m*;
  spingere
pushing intraprendente
pusillanimous pusillanime
put mettere; porre;
  posare; proporre; por-
  tare; obbligare; -
  down deporre; - off
  differire; svestire; - on

vestire mettere; — out
spegnere; tormentare;
— together metter in-
sieme; — in entrare;
(mar) approdare; — to
sea spiegare la vela;

Q

quadrangle quadrato m;
  corte interna f
quadrille quadriglia f
quadroon quartone m
quaint ricercato   [tarsi
quake tremare
quaker quacquero m
qualification qualifica-
  zione
qualified qualificato;
  atto; moderato
qualify qualificare
quality qualità f
qualm schifo; scrupolo m
quandary incertezza f
quantity quantità f
quarantine quarantena f
quarrel rissa f; altercare;
  — some irascibile
quarry cava di pietre;
  preda f
quart boccale; quarto m;
  — er quarto; trimestre;
  quartiere m; grazia f;
  dividere in quarti;
  alloggiare; — erly in
  quarto; quartale; ogni
  tre mesi; — ermaster
  quartiermastro m; — ern
  loaf pane di quattro
  libbre; — ers quartiere m;
  —ette quartetto m; — z
  quarzo m
queen regina; dama f
queenly da regina
queer strano; bizzarro
quell reprimere; domare

quench spegnere; estin-
  guere
query domanda f [ente
querulous querulo; dol-
query, question questione
  f; interrogare; — able
  dubbioso; incerto
quibble arguzia f
quick vivo; rapido;
  presto; — en vivificare;
  — lime calce viva f;
  — ness prestezza; rapidità; — silver mercurio m
quiet quieto; calmo;
  calma f; calmare
quill penna f
quit pagare: abbandon-
  are; lasciare
quite interamente; affatto

quits quitanzato; pace!
quiver faretra f; trem-
  olare; vibrare
quoin canto; cuneo m
quoit disco m
quotation citazione f;
  corso m
quote citare; quotare

R

rabbet incavatura f
rabbi rabbino m
rabbit coniglio m
rabble canaglia f
rabid rabbioso
race razza; corsa f;
  correre con velocità;
  — iness forza f
rack ruota f; rastrello m;
  tortura f; arrotare; tor-
  turare; spremere; — et
  schiamazzo m; rac-
  chetta f
radiance splendore m
radiant radiante

radiate radiare
radical radicale *m*
radish ravanello *m*;
  horse - ramolaccio *m*
radius raggio *m*
raffle tombola *f*
raft zattera *f*
rafter trave *f*
rag cencio *m*
rage rabbia; collera
rail sbarra *f*; cancello *m*;
  rotaia *f*; - **lery** motteg-
  gio *m*; - **road**, - **way**
  ferrovia *f*
rain pioggia *f*; piovere;
  - **bow** arcobaleno *m*;
  - **y** piovoso
raise alzare; levare;
  coltivare; aumuntare
raison uva passa *f*
rake rastrello; libertino
  m; rastrellare
rally raccolta *f*; raccogliere; ricuperare
ram ariete; montone *m*;
  impinzare
ramble giro *m*; vagare
rambling errante [zione *f*
ramification ramifica-
rampart bastione *m*
rancid rancido
rancour rancore *m*
random caso *m*; **at** - **a**
  caso
range ordine; giro *m*;
  fila; catena; ordinare
rank grosso; rango *m*
rankle inviperarsi
ransack frugare
ransom riscatto *m*

rape ratto *m*
rapid rapido; celere
rapture estasi *f*
rare raro; esimio
rasp grattugia *f*; grattugiare
raspberry lampone *m*

rat topo; ratto *m*
rate prezzo *m*; tariffa;
  velocità *f*
rather piuttosto
ratify ratificare
ratio ragione *f*
rational razionale
rattle sonaglio *m*; strep-
  itare; - **snake** serpente
  a sonagli
reach portata; estensione
  f; giungere (a); esten-
read leggere   [dere
readable leggibile
ready pronto; lesto;
  - -**made clothes** abiti
  fatti *m pl*
real reale; vero
reality realtà *f*
realize realizzare
really realmente
realm reame *m*
ream risma *f*
reap raccogliere
reaper mietitore *m*
rear indietro; di dietro;
  retroguardia *f*; innal-
  zare; coltivare
reason ragione *f* motivo;
  m; ragionare; - **able**
  ragionevole
reassure riassicurare
rebel ribelle *m* & *f*;
  insorgere
rebellion rivolta *f*
rebuke riprensione; riprendere
rebus rebus
recall revocare
recant ritrattare
recantation ritrattimento
recede recedere   [*m*
receipt *m*; quitanza
  ricetta *f*
receive ricevere
receiver ricevitore *m*
recent recente; fresco

receptacle ricettacolo *m*
recite recitare; citare
reckless temerario
reckon contare
reckoning conto *m*
reclaim riformare
recline inclinarsi
recognition ricognizione *f*
recognize riconoscere
recoil indietreggiare
recollect riconoscere
recollection ricordanza *f*
recommend raccomand-
are [andazione *f*
recommendation raccom-
record registrare; inscrivere; raccontare; rappor-
to; registro *m*; memoria
f; – s archivi *m* *pl*
recourse ricorso *m*
recover ricuperare
recovery ricupero
recreant poltrone
recreation ricreazione *f*
recriminate recriminare
recruit recluta *f*
recumbent giacente
recur ricorrere
recurrence ritorno *m*
red rosso *m*; – breast
pettirosso *m*; – den
arrosire; –ish rossatro;
– -hot rovente; – ness
rossezza *f*
redeem redimere; liber-
are; mantenere; – able
redimibile [riscatto *m*
redemption ridenzione *f*;
reduce ridurre
reduction riduzione *f*
reed canna *f*
reel aspo; rocchetto *m*;
annaspare; barcollare
re-elect rielleggere
re-establish ristabilire
refectory refettorio *m*
refer riferire; – ee arbitro

100

m [erenza *f*
reference menzione; ref-
refine raffinare; – ry
raffineria *f*
refresh rinfrescare
refreshment rinfresco *m*
refrigerator refrigeratore
m
refuge rifugic; asilo *m*
refusal rifiuto *m*
refuse rifiutare; rifiuto *m*
refute confutare
regenerate rigenerare
regeneration rigenera-
zione *f*
regent reggente *m* & *f*
regiment reggimento *m*
region regione *f*
register registro *m*;
registrare
registrar registratore *m*
regret rincrescimento *m*;
rincrescere
regular in regola
regularity regolarità *f*
regulate regolare
regulation regolamento *m*
rehearsal prova *f*
rehearse provare
reign regno *m*; regnare
reimburse rimborsare
rein redina *f*
reindeer renna *f*
reinforce rinforzare
reiterate reiterare
reject rigettare
rejoice giubilare
rejoin raggiungere
relapse ricaduta *f*; rica-
relate raccontare [dere
related affine; parente
relation relazione *f*;
parente *m* & *f*
relative relativo *m*
relax rilasciare; mitigare
relaxation *m*; ricreazione
relay posta *f* [*f*
release liberare; libera-

zione *f*
relegate relegare
relent rallentare
relentless inflessibile
relevant applicabile
reliance fiducia; fede *f*
relief sollievo; aiuto *m*
relieve alleviare; soccor-
religion religione *f* [rere
religious religioso
relinquish rinunziare (a);
  abbandonare
relish gusto *m*; gustare
reluctance riluttanza *f*
reluctant avverso
rely fidarsi
remain restare; rimanere
remainder resto *m*
remark osservazione *f*;
  osservare
remarkable rimarchevole
remedy rimedio *m*; rim-
  ediare
remember riconoscere
remembrance ricordo *m*
remind rimembrare
reminiscence reminis-
  cenza *f*
remiss négligente
remission remissione *f*
remissness negligenza
remit rimettere
remittance rimessa *f*
remote rimoto
removal trasporto *m*
remove rimuovere
render rendere
renew rinnovare
renewal rinnovamento *m*
renounce rinnegare
renovate rinnovare [*m*
renovation rinnovamento
renown rinomanza; fama
  f   [affittare
rent pigione *f*; affitto *m*;
renunciation rinuncia *f*
repair ripara *m*; riparare

repeal revoca *f*; rivocare
repeat ripetere; — edly
  ripetutamente
repel respingere
repent pentirsi
repentance pentimento *m*
repentant penitente
repetition ripetizione *f*
repine gemere
replace rimettere; sosti-
  tuire
reply replica; risposta *f*;
  replicare; rispondere
report rapporto; rumore;
  scoppio *m*; rapportare;
  raccontare
repose riposo *m*; riporre
reprehensible riprensibile
represent rappresentare
representation rappresen-
  tazione *f*
representative rappresent-
  ante *m* & *f*; rappre-
  sentativo
repress reprimere
reprieve dilazione *f*
reprimand riprensione *f*
  riprendere   [tampare
reprint ristampa *f*; ris-
reproach rimprovero *m*;
  rimproverare

reproduce riprodurre
reproof rimprovero *m*
reprove rimproverare
reptile rettile *m*
republic repubblica *f*
republican repubblicano
reputation reputazione *f*
repute reputazione *f*
request richiesta; dom-
  anda; richiedere
rescue riscossa; libera-
  zione *f*; salvare; liberare
research ricerca *f*
resemblance rassomigli-

anza *f*
resemble rassomigliare
resent risentire
resentful vendicativo
resentment risentimento
reservation riserva *f* [*m*
reserve riserva *f*; conservare
reservoir serbatoio *m*
reside risedere; abitare
residence residenza *f*; domicilio *m*
resident residente *m & *
resign rassegnare
resignation rassegnazione
resort ridotto; luogo frequentato *m*; frequentare
resource risorsa *f*
respect rispetto; riguardo; rapporto *m*; guardare; concernere; − **ability** rispettabilità *f*; − **able** rispettabile; − **ful** rispettuoso; − **ive** rispettivo
respiration respirazione *f*
respond rispondere
respondent convenuto *m*
response risposta; replica *f*
responsibility responsabilità *f*
responsible responsabile
rest riposo; resto *m*; pace; pausa *f*; riposare; restare
restaurant ristorante *m*
restitution restituzione *f*
restless inquieto
restoration ristoramento *m*; restituzione *f*
restore rendere; restituire; ristorare
restrain reprimere
restraint freno *m*
restrict restringere

restriction restrizione *f*
result risultato *m*; risultare; seguire
resume ripigliare
resurrection risurrezione *f*
retail minuto; dettaglio *m*; vender al minuto; spacciare; − **er** dettagliante *m & f*
retain ritenere
retaliate contraccambiare
retaliation pariglia *f*
retard ritardare
retire ritirarsi
retirement ritiratezza
return ritorno; rinvio *m*; ritornare; rendere
reveal rivelare
revel festa *f*; festeggiare; − **ation** rivelazione *f*;
revenge vendetta *f*; vendicare; − **ful** vendicativo
revenue reddito; fisco *m*
reverend reverendo
reverent riverente
reverse rovescio; disastro *m*; rovesciare; rivocare
review rivista; critica *f*
revise rivedere
revision revisione *f*
revival ravvivamento *m*
revive ravvivare
revoke rivocare
revolt rivolta *f*; rivoltarsi
revolution rivoluzione *f*
revolve rivolgere
revolver rivoltella *f*
reward ricompensa *f*; ricompensare
rheumatic reumatico
rheumatism reumatismo
rhyme rima *f*; rimare
rib costola; balena (ombrello) *f* [cia

ribbon nastro *m*; rettuc-
rice riso *m*
rich ricco; fertile
riches ricchezza *f*
ride cavalcata; passeggiata *f*; cavalcare; passeggiare   [cillo *m*
rider cavallerizzo; codi-
ridge cima *f*; dorso *m*
ridicule ridicolo *m*
rife comune
rifle carabina *f*; spogliare
rigging sartiame *m*
right retto; diritto;
destro; bene; assai;
diritto *m*; giustizia;
– **eous** giusto; – **ly**
bene; giustamente; –
ful legittimo

rind scorza; crosta *f*
ring anello; cerchio;
suono; tintinnio *m*;
suonare; circondare;
– **leader** caporione *m*
rinse sciacquare   [tuare
riot baccano *m*; tumul-
ripe maturo
ripen maturare
ripple increspatura *f*;
increspare
rise ascensione; eminenza
f; avanzamento *m*;
levarsi; sorgere
risk rischio *m*; avven-
rite rito *m*   [turare
rival emulo; competitore
m; rivaleggiare
river fiume *m*   [dire
rivet ribaditura *f*; riba-
road strada; via *f*;
cammino *m*
roam percorrere
roar ruggito; rombo *m*;
roast arrostire   [ruggire
rob rubare
robber ladro *m*
robbery ruberia *f*

robe toga; roba *f*;
vestire
robust robusto
rock roccia; rocca *f*;
dondolare; – **er** culla *f*;
roll rotolo; ruolo; registro; rullo (tamburo);
panino *m*; rotolare;
girare; rullare;
romance romanzo *m*
romantic romantico
roof tetto *m*
rook cornacchia *f*; rocco
(scacchi) *m*
room stanza; camera *f*;
spazio *m*; – **y** spazioso
roost pollaio *m*; appollaiarsi
root radice; origine *f*;
fissare; grufolare
rope fune; corda *f*;
rosary rosario *m*
rose rosa *f*
rot putrefazione *f*; in-
fracidire; putrefare
rotate rotare
rotation rotazione *f*;
giro *m*
rotatory rotatorio
rotten putrefatto
rough aspro; rozzo;
violento; – **ness** ruvidezza *f*
round rotondo; circo-
lare; tondo; cerchio;
giro; rondò *m*; ronda
m; ronda *f*; arroton-
dare
rouse svegliare
rout sconfitta; rotta *f*;
metter in rotta
route via; strada *f*
routine uso *m*
rove errare; viaggiare
row fila; distesa; or-

dine *f*
row baruffa; rissa; cag-
nara *f*
row remare
royal reale; regale; — ist
realista *m & f*; — ty
dignità reale *f*
rub attrito *m*; fregare
rubber fregatoio *m*;
gomma elastica *f*
rubbish robaccia *f*
ruby rosso; rubino *m*
ruffle manichino *m*;
increspare; turbare;
rug bigello *m* [disordinare
rugged scabro; ruvido
ruin rovina *f*; desolare
ruinous rovinoso
rule regola; norma *f*;
precetto *m*; governare;
regolare
ruler reggitore *m*; riga *f*
rum rum *m*
rumble rombare
rumbling rombante ;
rombo *m*
ruminate ruminare
rumour fama *f*
rummage rimuovere
run corsa; durata *f*;
correre; fuggire; — away
fuggitivo *m* [pere
rupture rottura *f*; rom-
rural rurale; rustico
rush slancio; urto;
giunco *m*; lanciarsi;
gettarsi; precipitarsi

S

sabbath Sabbato *m*;
Domenica *f*
sable nero; zibellino *m*
sacrament sacramento *m*
sacred sacro; santo
sacrifice sacrificio *m*;
sacrificare [religio·*m*

sacrilege, sacrilegious sac-
sad tristo
sadness tristezza *f*
safe sicuro; salvo; cassa
forte *f*; guarda-vivande
safety sicurezza *f* [*m*
sagacious sagace
sagacity sagacia *f*
sage saggio; savio *m*;
salvia *f* [giare
sail vela; ala *f*; veleg-
sailor marinaio *m*
saint(ly) santo
sake causa *f*
salad insalata *f*
salary salario *m*
sale vendita *f*
salesman venditore *m*
saliva saliva *f*
salmon salmone *m*
saloon salone *m*
salt salato; sale *m*;
salare;
salute saluto *m*
salvage salvataggio *m*
salvation salvazione *f*
salve unguento; balsamo
salver vassoio *m* [*m*
same medesimo; stesso
sample mostra *f*
sanctify santificare
sanction sanzione *f*;
sanzionare
sanctity santità *f*
sanctuary santuario;
sand sabbia *f* [asilo *m*
sandwich panino gravido
m; —-man portaffissi *m*
sandy sabbioso
sanguinary sanguinario
sanguine sanguigno
sanity sanità *m*
satellite satellite *m*
satiety sazietà *f*
satin raso *m*
satire satira *f*
satisfaction soddisfazione;

riparazione *f*
satisfactory soddisfacente
satisfy soddisfare
saturate saturare
sauce salsa *f*; condimento *m*; − **pan** cazzarola *f*; − **r** sottocoppa *f*
saucy impertinente
saunter girandolare
sausage salsiccia *f*
savage selvaggio
save salvare
saving economo; risparmio *m*; − **s-bank** cassa di risparmio *f*
saviour salvatore *m*
savoury aporito
saw ega *f*; proverbio *m*; segare
scallop petonchio *m*
scaly squamoso
scamper correre
scandal scandalo *m*
scandalous scandaloso
scanty scarso
scar cicatrice *f*
scarce scarso; raro
scarcity scarsezza *f*
scare spaventare
scarecrow spauracchio *m*
scarf ciarpa *f*; velo *m*
scarlet scarletto *m*; − **fever** febbre scarlatina *f*
scatter spargere
scavenger letamaiolo *m*
scene(ry) scena *f*; scenario *m*   [odorare
scent odore; profumo *m*;
sceptical scettico
sceptre scettro *m*
schedule cedola
scheme schema *f*
scholar scolare *m*
school scuola *f*; − **fellow** compagno di scuola *f*; − **master** maestro *m*

science scienza *f*
scientific scientifico
scissors forbici *m pl*; cesoie *f pl*
scoff beffeggiare
scold sgridare
scoop votazza *f*
scope scopo *m*
scorch bruciarsi
score scotto; conto *m*; segnare
scorn sdegno *m*; sdegnare; − **ful** sdegnoso
scoundrel scellerato *m*
scout spia *f*
scramble contesa *f*; sforzo *m*; arrampicarsi
scrap frammento *m*
scrape raschiatura; difficoltà *f*; raschiare
scratch graffio *m*; graffiare   [scarabocchiare
scrawl scarabocchio *m*;
scream strido; grido acuto *m*; stridere
screen parafuoco; paravento *m*
screw vite *f*; spilorcio *m*; invitare; torcere
scribble scarabocchio *m*; scarabocchiare
scrip sacchetto *m*; cedola *f*; azioni *f pl*
Scripture Scrittura *f*
scroll ruolo *m*
scrub fregare fortemente
scruple scrupolo *m*
scrupulous scrupoloso
scrutinize scrutinare
scrutiny scrutinio *m*
scuffle zuffa *f*
scull cranio; remo piatto *m*; remare
sculptor scultore *m*
sculpture scultura *f*
sea mare; oceano *m*

seal foca *f*; sigellare
search ricerca *f*; cercare
sea-sickness mal di mare
season stagione *f*; tempo *m*; stagionare; abituare condire; – **able** opportuno; – **ing** condimento
seat sede *f*; banco   [*m*
sea-weed alga *f*
secede separarsi
secluded ritirato
second secondo; secondo *m*; – **ary** secondario; – **-hand** di seconda mano; d'occasione; – **ly** in secondo luogo
secrecy segretezza
secret segreto *m*
secretary segretario *m*
secrete nascondere
secretion secrezione *f*
sect setta *f*
section sezione *f*
secular secolare
secure sicuro;   certo
seduction seduzione *f*
seductive seducente
see vescovato *m*; vedere
seed seme *m*
seek cercare
seem sembrare
seemly convenevole
seethe bollire
seize afferrare
seizure presa *f*
seldom raramente
select scelto;   eletto; scegliere
selection scelta *f*
self stesso;   medesimo; – **-denial** abnegazione di se stesso *f*; – **ish** egoista;
send mandare
senior seniore *m*
sensation sensazione *f*
sense senso; intelletto *m*; – **less** insensato

sensibility sensibilità *f*
sensible sensibile
sensitive sensitivo
sensual sensuale
sensuality sensualità *f*
sentence sentenza *f*
sentiment sentimento *m*
separate separato; separare
separation separazione *f*
sequel sequela *f*
serenade serenata *f*
serene serno
serenity serenità *f*
series serie; sequela *f*
serious serio
sermon sermone *m*
serpent serpente; serpe *m*
servant domestico *m*
serve servire
service servizio *m*

set fisso; fermo; assortimento; servizio *m*
set mettere; porre
settle panca *f*; sedile *m*; fissare; decidere
settlement regolamento; colonia *f*
seven sette *m*; – **fold** settuplo; **teen** diciassette *m*; – **teenth** diciassettesimo *m*; – **th** settimo *m*; – **tieth** settantesimo *m*; – **ty** settanta *m*
sever staccare
several parecchi
severe severo
severity severità
sew cucire
sewer fogna *f*: condotto sotteraneo *m*; – **age** fognatura *f*
sex sesso *m*
sexton beccamorti *m*
sexual sessuale
shabby mal vestito

shackle incatenare
shad cheppia; laccia *f*
shade ombra; tinta *f*; ombrare
shadow ombra *f*
shake scossa; stretta *f*; trillo *m*; scuotere; agitare
shame vergogna *f*; pudore *m*; svergognare;
shape forma *f*; modello *m*; formare; modellare
share porzione; parte *f*; partecipare (a); distribuire; --**holder** azionista

sharp acuto; tagliente; acido; — **en** affilare;
shatter fracassare
shave radere
shawl scialle *m*
she essa; ella; femmina (d'animali)
sheaf covone; facsio *m*
shear tondere
shears forbici grosse *f pl*
sheath fodero *m*; guiana *f*
shed tettoia *f*   [*m*
sheep pecora *f*; montone
sheet lenzuolo; foglio; specchio (d'acqua) *m*
shelf palchetto; scaffale; scoglio *m*
shell nicchio *m*; bomba *f*; sbaccellare; bombardare
shining rifulgente
ship nave *f*; imbarcare; —**ment** imbarco *m*; — **per** speditore *m*; — **wreck** naufragio *m*
shirt camicia *f*; — **ing** tela da camici

shiver scheggia *f*; frammento *m*; tremare
shoal poco profondo; frotta; folla *f*

shock cozza *f*; urto *m*; urtare; offendere; — **ing** ributtante; orrido
shoe scarpa *f*; ferro *m*; ferrare; --**black** lustrino *m*; — **maker** calzolaio *m*
shoot gettone; rampollo *m*; fucilare; lanciare; tirare; — **ing** tiro *m*
shop bottega *f*; — **keeper** mercante *m & f*
shore lido *m*; riva *f*
short corto; breve; — **coming** insufficienza;
shove spinta *f*
shovel pala *f*
show mostra; esposizione *f* mostrare
shower rovescio; nembo
shrewd fino; sagace; —**ness** astuzia *f*
shriek strido *m*; stridere
shrill acuto
shrimp squilla *f*
shrine reliquario *m*
shrink raggricchiare

shrug stretta di spalle *f*
shudder tremito *m*; fremere   [colare
shuffle inganno *m*; mescshun evitare
shut chiudere; serrare
shutter anta *f*
shy timido
sick malato; —**en** rendere infermo; — **le** roncola *f* — **ly** malsano; — **ness** malattia *f*
side lato; canto *m*; — **board** credenza; — **walk** marciapiede
sigh sospiro *m*; sospirare
sight vista; veduta *f*; spettacolo *m*; — **less** ceco
sign segno *m*; segnare
signal segnale; segnalare

signature firma; segnatura *f*;

signify significare

silence silenzio; tacere *m*; far tacere

silent silenzioso

silk seta *f*; – **en** di seta; serico; – **-worm** baco *m*

silly sciocco; goffo

silver argento *m*; argenteria *f*; inargentare;

similar simile; similare

similarity similarità *f*

simile similitudine *f*

simple semplice

simplify semplificare

simultaneous simultaneo

sin peccato *m*; peccare

since da; dopo; da chè

sincere sincero

sincerity sincerità *f*

sing cantare; lodare; – **er** cantante *m* & *f*

singe bruciar leggiermente   [celibe *m*

single solo; semplice;

singular singolare

singularity singolarità; rarità *f*   [affondare

sink fogna *f*; acquaio *m*;

sinner peccatore *m*

sip sorso *m*; sorseggiare

siphon sifone *m*

sister sorella; monaca *f*; – **-in-law** cognata *f*;

sit sedere [– **ly** di sorella

site sito; luogo *m* situazione *f*

situate(d) situato

situation situazione *f*

six sei *m*; – **teen** sedici *m*; – **teenth** sedicesimo *m*; – **th** sesto *m*; – **thly** in ϵesto luogo; – **tieth** sessantesimo *m*; – **ty** sessanta *m*

size grandezza; colla *f*

skate pattino *m*; pattinare

skeleton scheletro *m*

sketch abbozzo; schizzo *m*; abbozzare; schizzare

skewer brocco *m*; schidionare

skid incastratura *f*

skiff palischermo *m*

skilful versato; abile; esperto

skill perizia; destrezza *f*

skim schiumare

skin cute *m*; pelle; buccia *f*; scorticare;

sky cielo; firmamento *m* – **-light** lanterna *f*

slab lastra; tavola *f*

slack allentato

slacken allentare

slake annacquare

slam chidure con violenza

slave schiavo *m*

slavery schiavitù *f*

sleep sonno *m*; dormire;

sleet nevischio *m*

sleeve manica *f*

slender esile

slice fetta; placca *f*; affettare   [ciolare

slide sdrucciolo *m*; sdruc-

slight tenue; sfregio *m*; negligenza *f*; spregiare

slim svelto

slip passo falso; sbaglio *m*; striscia; scivolare; – **shod** negletto

slipper pantofola *f*

slippery sdrucciolevole

slit fessura *f*; fendere; fendersi

slope pendio *m*; pendere

sloping pendente

slow lento; tardo

sluggard dormiglione *m*
sluggish pigro [nacchiare
slumber sonno *m*; son-
slur sfregio *m*
sly astuto; malizioso
smack schiafed; bacio *m*
small piccolo; minuto;
 – **pox** vaiolo *m*
smart vivo; bello
smash fracasso *m*; fran-
tumare
smear imbrattare
smell odore *m*; sentire
smelt eperlano *m*; fondere
smile sorriso *m*; sorridere
smith fabbro *m*   [*m*
smock camicia *f*; saione
smoke fumo *m*; fumare
smoking - compartment,
 – **-room** fumatoio *m*
smoky fumoso
smooth piano; liscio;
 lisciare
smother soffocare
smuggle contrabbandare;
 – **r** contrabbandere *m*
smut fiocco di fuliggine *m*
snail lumaca *f*
snake serpe *m*
snap rottura *f*; fermaglio
 m; rompere [polare
snare trappola *f*; trap-
snarl ringhiare
snatch presa *f*; sforzo
sneak sornione *m*
sneer sogghigno *m*
sneering beffardo
sneeze starnuto *m*; starnutare   [*m*; russare
snore, snort russamento
snout grugno; muso *m*
snow neve *f*; nevicare;
 – **ball** palla di neve; –
 drop foraneve *f*; – **y**
 nevoso

snuff tabacco da naso *m*;
 smoccolare; fiutare
snuffers smoccolatoio *m*
so cosi; si; sia
soak ammollare; bagnare
soap sapone *m*
soar alzarsi [hiozzare
sob singhiozzo *m*; sing-
soft molle; tenero; dolce;
 – **en** ammollare; – **ness**
 morbidezza *f*
soil suolo *m*; macchiare
sojourn soggiorno *m*
solace sollievo *m*; con-
solder saldare   [solare
soldier soldato *m*
sole pianta; soglia *f*;
 solo; unico
solemn solenne
solemnity solennità *f*
solicit sollecitare
solicitor avvocato *m*
solid solido
soliloquy soliloquio *m*
solitary solitario; isolato
solution soluzione *f*
solve risolvere
solvency solvibilità *f*
some qualche; alcuno;
 certi *pl*; circa; del;
 – **body** qualcuno; – **how**
 in qualche modo; –
 thing qualche cosa *f*;
 un che *m*; – **times**
 qualche volta; – **what**
 un poco; alquanto *m*;
 – **where** in qualche
 luogo   [genero *m*
son figlio *m*; – **-in-law**
song canto *m*
soon tosto; presto
soot fuliggine *f*
sorcery stregoneria *f*
sordid sordido
sore doloroso; ulcera *f*
sorrow dolore *m*;

sorry tristo; dolente;
sort sorta; specie *f*;
  classificare
soul anima *f*; spirito *m*
sound sano; valido;
  suono *m*; snoare
soup zuppa *f*
sour agro; acido
source fonte; origine *f*
south sud *m*; – erly del
  sud; meridionale
souvenir ricordo *m*
sovereign sovrano
space spazio *m*
spacious spazioso
spade vanga; picca (carte)
span spanna *f*   [*f*
spaniel cane spagnuolo *m*
spar pertica *f*; alberetto
  m   [magro
spare parco; frugale;
sparing economico
spark scintilla *f*
sparkle scintillare
sparrow passero *m*
spasm spasmo *m*
spawn fregola *f*; uova *f pl*
speak parlare   [tore *m*
speaker favellatore; ora-
spear lancia ; asta *f*
special speciale
speciality specialità *f*
specie moneta contante *f*
species specie; classe *f*

specific specifico *m*
specification specifica-
  zione *f*
specify specificare
specimen esemplare *m*

speculate speculare
speech parola; favella *f*;
  – less senza parola
peed fretta; rapidità *f*;
  affrettare; – y rapido;
  pronto; celere
spell incanto; tempo *m*;

compitare
spend spendere
spendthr ft prodigo *m*
sphere sfera *f*; globo *m*
spice spezie *f pl*
spider ragno *m*
spike spiga *f*; inchiodare
spill versare
spin filare
spinach spinaccie *f pl*
spindle fuso *m*
spine spina *f*
spinster zitella *f*
spiral spirale
spire guglia *f*
spirit spirito; coraggio;
  brio *m*; – ed spiritoso;
  – less senza spirito;
  – ual spirituale; – uou
  spiritoso
spit schidione *m*; sputare
sponge spugna *f*
spongy spugnoso
spontaneous spontaneo
spoon cucchiaio *m*
spoonful cucchiaiata *f*
sport trastullo; giuoco *m*
  – ive festevole; – sman
  amatore delle corse
spot macchia *f*; punto *m*;
  macchiare
spotless immacolato
spout doccia; tromba *f*
sprain storta *f*; storcere
sprat palamita *f*
sprawl stendersi
spray fresca; schiuma *f*
spread stendere
spring fontana; sorgente;
  molla *f*; lancio; sbalzo
  m; scaturire; proce-
  dere; sorgere; – y elas-
sprinkle spargere   [tico
sprout germoglio; broc-
  colo *m*; germogliare
spy spia *f*; spiare
squadron squadra *f*

110

square quadrato; pari quadro *m*; piazza *f*; quadrare; bilanciare

squeak strillo *m*; cigolare

squeamish fastidioso

squeeze serrare

squint esser guercio

squirrel scoiattolo *m*

squirt siringa *f*; siringare

stab stillettare

stability stabilità *f*

stable stabile; scuderia *f*

stack mucchio *m*; ammucchiare

staff bastone *m*

stag cervo *m*

stage palco; treatro *m*

stagger barcollare

stain macchia; tinta *f*; macchiare; tingere;

staircase, stairs scala *f*

stake palo; premio *m*; posta *f*

stale stantio; vecchio

stamp stampa; marca *f*; francobollo; punzone *m*; stampare; imprimere

stand posto; banco *m* resistenza *f*; stare; sostenere [bandiera *f*

standard di norma;

staple principale; rampone

star stella *f*; astro *m*

starch amido *m*; inamidare [dentemente

stare guardare impu-

start scossa *f*; motto involontario

start trasalire; partire

startle trasalire

starvation inedia; fame;

starve affamare

state stato ; *m*; condizione; pompa *f*;

dire; constatare; – **ly** maestoso; – **ment** rapporto *m*; – **sman** statista; politico *m*

stay soggiorno *m*

stay soggiornare; stare

stead vece *f*; luogo *m*; – **fast** fermo; – **iness** fermezza *f*; – **y** fermo

steak fetta di carne *f*

steal rubare [di soppiato

stealth segreto *m*; by – **stealthy** furtivo; fatto di soppiatto

steam vapore; fumo *m*; fumare; – **boat** battello a vapore *m*; – **-engine** macchina a vapore *f*

steel acciaio *m*

steep erto; scosceso

steep immollare

steeple campanile *m*

steer manzo *m*; governare; – **sman** timoniere

stem stelo; ceppa; tronco *m*; prua *f*; arrestare

step passo; gradino *m*; – **-brother** fratellastro *m*; – **-daughter** figliastra *f*; – **-father** patrigno *m*; – **-mother** matrigna *f*; – **ping-stone** passatoio *m*; – **-sister** sorellastra *f*; – **-son** figliastro *m*

stern severo; poppa *f*

stew stufato *m*; stufare

steward fattore *m*

stick mazza; bacchetta *f*; aderire; incollare; – **y** glutinoso

stiff rigido; ostinato; – **en** indurire; – **ness**

stifle soffocare [rigidezza *f*

stile barriera *f*

still sereno; immobile,

pertanto; lambicco *m*;
quetare; calmare
stimulant stimolante *m*
stimulate stimolare
sting morsicatura *f*
stingy meschino
stink fetore *m*; puzzare
stipulate stipulare
stir moto *m*; muovere;
stock tronco; blocco;
capitale *m*; fornire;
– **broker** agente di cam-
stocking calza *f* [bio *m*
stomach stomaco *m*
stone pietra *f*; sasso *m*;
lapidare; – **y** pietroso
stool scranna; seggetta *f*
stoop inclinazione *f*;
piegare
stop fermata; posa *f*;
fermare; arrestare
stopper turacciolo *m*
store provvigione; riserva
f; magazzino *m*; ap-
provvigionare; accu-
mulare
stork cicogna *f*
storm temporale *m*;
burrasca *f*; – **y** tempestoso [*m*; bugia *f*
story storia *f*; racconto
stout grassotto
stove stufa *f*; fornello *m*
straight diritto
strain sforzo *m*; tensione *f*; sforzare; colare;
strange strano
stranger straniero *m*
strangle strangolare
strawberry fragola *f*
stray smarrire; vagare
streak screziatura *f*;
screziare
stream corrente; corso *m*
street via; strada *f*
strength forza *f*; vigore *m*
– **en** rinforzare

strenuous vigoroso
stress forza *f*
stretch tensione; estensione *f*; stendere
strike battere; colpire
string corda; stringa *f*
stringent stringente; duro
strip denudare
stripe striscia *f*; rigare
strive contendere
stroke botta *f*
stroll girata *f*; girare
strong forte; vigoroso
stubborn ostinato
stud bottoncino *m*
student studente *m*
studious studioso; stu-
study studio *m* [diare
stuff stoffa; imbottire
stumble inciampare
stump moncone *m*
stun stordire
stupefy stupefare
stupendous stupendo
stupid stupido
stupor stupore *m*
sturdy tarchiato
stutter balbettare
style maniera *f*; stile *m*
subdue soggiogare
subject soggetto
sublime sublime
submerge sommergere
submersion sommersione
submission sommessione
subside abbassarsi
subsidy sussidio· *m*
subsist sussistere
subsistence sussistenza
substance sostanza *f*
substantial sostanziale
substantiate provare
substantive sostantivo *m*
substitute sostituto *m*;
sostituire
subtle sottile
subtract sottrarre

subtraction sottrazione *f*
suburb sobborgo *m*
subvert sovvertire
succeed succedere
success successo; − ful
  felice; fortunato; − ion
  successione; serie *f*;
  − ive successivo; con·
  secutivo;
suck succhiare
sucker pollone; rampollo
suckle allattare   [*m*
sudden subito
sue processare
suet grasso (bove) *m*
suffer soffrire; − er vittima *f*; − ing pena *f*
suffice bastare
sufficient sufficiente
suffocate soffocare
sugar zucchero *m*
sugary zuccheroso
suggest suggerire
suggestion suggestione *f*
suicide suicidio *m*
suit assortimento *m*;
  convenire;   adattare;
  − able convenevole; − or
  postulante *m*
sum somma *f*; sommare;
  − mary sommario *m*;
  − mer estate; state; *f*;
  − mit cima *f*; − mon
  convocare;   citare;   −
  mons chiamata *f*;
  − ptuous suntuoso
sun sole *m*
sundry diversi
sunny solatio
sunrise il levar del sole *m*
sunset tramonto del sole
  m
sunshine luce del sole *f*
superintend sorvegliare
superintendent dirrettore
  m

superoir superiore *m & f*
  − ity superiorità *f*
superlative superlativo
supernatural sopranatur-
  ale
supersede sostituire   [*f*
superstition superstizione
superstitious superstizioso
supervise sorvegliare
supervisor sopraintend-
supper cena *f*   [ente *m*
supplant soppiantare
supple flessibile
supplement supplemento
  m; aumentare
supplementary supple-
  mentare   [*& f*
supplicant supplicante *m*
supplicate supplicare
supply provvigione *f*;
  assortimento *m*; prov-
  vedere; approvvigion-
  are
support sostegno *m*;
  sostenere; − able sop-
  portabile
suppose supporre
supposition supposizione *f*
suppress sopprimere
suppression soppressione
  f
supremacy supremazia *f*
supreme supremo
surcharge sopraccaricare
sure sicuro; certo
surety sicurezza *f*; gar-
  ante *m & f* [spuma *f*
surf cavalloni *m pl*;
surmise congettura *f*;
  congetturare
surmount sormontare
surname cognome *m*
surpass sorpassare
surplus soprappiù *m*
surprise sorpresa *f*; sorprendere

113

surround circondare
survey esame *m*; vista *f*
 esaminare; misurare
surveyor agrimensore *m*
survive sopravvivere
susceptibility suscettibil-
 ità *f*
susceptible suscettibile
suspect sospettare
suspend sospendere
suspense sospensione *f*
suspicion sospetto *m*
suspicious sospettoso
sustain sostenere
sustenance alimento *m*
suzerainty signoria *f*
swagger vantarsi
swallow rondine *m*; gola
 f; inghiottire
swamp palude *f*
sway brandire; dominare
swear giurare; testificare
sweat sudore *m*; sudare
sweep spazzacamino *m*;
 spazzare; – ings spaz-
 zatura *f*
sweet dolce; amabile;
swell enfiare; gonfiare;
 crescere; ingrandire; en-
 fiarsi
swelling gonfiamento *m*
swerve sviarsi
swift rapido; celere
swiftness rapidezza *f*
swim nuotare
swindle truffa *f*; truffare
swing oscillamento; don-
 dolo *m*; branda *f*; dondolare
sword spada *f*
sworn giurato
sycamore sicomoro *m*
syllable sillaba *f*
symbol simbolo *m*
symmetry simmetria *f*
sympathetic simpatico
sympathize simpatizzare

sympathy simpatia *f*
symphony sinfonia *f*
symptom sintomo *m*
syndicate sindicato *m*
synthesis sinthesi *f*
syphilis sifilide *f*
syphon sifone *f* [are
syringe siringa *f*; siring-
syrup sciroppo *m*
system sistema *m* – atical
 sistematico; – atically
 sistematicamente

T

tabernacle tabernacolo *m*
table tavola; lista *f*
 -cloth tovaglia *f*;
tack bulletta; amura;
 bordata; attaccare;
 appiccare
tackle girella *f*; attiraglio
 m; attaccare; pigliare
tact tatto *m*
tail coda *f*
tailor sarto *m*
taint macchia; infettare
take prendere
talent talento *m*
talented dotato
talk parlare *m*; parlare
talkative loquace
tall alto; grande
tame domestico; domare
tamer domatore *m*
tamper subornare
tan concia *f*; bruciare
tangible tangibile
tank cisterna *f*
tanner conciaiolo *m*
tantalize tantaleggiare
tap chiave; cannella *f*;
 colpo leggiero *m*
tape cordellina *f*; – r cero
 m; terminarsi in punta;
 – ring conico; – stry tap-

114

pezzeria *f*; − **worm** verme solitario *m*

tar catrame *m*; pece *f*; catramare

tarantula tarantola *f*

tardy lento; tardivo

tare tara *f*

tardiness lentezza *f*

target bersaglio *m*

tariff tariffa *f*

taste gusto; sapore *m*; inclinazione *f*; gustare; − ful gustoso; elegante; − less senza gusto

tasty di buon gusto

tatter straccio *m*

tattle ciancia *f*; cianciare

tattoo ritirata *f*; screziare

taunt insulto *m*; insultare

tavern osteria ; taverna *f*

tawdry di lustro falso

tawny olivastro

tax tassa; imposta *f*; tassare; accusare − ation tassazione *f*

tea tè *m*; − **kettle** cogoma *f*; − **things** servizio da tè

teach insegnare; istruire; − er maestro; istitutore *m*; − ing insegnamento

team fila *f*   · [*m*

tear lagrima *f*; − s pianto *m*; stracciatura *f*; stracciare; lacerare

tease seccare; importunare

telegram telegramma *m*

telegraph telegrafo *m*; telegrafare

telephone telefono *m*; telefonare

telescope telescopio *m*

tell ·dire; raccontare

temper tempera; collera *f*; temperare; mescolare

temperance temperanza *f*

temperate sobrio   [*f*

temperature temperatura

tempest tempesta *f*

tempestuous tempestoso

temple tempio *m*

tempt tentare

temptation tentazione *f*

tempter tentatore *m*

ten dieci *m*

tend custodire; tendere

tendency tendenza *f*

tender tenero; ⁄ dolce; offerta *f*; offerire; − ness tenerezza; cura *f*

tennis, − -**court** pallacorda *f*

tenor tenore; senso⁶ *m*

tense rigido; tempo *m*

tension tensione *f*

tent tenda *f*; padiglione

tenth decimo *m*   [*m*

term termine; semestre *m*; durata *f*

terminate terminare   [*f*

termination terminazione

terrace terrazzo *m*

terrible terribile

terrier bassotto *m*

terrific spaventevole

terrify atterrire

territory territorio *m*

terror terrore *m*

terse terso; lindo

test saggio *m*; prova *f*; provare

testament testamento *m*

testicle testicolo *m*

testify attestare   [*f*

testimonial testimonianza

testimony testimonianza *f*

testy ringhioso

tether pastoia *f*; impas-

text testo *m*   [toiare

textile tessile

texture tessitura *f*; tes-

than che; di   [suto *m*

thank ringraziare; − ful

grato; – **fulness** riconoscenza *f*; – **less** ingrato; – **s** grazie *f pl*

that quello; quella; ciò; sia; che; perche; che; il quale; la quale; chi; quegli; colui

the il; lo; la; i; gli; le

theatre teatro *m*; scena *f*

theatrical teatrale

thee te; ti

theft furbo *m*

their. – **s** il loro; la loro; i loro; le loro

them li; le; loro; essi

themselves si; se stessi

theme tema *m*

then allora; poi; dunque

there li; là; vi; ci; ivi; – **is** c'è; ecco – **about** là intorno; – **after** dopo ciò; – **by** da ciò; – **fore** quindi; perciò; – **from** da ciò; – **in** in ciò; entro; – **on** su di ciò; – **with** con ciò   [*m*

thermometer termometro

these questi; queste

they essi; esse; loro

thick spesso; grosso

thicken spessire; raddoppiare; oscurarsi

thief ladro *m*

thieve rubare

thievish da ladro

thigh coscia *f*

thimble ditale *m*

thin sottile;   magro; assottigliare

thine il tuo; la tua ; i

thing cosa *f* [tuoi; le tue

think pensare

third terzo *m*

thirst sete *f*

thirsty assetato

thirteen tredici *m*

thirty trenta *m*

this questo

thorough fondato; completo;

though sebbene; benchè

thought pensiero *m*; idea *f*; – **ful** pensieroso; – **less** spensierato; –

thousand mille *m*

thrash trebbiare

thrashing bastonata *f*;

thread filo; refe *m*; infilare;

threat minaccia *f*

threaten minacciare

three tre *m*

thrift economia *f*

thrifty frugale   [tare

thrill sussulto *m*; sussu-

thrilling toccante

thrive prosperare

throat gola; strozza *f*

throb palpitare

throne trono *m*

through attraverso; per – **out** in ogni parte

throw getto; colpo *m*; gettare; lanciare

thrush tordo *m*

thrust spinta *f*; spingere

thumb pollice *m*

thunder tuono *m*; fulminare; – **bolt** fulmine

thus così; in questo modo

thwart attraversare

tide marea *f*

tidy pulito

tie legame *m*; cravata *f*;

tier rango *m* [legare

tiger tigre *m*

tight tirato; serrato; – **en** stringere; – **ness** strettezza *f*; – **s** calzoni

tile tegola *f* [*m pl*

till cassa *f* coltivare

timber legname *m*;

time tempo *m*; epoca *f*

timely opportuno

116

timid timido

tin stagno *m*; latta *f*; stagnare

tincture tintura; tinta *f*

tinge tingere

tingle pizzicare [tinnire

tinkle tintinno ; tin-

tinsel orpello *m*

tint tinta *f*; tingere

tiny piccino

tip punta *f*; regalo *m*:

tire cerchio *m*; stancare

tiresome seccante

tissue tessuto *m*

tissue paper carta velina *f*

tit ronzino *m*

tithe decima *f*

title titolo; nome *m*; intitolare [nare

titter risolino *m*; sogghig-to a; verso; su; per

toad rospo *m*

toast pane abbrustolita *f*; brindisi *m*; abbrustolire; to-day oggi

toe dito (del piede) *m*

together insieme

toil pena *f*; travagliare

toilet toeletta *f*

token segno *m*

tolerable tollerabile

tolerant tollerante

tolerate tollerare

toleration tolleranza *f*

toll pedaggio *m*; rintoc-care

tomato pomidoro *m*

tomb tomba *f*

tomb-stone lapide *m*

ton tonnellata *f* [= 1015 kilogrammes)

tone tono; suono *m*

tongs molle *f pl*

tongue lingua *f*; linguag-

tonic tonico *m* [gio *m*

to-night stanotte

tonsil tonsilla *f*

tonsure tonsura *f*

too troppo; anche

tool arnese; strumento *m*

tooth dente *m*; - -ache mal di denti *m*;

torch torcia *f*

torment tormento *m*; tormentare [*m*

tormentor tormentatore

tornado uragano *m*

torpedo torpedine *m*

torture tortura *f*; tor-turare

toss trabalzare; lanciare

total totale *m*

touch tatto; contatto *m*; toccare; - stone pietra di paragone

touching toccante

tough tenace

toughness durezza *f*

tour giro; viaggio *m*; - ist viaggiatore *m* [*m*

tournament torneamento

tow stoppa *f*; rimorchiare

towards verso; per; a

towel tovagliolo *m*

tower torre *f*; torreggiare; dominare

town città *f*; borgo *m*; -hall casa della città *f*

toy giocattolo *m*; giocol-are

trace traccia *f*; vestigio *m*; tirella *f*; tracciare

track traccia; marca *f*; tracciare [regione *f*

tract trattatello *m*;

trade commercio; nego-zio; *m*; negoziare; - ing mercantile; mercatura *f* -r mercante *m*

tradition tradizione *f*

traffic traffico *m*; traffi-care

tragedy tragedia *f*

tragic(al) tragico

trail traccia *f*; strascinare

train treno *m*; addestrare; istruire

trait tratto *m*

traitor traditore *m*

tranquil tranquillo

tranquillize calmare

transact negoziare

transaction transazione *f*

transcribe trascrivere

transfer trasporto *m*; trasferire

transferable trasferibile

transformation trasformazione *f*   [violare

transgress trasgredire;

transgressor trasgressore; peccatore *m*

transient passeggiero

transitory transitorio

translate tradurre

translation traduzione *f*

transmission trasmissione

transmit trasmettere   [*f*

transparent trasparente

transpire traspirare

transplant trapiantare

transport trasporto *m*; trasportare; deportare

transpose trasporre

trap trappola; carozza *f*; trappolare; − -door botola; *f* − pings livrea *f*

travel viaggio *m*; viaggiare; − ler viaggiatore; commesso *m*

traverse taversare

tray vassoio *m*

treacherous perfido

treachery tradimento *m*

treason tradimento *m*

treasure tesoro *m*; tesoreggiare; ammassare; − r tesoriere *m*

treasury tesoreria *f*

treat regalo *m*; cosa squisita *f*; trattare;

tree albero *m*

tremble tremare; fremere

tremendous tremendo

tremor tremore *m*

trench trincea *f*; fosso *m*; trincerare

trepidation trepidazione *f*

trespass peccato; trapasso *m*; trasgredire

triangular triangolare

tribe tribù; orda *f*

tribunal tribunale *m*

tributary tributario *m*

tribute tributo *m*

trick tiro *m*

trickery birbonata *f*

tricycle triciclo *m*

trigger grilletto *m*

trill trillo *m*; trillare

trim lindo; parare; guarnire

trinity trinità *f*

trinket ciondolo *m*

trip inciampo *m*; gita *f*; inciampare

tripe trippa *f*

triple triplo

triumph trionfo *m*;

trivial triviale

trombone trombone *m*

troop truppa; banda *f*; − er soldato di cavalleria *m*

trophy trofeo *m*

tropical tropicale

tropics tropici *m pl*

trot trotto *m*; trottare

trouble pena *f*; molestare; − some seccante

trough truogolo *m*

trousers pantaloni *m pl*

trousseau scherpa *f*

trout trota *f*

trowel cazzuolo *f*

truant pigro *m*

truce tregua *f*

truck carretta *f*

118

truculent truce; feroce
trudge marciare con fatica [cero
true vero; verace; sin-
trunk tronco *m*; pro- boscide *f* (d'élefante)
– -maker cofanaio *m*
trust fiducia; fede *f*; credito *m*; fidare; credere a; – ee deposi- tario *m*; – worthy fido; fidato [verace
truth verità *f*; – ful
try tentare; provare
tub tino *m*
tube tubo *m*
tug stiracchiamento *m*; rimorchiatore *m*; stir- richiare

tune tono *m*; aria *f*; accordare; – ful armo-
tunnel galleria *f* [nioso
turbot rombo *m*
turbulent turbolento
turf erba; torba *f*
turkey tacchino; pollo d'India *m*
turmoil imbroglio *m*
turn giro *m*; girare; volgere ; –er tornitore *m*; – ing giro *m*; – ing-
turquoise turchese *f*
turret torricella *f*
turtle tortora *f*
tusk zanna *f*
tutor maestro *m*
twang suono acuto *m*; pronunzia nasale *f*
tweezers pinzette *f pl*
twelfth duodecimo *m*
twelve dodici *m*
twentieth ventesimo *m*
twenty venti *m*
twice duo volte; doppia-
twig virghetta *f* [mente
twilight crepuscolo *m*

twin gemello *m* [chiare
twine spago *m*; avvitic-
twinge spasimo *m*
twinkle scintillare
twirl girar rapidamente
twist torcitura *f*; tor-
twitter garrire [cere
two due *m*
typhus fifo *m*
typical tipico
typography tipografia *f*
tyrannize tiranneggiare
tyranny tirannia *f*
tyrant tiranno *m*

U

ubiquitous onnipresente
ubiquity ubiquità *f*
udder tetta; poppa (animale)
ugliness laidezza *f*
ugly bruto; laido
ultramarine oltremarino
umbrage ombra *f* [*m*
umber terra d'ombra *f*
umbrella ombrella *f*; – -stand posaombrelle *m*
umpire arbitro *m*
unabashed non confuso
unable incapace [bile
unacceptable inaccetta-
unaccountable inespli- cabile [tuato
unaccustomed poco abi-
unacquainted ignaro (di)
unadorned disadorno
unadvisable imprudente
unaffected sincero
unaided senz'assistenza
unalterable inalterabile
unaltered non alterato
unanimity unanimità *f*
unanimous unanime
unanswerable incon-

unapt inetto [testabile
unarmed senza armi
unashamed senza vergogna
unasked non richiesto
unassuming senza pretesa
unattainable fuori mano
unattended solo [ente
unattractive poco attraunavailing inefficace
unavoidable inevitabile
unaware non avvertito;
 – s all'improvviso
unbecoming disdicevole
unbelief incredulità f
unbeliever infidele m & f
unburden scaricare; aprisi
unbutton sbottonare
unceremonious senza cermonie
uncertain incerto
uncertainty incertezza f
unchangeable immutabile
unchristian poco cristiano
uncivil incivile
uncivilized barbaro
uncle zio m

uncomfortable incomodo
uncommon non comune
unconcern indifferenza f
unconcerned indifferente
unconnected non connesso
unconscionable irragionevole
unconscious inconscio
unconstrained libero
uncontrollable incontroluncork stappare [labile
uncouth goffo; bizzarro
uncover scoprire; svelare
undefinable indefinibile
undefined indefinito
undeniable innegabile
under sotto; al di sotto
underbid offerire meno
underdone poco cotto

undergo subire
underground sotterraneo
underhand sottomano
underline sottolineare
understanding comprensione f; accordo m
undertake intraprendere
undertaker impresario (di pompe funebri) m
undertaking intraprendenza f [di
undervalue far poco conto
underwrite assicurare m
underwriter assicuratore
undeserved immeritato
undesirable da non desiderarsi
undetermined indeciso
undignified senza dignità
undisciplined indisciplinato [cherato
undisguised non masundisturbed tranquillo
undivided indiviso
undo disfare
undoubted indubbio
undress abito di camera m; svestirsi
undressed non vestito
undue indebito
undulation ondulazione f
uneasiness inquietudine f
uneasy inquieto
uneducated non educato
unemployed disoccupato
uneven ineguale
unexpected inaspettato
unfailing infallibile
unfair non equo
unfaithful infido
unfasten slegare [bile
unfathomable impenetraunfavourable sfavorevole
unfeeling insensibile
unfeigned sincero
unfinished incompleto
unfit inetto

120

unfold spiegare
unforeseen impreveduto
unforgiving implacabile
unfortunate sfortunato
unfounded infondato
unfriendly non amiche-
vole
unfruitful infruttuoso
unfurl spiegare   [ato
unfurnished non mobili-
ungenerous ingeneroso
ungrateful ingrato
unguarded sconsiderato
unhappiness miseria f
unhappy infelice
unharness levaregli arnesi
unhealthy malsano
unheard inaudito
uniform uniforme; uni-
forme f
unimaginable inimmag-
ginabile   [tante
unimportant poco impor-
union unione
unique unico
unison unisono m
unit unità f
unite unire
unity unità f
universal universale
universe universo m
university università f
unjust ingiusto
unjustifiable ingiustifica-
bile
unkind non benigno
unknown incognito
unlace slacciare
unlawful illegale
unlearned illetterato
unless meno che; fuorché
unlike dissimile
unlikely improbabile
unlimited illimitato
unload scaricare
unlock aprire

unloose slegare
unlucky sfortunota
unmanageable intratta-
bile
unmanly effeminato
unmannerly mal creato
unmarried celibe
unmeaning insensato
unmerciful inumano
unmindful immemore
unmixed puro
unmoved immorto
unnatural non naturale
unnecessary non neces-
sario
unnoticed inosservato
unoccupied disoccupato
unoffending innocente
unpack sbalare
unpaid non pegato [gusto
unpalatable sgradevole al
unparalleled incompara-
bile   [abile
unpardonable imperdon-
unpleasant spiacevole
unpolished rozzo
unpopular impopolare
unprepared impreparato
unprincipled senza prin-
cipii
unproductive infruttuoso
unprofitable inutile
unreasonable irragione-
vole   [ciliabile
unreconcilable irrecon-
unrelenting inesorabile
unreliable indegno di
fiducia   [franco
unreserved senza riserva;
unsalable invendibile
unsatisfactory non sod-
disfacente
unsavoury non saporito
unscrew svitare
unseasonable fuori di
stagione; intempestivo

unserviceable inutile
unsettle dissestare
unsettled dissestato
unshaken fermo
unsightly difforme
unskilful inesperto
unskilled imperito
unsociable insociabile
unsold invenduto
unspeakable indicibile
unstable instabile; in-costante
unsteady mal fermo
unsuccessful non riuscito
unsuitable disadatto
untidy non pulito
untie snodare   [che
until sino a che: tanto
untrained inesercitato
untried non provato
untrue falso; sleale
untwist strigare
unusual insolito
unveil rilevare   [rizzato
unwarranted non auto-
unwary incauto
unwearied indefesso
unwelcome mal accolto
unwell non bene
unwholesome malsano
unwieldy pesante
unwilling mal disposto
unwind annaspare
unwise mal accorto
unwonted insolito
unworthy indegno
unwrap scoprire
unyielding inflessibile
up su; sopra; sopra di;
uphill difficile [in alto
uphold sostenere
upholsterer tappezziere *m*
uplift elevare
upon sopra
upper superiore; più alto

uproar tumulto *m*
uproot sradicare

upset capovolgere
upside-down sossopra
upstart spaccone *m*
upwards su; in su; in alto; più (di)
urge stimolare
urgency urgenza
urgent urgente
urine urina *f*
urn urna *f*
us ci; ce; ne; noi
usage uso
use uso *m*; usare; – ful utile; – fulness utilità *f*; – less inutile; – less-ness inutilità *f*
usual usuale
utensil utensile *m*
utility utilità *f*
utmost estremo   [ciare
utter assoluto; pronun-
utterance pronunzia *f*
utterly totalmente

V

vacancy vacanza *f*; spazio vuoto *m*
vacant vacante
vacate lasciar vacante
vacation vacanza *f*
vaccinate vaccinare [*f*
vaccination vaccinazione

valet valetto; giovano servitore *m*
valiant valoroso
valid valido
validity validità *f*
valour valore *m*
valuable prezioso
valuation valutazione *f*
value valore; prezzo *m*; valutare; – d valutato; – less senza valore
valve valvola *f*
vamp rappezzare

vampire vampiro
van carrettone *m*; avan-
 guardia *f*
vane banderuola *f*
vandalism vandalismo *m*
vanilla vaniglià *f*

vanish svanire
vanity vanità *f*
vanquish vincere
vantage vantaggio *m*
variable variabile
variableness variabilità *f*
variance variazione *f*
variation variazione *f*
varied variato
variegate variare
variety varietà *f*
various vario; diverso
varnish vernice *f*; verni-
 ciare
vary variare
vase vaso *m*
vault volta *f*; salto *m*;
 volteggiare
veal vitello *m*
veer girare   [gume *m*
vegetable vegetabile; le-
vegetate vegetare
vegetation vegetazione *f*
vehemence veemenza *f*
vehement veemente
vehicle veicolo *m*
veil velo *m*; velare
vein vena *f*
velocity velocità *f*
velvet velluto *m*
vendor venditore *m*
venereal venereo
vengeance vendetta *f*
vengeful vendicativo
venison selvaggina *f*
venom veleno *m*
venomous velenoso
vent vento; sbocco *m*;
 sfogare; – ilate ventilare
 – ilation ventilazione *f*;

– riloquist ventriloquo *m*
venture ventura *f*; av-
 venturare;
verb verbo *m*
verbal verbale; orale
verdict verditto *m*
verdigris verdame *m*
verdure verdure *m*
verge bordo; orlo *m*;
 tendere verso
verification verificazione *f*
verify verificare
verily in verità
veritable vro; attuale
verity verità *f*
vespers vespri *m pl*
vessel vaso; vascello *m*
vest camiciola *f*; veste *f*

vestige vestigio *m*
vestment vestito *m*
vestry vestiario *m*; sac-
 ristia *f*
veteran veterano *m*
veterinary veterinario *m*
veto veto *m*
vex irritare   [*f*
vexation vessazione; noia
vexatious vessante
vial caraffina *f*
viands vivanda *f*
vibrate vibrare
vibration vibrazione *f*
vicar vicario *m*
vice vizio *m*; morsa *f*;
 – -admiral vice-ammir-
 aglio *m*; – roy vicerè *m*
vicious vizioso
vicissitude vicissitudine *f*
victim vittima *f*
view vista *f*; guardare
vigilance vigilanza *f*
vigilant vigilante
vigorous vigoroso
vigour vigore *m*
vile vile
vilify avvilire
villa villa *f*

123

village villaggio *m*
villager villico *m*
villain scellerato *m*
villainous villano
villainy scelleratezza *f*
vindicate difendere [*f*
vindication giustificazione
vindictive vendicativo;
 – ness carattere vendi-
 cativo *m*
vine vite; vigna *f*
vinegar aceto *m*
vineyard vigna *f*
vinous vinoso
vintage vendemmia *f*
viol viola *f*
violate violare
violation violazione *f*
violence violenza *f*
violent violento
violet viola *f*
violin violino *m*
violinist violinista *m & f*
violoncello violoncello *m*
viper vipera *f*
virago virago *f*
virgin vergine *f*
virginity verginità *f*
virtual virtuale
virtue virtù *f*
virtuous virtuoso
virulent virulento
visage viso *m*
viscera viscere *f pl*
viscount visconte *m*
viscous viscoso
visible visibile
vision visione; vista *f*;
 – ary visionario
visit visita *f*; giro *m*;
 visitare;
vital vitale
vivacious vivace [zione *f*
vivacity vivacità *f*
vivid vivo
vocabulary vocabolario *m*
vocal vocale

voice voce *f*
void vuoto; vacuo *m*
volatile volatile
volcanic vulcanico
volcano vulcano *m*
volley scarica; salva *f*
volt vólta *f*
volubility volubilità *f*
voluble volubile [*f*
volume volume *m*: massa
vomit vomitare *f*
vote voto; suffraggio *m*;
 votare; – r votante
vouch attestare;
vow voto *m*; giurare
vowel vocale *f*
voyage viaggio *m*
vulgar volgare
vulgarity volgarità *f*
vulnerable vulnerabile

voluminous voluminoso
voluntary volontario
volunteer volontario *m*;
 offrire
voluptuous voluttuoso;
 – ness voluttà *f*

W

wabble esitare; vacillare
wad fascio di paglia;
 mettere lo stopaccio;
 – ding ovatta *f*; – dle
 ciondolare
wade guadare
wafer cialda; ostia *f*
wag piacevolone *m*; scuotere
wage scommettere; – r
 scommessa *f*; scom-
 mettere; – s salario *m*
waist vita *f*; busto *m*;
 – band cintura *f*; – coat
 gilè *m*
wait aspettare; – er
 garzone *m*; – ing attesa

124

wake seguito *m*; veglia *f*;
funerale *m*; svegliarsi;
– ful vigilante; – n svegliare   [*f*; camminare
walk camminata; strada
wall muro *m*

waltz valzer; *m* ballar il
wan smorto   [valzer
wand bacchetta *f*
wander vagare; – er gir-
ovago *m*; – ing errante
wane decadenza *f*; declinare
want mancanza *f*; bisogno *m*; indigenza *f*;
mancare; aver bisogno
di   [zioso
wanton sboccato; licen-
war guerra *f*; far guerra
warble trillare
ward guardia *f*; rione;
pupillo *m*; parare;
proteggere; – – er guar-
diano *m*; – robe guarda-
roba *f*
ware mercanzia *f*
warehouse magazzino *m*;
immagazzinare
warm caldo; vivo; scaldare
warmth caldo; ardore *m*
warn avvertire
warning avviso; avverti-
mento *m*   [torcere
warp far piegare; con-
warrant mandato *m*;
garanzia *f*; autorizzare;
garantire;
wart porro *m*
wary avveduto
wash lavatura; lozione *f*;
lavare; bagnare; – up
rigovernare; – erwoman
lavandaia *f*;   – ing
bucato *m*; lavanda *f*;

wasp vespa *f*

waste incolto; inutile;
sciupio; scialacquo *m*;
perdita; spesa inutile;
terra incolta *f*; deserto;
scarto *m*; sciupare;
prodigare; devastare;
sperperare;
watch veglia *f*; orologio
m; vigilare; sorvegliare;
– ful vigilante; – fulness
vigilanza; – maker oro-
logiaio *m*; – man guard-
ia notturna *f*; – word
parola d'ordine *f*
water acqua *f*; adacquare
– -fall cascata *f*; – fowl
uccello acquatico; – ing-
place i bagni *m pl*;
– ing-pot annaffiatoio *m*;
– -jug mesciacqua *f*;
– -lily ninfea *f*; – proof
impermeabile *m*;   –
wave onda *f*; flutto *m*;
far fluttuare; ondeg-
giare
waver fluttuare; vacillare
wavering esitante
wavy ondoso
wax cera *f*; crescere
way via; strada *f*; modo
m – lay sorprendere;
we noi
weak debole; – en indebolire:-ness debolezza *f*
wealth richezza *f*
wealthy ricco; opulento
wean svezzare
weapon arma; difessa *f*
wear logoro; servizio;
uso *m*; portare; aver
addosso
wearied stanco, infasti-
weariness fatica *f* [dito
wearisome faticoso
weary lasso; stanco
f; faticare

weasel donnola *f*

weather tempo *m*; temperatura *f*; resistere;

web tela *f*

wed sposare; maritarsi; sposarsi; – -lock matrimonio *m*

wedding nozze *f pl*; sposalizio *m*

wedge zeppa *f*; zeppare

wee piccolo [chiare

weed malerba *f*; sar-

week settimana *f*; otto giorni *m pl*; – day giorno feriale *m*; – ly settimenale

weep lacrimare

weigh pesare; ponderare

weight peso; pondo *m*

weighty pesante; grave

welcome benevenuto *m*; dare il ben venuto (a)

weld saldare

welfare ben essere; bene *m*; felicità *f*

well pozzo *m*; fontana *f*; bene; – -bred ben educato – -wisher amico

west occidentale; verso l'ovest; occidente; ovest *m*; – erly, – ern d'occidente; – ward a ponente

wet umido; piovoso; umidità *f*; inumidire;

what cio che; quel che; quale; che; – ever; – soever tutto cio che, qual si sia; qualunque

wheat frumento; grano *m*

wheel ruota *f*; rotare; – barrow carriola *f*;

when quando; allorchè; mentre; ove; allora

where dove; ove; – about

in che luogo; di cui; – as mentre; mentre che; invece di; – at al che; su di che; – by per cui; pel qual mezzo; – fore per ció; quindi; onde; – in in che; nel quale; – of del quale; di cui; – on, – upon su di che; sopra di che; – soever in qualunque luogo; – with con che; con quale; di cui

whet aguzzare; affilare

whether se; sia; che; quale dei due

whey siero di latte

which che; il che; quale; chi

whichever qualunque; quello; quale

whiff soffio; buffo *m*

while tempo; attimo *m*; passare [che; finchè

whine gagnolamento; gemito *m*; gagnolare; gemere [frustare

whip frusta; sferza;

whirl giro rapido *m*; rotare rapidamente; – pool vortice *m*; – wind buffera *f*

whiskers fedine *f pl*; baffi *m pl* (di gatto)

whiskey acquavite (d'orzo) *f* [bisbigliare

whisper sussurro *m*;

whist wist *m*

whistle fischietto *m*; fischiare

white bianco; – n imbiancare; – ness bianchezza

who che; il quale; la quale; i quali; le quali; chi [chessia

whoever chiunque; chic-
whole intero; totale;
tutto *m*; - **sale** all'
ingrosso; grosso *m*;
whom che; il quale;
cui; a chi; chi
whomsoever chiunque
whoop urlo *m*; urlare
whopping-cough tosse
canina *f*
whore prostituta *f*
whose di cui; del quale;
dei quali; delle quali;
why perchè [di chi
wick lucignolo *m*
wicked malvagio; cat-
tivo; - **ness** malvagità *f*
wicker di vinco; vinco *m*
wide largo; vasto
widen allargare
widow vedova *f*
widower vedovo *m*
width larghessa *f*
wife moglie; sposa *f*
wig parrucca *f*
wild selvaggio; furioso
wilderness deserto *m*
wilful testardo
will volontà *f*; testamento *m*; volere; leg-
are; - **ing** disposto (a);
- **ingly** volentieri; - **ing-
ness** buona volontà *f*
willow salice *m*
wily furbo; fino
win vincere; guadagnare
wind vento; fiato *m*;
avvolgere; torcere; -
- **up** liquidare; caricare
(orologio); - **ing** avvol-
gimento *m*; sinuosità *f*;
wine vino *m*; —**merchant** vinaio *m*; - -**press**
wing ala *f* [follatoio *m*
winged alato
wink batter d'occhio *m*;

ammiccare
winner vincitore *m*
winnings vincita *f*
winnow spagliare [are
winter inverno *m*; svern-
wisdom saggezza; sapi-
wise savio; saggio [enza *f*
wish desiderio *m*; voglia
f; desiderare; volere
wisp pagliola *f*; pugnon *m*
wistful attento
wit spirito *m*; sagacia *f*
witch strega; maga *f*
witchcraft stregoneria *f*
with con; per; contro;
fra; presso; di; - **draw**
ritirare; levare; - **drawal**
retiro *m*; - **er** appassire;
- **ered** appassito; - **hold**
ritenere; - **in** indentro;
in casa; - **out** fuori;
senza; fuori; - **stand**
resistere (a)
witness testimonio *m*;
testimonianza *f*; testificare; esser testimonio di
wizard stregone; mago *m*
woe guaio; dolore *m*
wolf lupo *m*
woman femmina; donna;
serva *f*; - **ish, ly** don-
nesco; - -**kind** bel sesso
womb seno *m*; matrice *f*
wonder maraviglio *f*;
prodigio *m*; maravig-
liarsi; - **ful** maraviglioso
wood bosco; legno *m*;
woof trama *f* [ante *m*
wool lana *f*; - **len** di
lana; lano; - **lens** lan-
eria *f*; - **ly** lanuto;
lanoso
word parola *f*
work lavoro *m*; opera *f*;
lavorare; operare; - **er**

127

lavorante *m & f*;
operaio *m*; – **house** casa
di lavoro *f*; – **ing-day**
giorno di lavoro *m*;
world mondo; universo
m; – **liness** mondanità

worry agitazione *f*; tormentare
worse peggiore; più male
worship sculto *m*; adorazione *f*; adorare
worst il peggio; il peggiore *m*; peggio
worst vincere
worsted filo di lana *m*
worth che vale; degno
di; uguale a; valore;
merito *m*; – **less** senza
valore; – **lessness** mancanza di valore; bassezza *f*; – **y** degno
wrap inviluppare
wrapper fascia; veste
da camera *f*
wrath collera; ira *f*
wrathful irato
wreak vendicare

wreath ghirlanda *f*
wreathe coronare

wreck naufragio *m*;
naufragare
wren reatino; liù *m*

wrench strappo *m*; chiave inglese *f*; strappare
write scrivere
writer scrittore *m*
writhe scontorcersi
writing scrittura; mano *f*
wrong malo; cattivo;
inesatto; torto; male;
danno *m*; ledere; nuocere; – **ful** ingiusto;
wry di traverso; – **neck**
torcicollo; – **ness** torsione

X

xylographic zilografico
xyster rastiatoio *m*
xystus zisto; portico *m*

Y

yacht iachetto; yacht *m*
yahoo selvaggio *m*
yankee Americano degli
Stati Uniti
yard cortile *m*; iarda
(·914 metri) *f*
yarn filo *m*
yawn sbadiglio *m*; sbadi-
yea sì; già   [gliare
year anno *m*; – **ling**
d'un anno; – **ly** annuale
yearn sospirare dietro
yeast lievito *m*
yell urlo *m*; urlare
yellow giallo *m*
yellowish gialliccio
yelp latrato *m*; latrare
yeoman piccolo proprietario *m*; guardia reale
yes sì   [a piedi *f*
yesterday ieri
yet ancora; anche; pure;
eppure: nondimeno
yield raccolto *m*; rendenza *f*; produrre;
rendere
yoke giogo *m*; aggriogare
yolk tuorlo; rosso d'uovo
you voi; vi; ve; te; a te
young giovane; giovani
m pl   [ragazzo *m*
youngster giovanotto;
your vostro; tuo; – **s**
il vostro; – **self**, – **selves**
voi stesso
youth gioventù *f*; – **ful**
giovanile; – **fulness** gio

128

vanezza *f*
Yule Natale *m*; – log

Z

zebra zebra *f*
zero zero *m*

zest fetta *f*; sapore *m*
zodiac zodiaco *m*
zone zona; cintura *f*
zoographer zoografo *m*
zoography zoografia *f*

zoological zoologico
zoologist zoologo *m*
zoology zoologia *f*

ITALIAN-ENGLISH
DICTIONARY

abbacare embroil; confuse

abbacchista *m* arithmetician

abbacinamento *m* blindness

abbagliamento *m* blindness; mistake [error

abbaglianza *f* illusion;'

abbagliare deceive

abbaglio *m* mistake; blunder; error

abbaiamento *m* barking

abbaiare bark; bore

abbaiatore *m* barker (*met.*) ·brawler [dow

abbaino *m* dormer-win-

abballare pack [tate

abbalordire *va* stun; irri-

abbambagiare trim; stuff

abbandonamento *m* abandonment

abbandonare abandon

abbaruffare mix; embroil

abbassamento *m* abasement [ate

abbassare lower; humili-

abbasso under; below

abbastanza enough; sufficiently

abbattere overthrow; demolish; deduct

abbattimento *m* ruin; dejection; chance

abbattitore *m* destroyer

abbattuffolare jumble

abbecedario *m* abecedarian

abbellare embellish

abbellimento *m* embellishment; ornament

abbiettare disgrace

abbiettezza *n* abjection

abbietto low; abject

abbiezione *f* abjection

abbigliamento *n* clothes; furniture [adorn

abbigliare dress; trim;

abbindolamento *m* dodge; fraud [cheat

abbindolare deceive;

abbindolatore *n* deceiver

abbiosciare fall down; – si lose courage

abbisognante needy

abbisognare be necessary; want

abbiurare *va* to abjure

abbiurazione *f* abjuration

abboscamento *n* intervie; colloquy

abboccare seize with the teeth; fill up; – si *n* have an interview

abboccato agreeable; deli-

abbocconare hash [cate

abbombarsi get drunk

abbominabile abomin-

abbominsre hate

abbonacciamento *n* calm

abbonacciare calm; pacify

abbonamento *n* amelioration; subscription

abbonare ameliorate; improve; subscribe for

abbondante abundant

abbondantemente abundantly

abbondanza *f* abundance

abbondare di abound in

abboracciare   bungle;
  botch
abbordare accost; board
abbozzare sketch   [line
abbozzo m sketch; out-
abbracciamento m; ab-
  bracciare, abbracciata f
  embrace   [tight
abbrancare clasp; hold
abbreviare abridge
abbreviatura f abbrevia-
abbrividiro shiver
abbrustolare toast
abbuiare darken
abbuono m improvement
abdicare abdicate
abete m fir
abietto abject
abile able; clever
abilità cleverness
abilitare qualify
abisso m abyss
abitabile habitable
abitante m inhabitant
abitare inhabit; dwell
abitatore m inhabitant
abitazione f dwelling
abito m habit; dress
abituale customary
abituarsi get accustomed
abluzione f ablution
abolire abolish
abolizione f abolition
abominare, aborrire detest
abominevole abominable
aborto m abortion
abrogare abrogate
abside f apsis
abusare misuse
abusivo abusive
abuso m abuse
accadere happen   [cuse
accagionare impute: ac-
accarezzare caress
accasamento m marriage
accasarsi marry

accatarrare catch cold
accedere approach
accelerare accelerate
accelerazione f accelera-
accendere kindle   [tion
accenditore m lighter
accennare beckon; hint
accenno m notice; hint
accento m accent; word
accentuare accentuate
accertare ascertain; affirm
accessibile accessible
accesso m access
accessorio accessory
accettabile acceptable
accettare accept
accettazione f acception
acchetare calm
acchiappare catch; grasp
acchiocciolarsi squat
acciabattare botch, daub
acciacco m insult; indis-
  position
acciaiare steel, harden
acciaieria f steel-works
acciaio m steel
acciaiuolo m fire-steel
acciappinarsi fatigue oneself
accidentale accidental
accidente m accident;
  apoplexy
accigliarsi knit the brows
accio, acciocchè in order
  that   [hair
acciuffare seize by the
acciuga f anchovy
acclamare applaud [tion
acclamazione f acclama-
acclimare acclimat(iz)e
accludere enclose
accoccolarsi squat
accoglienza f reception
accogliere welcome
accollare lade
accolta f assembly

133

accoltellare stab [ment
accomodamento m agree-
accomodare settle; ar-
range; – si sit down
acconcio m advantage;
arranged
acconto m part-payment
accoppiare match
accorciare shorten
accordare grant; tune;
reconcile; agree
accordo m accord; con-
accorgersi perceive [cord
accorrere run; hasten
accorr'uomo help! help!
accorto prudent
accostare approach
accosto near, beside
accostumare accustom
accozzare heap; gather
accreditare accredit
accrescere increase
accrescimento m increase
acido sour; m acid
acino m grain; grape-
stone
acqua f water; – cedrata
lemonade; – di latte
whey; – forte aqua for-
tis; – dolce fresh water;
– di mare sea-water
acquapendente f water-
acquartierare lodge [shed
acquatico aquatic
acquavite f brandy
acquazzone m shower
acquerellare paint in
water-colours
acquerellista m water-
colour painter
acquerello m water-col-
our painting
acquidotto m acqueduct
acquiescenza f acquies-
cence
acquisizione f acquisition
acquistare acquire

adamante m diamond
adattare adapt
adatto convenient
addarsi apply one's self
addentro inside; within
addestrare teach; drill
addetto attached
addietro behind
addio farewell
addirsi suit; become
addirizzare direct; cor-
rect
addizionale additional
addizione f addition;
supplement
addobb(ament)o m orna-
ment; furniture
addobbare adorn
addolcire soften
addolorato afflicted
addome m abdomen
addomesticare tame
adempiere perform
aderente adherent
aderire adhere
adescare bait; allure
adesione f adhesion
adesso now
adiacente adjacent
adiposo adipose; fat
adirare irritate; make
angry
adoperare employ; exert
adorabile adorable
adorare adore
adoratore m adorer
adorn(ament)o m orna-
adornare adorn [ment
adottare adopt
adott(at)ivo adoptive
Adriatico m Adriatic
adulare flatter
adulatore m flatterer
adulazione flattery
adulterare adulterate
adultero adulterous
adulterio m adultery

adulto adult
adunanza *f* meeting
adunare assemble
aere *m* air; **aereo** aerial
affaccendato very occupied
affacchinarsi drudge
affacciare show
affamare famish
affannare grieve; provoke
affanno *m* grief
affare *m* affair
affascinare fascinate
affaticare tire
affatto quite; entirely
affettazione *f* affectation
affetto *m* love   [self
affezionarsi attach one's
affezionato affectionate
affezione *f* affection; love
affibbiare buckle   [hole
affibbiatoio *m* button-
affidare confide; trust
affilare sharpen
affinare refine
affinchè in order that
affinita *f* affinity
affissione *f* posting
affisso *m* placard, poster
affittare let; hire
affitto *m* rent
affliggere afflict
afflizione *f* affliction
affluente abundant; affluent
affluenza *f* abundance
affocare set fire to
affogare suffocate; drown; be drowned
affollare tread; press; crowd
affrettare hasten
affrontare attack
affronto *m* insult
affum(ic)are smoke
affusto *m* gun-carriage
agata *f* agate

135

agente *m* agent
agenzia *f* agency
agevole easy
aggiustare adjust, settle
aggomitolare wind up
aggradevole agreeable
aggradire agree with, like
ıgrandimento *m* increase
aggrandire increase; enlarge   [tion
aggravamento *m* aggrava-
aggravare aggravate; overload
aggregare aggregate
aggressione *f* agression
aggressore *m* agressor
aggrinzare wrinkle
aggrottare frown
agguagliare compare
agguaglio *m* comparison
agiato comfortable; rich
agile agile; nimble
agilità *f* agility
agio *m* ease
agire work; operate
agitare agitate; shake
agitatore *m* agitator
agitazione *f* agitation
aglio *m* garlic
agnello *m* lamb
ago *m* needle
agonia *f* agony
agonizzare agonize
Agostino Augustine
Agosto August
agricoltura *f* agriculture
agro sour; — **dolce** sweet and sour
agrume *m* fruits like oranges, lemons, etc.
aguzzare sharpen
aia *f* governess
aio *m* tutor   [floor
aiuola *f* small threshing-
aiutare **aiuto** *m* aid; help
ala *f* wing; — **to** winged

alabastro _m_ alabaster
alacrità _f_ alacrity
alba _f_ dawn; day-break
albagia _f_ pride
albeggiare dawn
albergare live; lodge
albergatore _m_ host; landlord
albergo _m_ hotel; inn
albero _m_ tree; mast
albicocca _f_ apricot
albicocco _m_ apricot-tree
albino albino
albo white
alitare pant
alito _m_ breath; breeze
allacciare lace; tie
allagare inundate
allargare enlarge
allarmare allarme _m_ alarm
allato contiguous; beside
allatare suckle; nurse
alleanza _f_ alliance
alleato allied
allegare allege
alleggerire lighten; relieve
allegrare cheer; rejoice
allegrezza _f_ gaiety
allegro cheerful; merry
allentare slacken
all'erta _f_ alarm; alert!
allesso _m_ boiled beef
allestare prepare
allettare allure
allettato bed-ridden
allevare bring up
alleviare alleviate
allieve _m_ pupil
allineare range into lines
allividire turn pale
alloggio _m_ dwelling
allontanamento _m_ removal
allontanare remove
allora then
alluminio _m_ aluminium.

allungamento _m_ enlargement
allungare lengthen
allusione _f_ allusion
almanacco _m_ almanack
almanco, almeno at least
alpestre, alpino alpine
alquanto a little
altalena _f_ swing; see-saw
altana _f_ balcony
altare _m_ altar
alterabile alterable
alterare alter; incense
altercare quarrel
alterezza alterigia _f_ haughtiness
alternare alternate
alternativo alternative
altero haughty
altezza _f_ height; highness
altitudine _f_ altitude
alto high; loud; _m_ height, high sea
altrettanto as much
altrove elsewhere
altrui other people
alzare raise; — si rise
amabile amiable
amabilità _f_ amiableness
amaca _f_ hammock
amante _m_ lover
amare love; like
amareggiare embitter
amarezza _f_ bitterness
amaro bitter; painful
amatore _m_ lover
ambasciata _f_ embassy
ambasciatore _m_ ambassador
ambedue both; the two
ambire desire ardently
ambizione _f_ ambition
ambizioso ambitious
amicare reconcile; make friends
amichevole friendly
amicizia _f_ friendship

amico *m* friend
amido *m* starch
ammaccare bruise
ammaestrare teach
ammalare fall ill
ammalato sick; ill
ammansare tame; do-
  mesticate
ammassare accumulate
ammasso *m* heap [bricks
ammattonare floor with
ammazzamento *m* slaugh-
ammazzare kill [ter
ammazzatoio *m* slaugh-
  terhouse
amministrazione *f* ad-
  ministration
ammirabile admirable
ammiragli(at)o *m* ad-
  miral(ty)
ammirare admire
ammiratore *m* admirer
ammirazione *f* admiration
ammissibile admissible
ammutinarsi mutiny
ammutire become dumb
amnistia *f* amnesty
amo *m* hook
amore *m* love
amoreggiare court; woo
amorevole amiable
amorino *m* little Cupid
amoroso amorous; lover
amovibile removable
ampio ample; copious
amplificare amplify
ampolla *f* phial
ampolliera *f* cruet-stand
amputare amputate
amputazione *f* amputa-
amuleto *m* amulet [tion
anagramma *m* anagram
analisi *f* analysis
analogo analogous
ananasso *m* pine-apple
anarchico anarchical;
  anarchist

anche too
ancora *f* anchor [though
ancora yet; still; – chè
ancoraggio *m* anchorage
andare go; suit; an-
  darsene go away
andata *f* step, walk; – e
  ritorno there and back
andito *m* lobby [corridor
androne *m* antechamber;
aneddoto *m* anecdote
anelare be out of breath
anello *m* ring
anemia anaemia [less
anemico anaemic, blood-
anfiteatro *m* amphiteatre
angelico angelical
angelo *m* angel
angolo *m* angle
angoloso angular
angoscia *f* anguish; grief
anguilla *f* eel
anguria *f* water-melon
angusto narrow
anice *m* anise
anima *f* soul
animale (*m*) animal
animo *m* mind; courage
animosità *f* animosity
animoso partial
anitra *f* duck
annata *f* year
annebbiato cloudy
annegare drown
annettere annex
annichilire annihilate
annidarsi nestle [sary
anniversario *m* anniver-
anno *m* year; Cape d'-
  anno New year's day
annodare tie; knot
annoiare annoy
annotare annotate [dark
annottarsi be night, get
annuale annual
annullare annul

annunziare announce
annunzio *m* announcement
annuvolare get cloudy
ano *m* anus
anonimo anonymous
ansietà *f* anxiety
ansioso anxious
antartico antarctic
antecedente antecedent
antecessore *m* antecessor
antenato *m* forefather
anteriore anterior
anticaglia *f* antiquities; rubbish
anticamera *f* antecham·
antichità *f* antiquity [ber
anticipare anticipate
antico antique, ancient
anzi before; rather
apatico insensible
ape *f* bee
aperto opened; open air
apertura *f* opening
apoplessia *f* apoplexy
apostata *m* apostate
apostolico apostolic
apostolo *m* apostle
apoteosi *f* apotheosis
appagare satisfy
appaiare match
appaltare let; farm
appalto *m* leasing [nish
appannare obscure tar-
apparécchiare prepare
apparente apparent
apparenza *f* appearance
apparire appear
apparizione *f* apparition
appartenere belong
appassionato passionate
appassire fade; wither
appello *m* call; appeal
appena scarcely
appendere hang on
appendice *m* appendix; feuilleton

appetito *m* appetite
appetitoso appetizing
appetto in front; in comparison
appianare level
appiccare attach; hang
appicciare tie; stick to
appiede at the foot of
appieno entirely
apportare bring
apposta expressly
apprendere learn
apprendista *m* apprentice
apprensione *f* apprehension
appresso near; after
apprestare prepare
apprezzare appraise; val-
approdare land [ue
approdo *m* boarding
approfittare profit by
approfondare deepen; investigate
appropriare appropriate
approssimativo approximative
approvare approve
appuntamento *m* agreement
appuntare sharpen
apuntellare prop [time
appunto precisely; in
appuzzare infect
aprire open
arancia *f* orange
aranciata *f* orangeade
arancio *m* orange-tree
arare plough
aratro *m* plough
arazzo *m* tapestry
arbitrario arbitrary
arbitrio *m* will; free will
arbitro *m* arbiter
arbusto *m* shrub
arca *f* chest; ark
arcangelo *m* archangel
arcano secret; arcanun

archeologo m archæologist
archetto m fiddlestick
architetto m architect
architettura f architecture
arcobaleno m rain-bow
ardente ardent
ardere burn; be ardent
ardire dare
arditezza f boldness
ardito bold
ardore m ardour
arduo arduous
area f area
arganello m turnstile
argano m crane; capstan
argentato silvered
argenteo of silver
argenteria f silver plate
argentino silvery
argento m silver; – vivo
 quick-silver
argilla f clay
argilloso clayey
argine f dyke
argomento m argument
arguire argue
arguto able; clever
arguzia f smartness
aridità f aridity
arido arid
aringa f herring
arioso airy; graceful
arista m pig's fillet
aristocratico aristocratic
aristocrazia f aristocracy
aritmetica f arithmetic
armellino m ermine
armeria f arsenal
armistizio m armistice
armonia f harmony
arnese m equipment, har-
arnione m kidney [ness
arrampicarsi climb up
arrecare bring; cause
arredare equip; furnish
arredo m equipment
arrenare strand

139

arrendere surrender; yield
arrestare arrest
arresto m arrest
arrichire enrich
arricciare curl; crisp
arringa(re) harangue
arrischiare risk; venture
arrivare arrive; reach
arrivista m ambitious
 person; place-hunter
arrivo m arrival
arrochire grow hoarse
arrogante arrogant
arroganza f arrogance
arrogare arrogate
arrolare enlist

arrossire redden; blush
arrostire roast; toast
arteria f artery
artesiano artesian
articolare articulate
articolo m article; joint
artificiale artificial
artificio m artifice;
 fuoco d' – fire-work
artigiano m artisan
artiliere m artilleryman
artiglieria f artillery
artista m artist
artistico artistic
asbesto m asbestos
ascella f arm-pit
ascendere go up; ascend
ascensione f ascension
ascensore m lift
ascesso m abscess
ascia f axe
asciolvere breakfast
asciugamano m towel
asciugare wipe, dry
asciutto dry
asma(tico) asthma(tic)
asparago m asparagus
aspergere besprinkle
aspettare expect; wait for
aspettazione f expectation
aspetto m aspect; sala

aspirante *m* candidate
aspirare aspirate; aspire
aspirazione *f* aspiration
aspro rough; harsh
assaggiare try; taste
assai much; very
assalire attack; assault
assalto *m* attack; assault
assassinare, assassinio *m*
 murder
assassine *m* murderer
asse *f* plank; axle
assediare besiege
assedio *m* siege
assegnare assign; appoint
assegno *m* rent
assembiare assemble
assemblea *f* assembly
assente absent
assentire consent
assenza *f* absence
assenzio *m* wormwood
asserire affirm; assert
asserzione *f* assertion
assetato thirsty
assettare settle
assieme together
assilio *m* horse-fly
assise *f pl* assizes
assistenza *f* assistance
assistere assist; help
asso *m* ace
associare accompany
associato *m* partner
associazione *f* association
assoggettare subdue
assoluzione *f* absolution
assolvere absolve
assomiglianza *f* resemblance   [compare
assomigliare resemble;
assopire make sleepy
assuefare accustom
assuetudine *f* custom
assumere assume
assunta, assunzione *f*

assumption
assurdità *f* absurdity
assurdo absurd
asta *f* stick; lance; auc-
astaco *m* lobster   [tion
astemio abstemious
astenersi abstain
asterisco *m* asterisk
astinente abstinent
astinenza *f* abstinence
astio *m* envy; hatred
astraere abstract
astratto abstract
astrazione *f* abstraction
astringere compel
astringente astringent
astro *m* star
astronomia *f* astronomy
astronomo *m* astronomer
astuccio *m* case; box
astuto cunning
astuzia *f* cunning
ateista *m* atheist
atlante *m* atlas
atomo *m* atom
atrio *m* vestibule
atroce atrocious
attagliarsi suit
atteggiamento *m* attitude
attempato elderly
attendere apply one's self
 await; mind
attenente belonging
attentare attempt; try
attentato *m* attempt
attento attentive
attenuare weaken
attenzione *f* attention
atterrare   overthrow;
 prostrate
atterrire frighten
attesa *f* expectation
atteso considering
attestare attest
attimo *m* moment
attirare attract
attitudine *f* attitude

attivita *f* activity
attivo active
attizzare poke; stir up
attizzatoio *m* poker
atto apt; *m* act; deed
attonito astonished
attore *m* actor
attorno around
attossicare poison
attrappare deceive
attrarre attract
attrattivo attractive
attraversare cross
attraverso through; across
attrazione *f* attraction
attrezzo *m* tool
attribuire attribute
attributo *m* attribute
attrice *f* actress
attuale actual
attuare perform
attuffare submerge; dive
audace audacious
audacia *f* audacity
augurare wish
augurio *m* omen; con-
  gratulation
augusto august
aumentare increase
austerità *f* austerity
austero, ra austere
australe austral; south-
  ern   [trian
austriaco, ca *m* & *f* Aus
austro *m* southern wind
autentica *f* authentica-
  tion   [tic
autenticare make authen-
autenticazione *f* authentication
autenticità *f* authenticity
autentico, ca authentic
autocrate *m* autocrat
autocrazia *f* autocracy
autografo *m* autograph
automa *m* automaton
autonomia *f* autonomy

autonomo autonomous
autopsia *f* autopsy
autore, trice author *m*;
  authoress *f*   [thority
autorevole accredited; au-
autorità *f* credit
autorizzare authorize
autunnale autumnal
autunno *m* Autumn
avacciare urge; hasten
avaccio in haste
avallo *m* guarantee
avantichè before that
avanzamento *m* advance-
  ment; progress [prove
avanzare advance; im-
avanzaticcio, cia rem-
  nant; scrap
avanzato *m* remainder
avanzo *m* remainder;
  profit
avaramente avariciously
avaria *f* damage
avarizia *f* avarice
avaro, ra avaricious
avello *m* tomb; tomb-
  stone
avena *f* oats; pipe
aventare grow
avere have; possess
averno *m* hell
aversione *f* aversion
avertere remove
avido, da greedy
avo, avolo *m* grandfather
avocare evoke
avola *f* grandmother
avoltoio *m* vulture
avorio *m* ivory   [age
avvallare lower; discour-
avvaloramento *m* courage
avvalorare encourage
avvampante burning
avvampare burn; be in-
  censed
avvantaggio *m* advantage

141

avvantaggioso, sa advantageous

avvegnachè as; when

avvelenamento m poison-

avvelenare poison [ing

avvelenato, ta poisoned

avvenimento m event; arrival [m future

avvenire happen; arrive;

avventamento m impetus

avventare rush; dash

avventatagine f inadvertence; imprudence

avventore m customer

avventura f adventure

avventurare venture; risk

avventurato, ti, roso, sa happy; lucky

avventuriere m adventurer; adventurous

avverare verify; aver

avverbiale adverbial

avverbio m adverb

avversamente unhappily; unluckily

avversare oppose

avversario, ria adversary

avversazione opposition; contest

avversità f adversity

avverso, sa adverse

avverso against

avvertente warned

avvertenza f warning;

avviare prepare; credit

avviato, ta attracted

avvicendare alternate

avvicendevole alternate

avvicinamento m proximity

avvicinare approach

avvilimento m humilia-

avvilire degrade [tion

avvilitivo, va degraded

avvilito, ta humiliated

avviluppare confuse; embroil

avvinacciato, ta drunk

avvinare mix with wine

avvinazzarsi get drunk

avvincere, vinchiare twist; tie [collision

avvisaglia f dispute;

avvisare inform

avvisatamente prudently

avvisatore m adviser

avviso m advice; advertisement

avvistare observe

avviticchiare twist; knot

avvivare revive

avvizzare, ire wither

avvocare practise; plead

avvocato m advocate

azione f act; deed; share

azoto m azote

azzampato, ta clawed

azzannare snap up; nal

azzardare risk

azzardo m hazard; chance

azzardoso, sa hazardous

azzeccare strike; beat

azzicare move

azzimare adorn; dress

azzimina f coat of mail

azzoppare become lame

azzuffamento m fight; collision

azzuffarsi dispute; fight; – colvino drink hard

azzuolo m dark blue

azzurro m blue

B

babbo m father

babbuino m baboon

babele babel; confusion

baccelliere m bachelor

baccello m pod; shell

baccheo a; chico, ca bacchic

bacchetta f wand; drum-

142

stick

bacchettone, .na bigot; hypocrite

bacchio *m* stick; pole

bacco; per – by jove!; **poffarbacco** by jove!

bacheca *f* show-case

baciamento *m* kiss; kissing   [bigot

baciapile *m* hypocrite;

baciare kiss; *m* kiss

bacile, no *m* basin; water-

bacio *m* kiss   [tax

baciozzo *m* kiss

baco *m* worm; **– da seta** silkworm

bacocco *m* imbecile

bacucco *m* hood; cowl

baffi *pl* moustache

bagaglia, glio *f & m* luggage

bagaglione *m* camp-follower

bagascia *f* prostitute

bagascione *m* bully

bagattella trifling

bagattelliere *m* mounte-

baggeo *m* booby   [bank

baggianata *f* trifle

baggiano *m* blockhead

baggiolare support

baggiolo *m* support; prop

bagliore *m* lightning

bagnaiuolo *m* bather; bath-keeper

bagnare bathe; water

bagnato, ta bathed;

bagno *m* bath   [watered

bagordo *m* seducer

baia *f* trick; bay; gulf

baiata *f* trifles; joke

baietta *f* taming; small

bailo *m* bailiff   [bay

baio, ia bay   [jester

baionaccio, baione *m*

baionnetta bayonet

balausta, tra, tro *f & m*

pomegranate-tree blossom

balaustrata *f* balustrade

balbettante stuttering

balbettare stammer

balbo, ba *m* stammerer

balbuzie *f* stammering

balconata *f* balcony

balcone *m* balcony

baldanza *f* courage

baldanzoso, sa daring

baldo. da audacious; bold

baldoria *f* Greek fire; bonfire

baldracca *f* prostitute

balena *f* whale

balenare be lightening

baleno *m* lightning

balia *f* nurse; power

balla *f* bale; pack

ballabile dancing

ballare dance

ballata *f* ballad; dance

ballerino *m* dancer

balsamo *m* balm

balza *f* rock; precipice

balzare jump

balzo *m* leap. jump

bambagia *f* cotton

bambinello *m* baby

bambino *m* child

bambola *m* doll

bambu *m* bamboo

banano *m* banana

banca *f* bank

bancarotta *f* bankruptcy

banchetto *m* banquet

banchiere *m* banker

banco *m* bench

banda *f* band; side

barattare exchange; barter   [switch

baratto *m* exchange

barba *f* beard

barbabietola *f* beet-root

barbaro barbarous

barbiere *m* barber

barbieria *f* barber's shop
barbone *m* water-spaniel
barbugliare stutter
barbuto bearded

barca *f* bark; boat
barcaiuolo *m* boatman
barchetta *f* small boat
barcollare vacillate; totter
bargello *m* sheriff
barile *m* barrel; hogshead
baritono *m* baritone
baroccio *m* car
barocco odd
barometro *m* barometer
barone *m* baron; sharper
barra *f* bar; cross-bar
barricata *f* barricade
barriera *f* barrier
baruffa *f* tumult; fray
basamento *m* pedestal
base *f* base; basis
Basilea Basle
basilica *f* basilica
bassezza *f* meanness
basso low; mean; *m* bass
bassorilievo *m* bas-relief
bassotto *m* terrier
basta enough! stop!

battaglione *m* battalion
batello *m* boat; – a
  vapore steamer
battere knock; beat; – le
  mani applaud
batteria *f* battery
battesimale baptismal
battesimo *m* baptism
battezzare baptize
batticuore, battito *m* pal-
Battista Baptist [pitation
battisterio *m* baptistry
baule *m* trunk
bava *f* slaver; foam
Bavarese Bavarian
bavero *m* collar
Baviera *f* Bavaria
bazar *m* bazar

bazzotto half-boiled
beatificare beatify [tion
beatificazione *f* beatifica-
beato happy, blessed
beffare joke, mock
beghino hypocrite
belare bleat
Belgio Belgium
belladonna *f* nightshade
belletto *m* paint (face)
bellezza beltà *f* beauty
bellico warlike; *m* navel
bellino pretty
bello beautiful
belvedere *m* belvedere
benché though
benda *f* band; – re bind
  up
bene well; *m* good;
  property
beneficenza *f* benevolence
beneficio *m* benefice
benefico beneficent
benessere *m* well-being
benevolenza *f* benevol-
  ence
benevolo benevolent
benigno benign; kind
bensì certainly
beone *m* drunkard
bere, bevere drink
bersaglio *m* mark; target
bertuccio *m* monkey
bestemmia *f* blasphemy
bestemmiare blaspheme
bestia *f* beast; – le bes-
bestiame *m* cattle [tial
bettola *f* tavern
betula *f* birch-tree
beva, bevanda *f* beverage
beveraggio *m* tip
bevitore *m* drinker
biacca *f* whitelead
biancheria *f* linen
bianchezza *f* whiteness
bianchire bleach
bianco white

144

biasciare mumble; munch
biasimare blame
bicchiere *m* glass; cup
bicicletta *f* bicycle
biciclista *m* bicyclist
bidello *m* beadle
bieco squinting
bietola *f* beet
bietta *f* wedge
biforcarsi fork
bigamo *m* bigamist
bigatto *m* silk-worm
bigio grey
bigliardo *m* billiards
biglietto *m* ticket
bigoncia *f* tub
bilanciare balance; weigh
bilanciere *m* beam; bal-
  ance-wheel
bile *f* bile; anger
bilioso bilious
bimbo *m* baby
binario *m* track
bindolo *m* sharper
binocolo *m* binocle
biografia *f* biography
biografo *m* biographer
birreria *f* brewery
bis! encore!   [father
bisavo(lo) *m* great-grand-
bisbigliare whisper
bisca *f* gambling-house
biscazzare gamble
biscia *f* snake
bisogna *f* business; affair
bisognare be necessary;
  want
bisogno *m* need; aver
  – di want; – so poor;
bisticciare dispute
bisticcio *m* pun
bistrattare ill-treat
bitume *m* bitumen
bivaccare   bivacco   *m*
  bivouac
bivio *f* cross-road

bizzarro capricious; odd
blandire flatter
blando soft; bland
blenoraggia *f* gonorrhœa
blocco *m* blockade; block
blu blue
boa *m* boa
boaro *m* cow-herd
bocca *f* mouth
boccale *m* jar; mug
boccata *m* mouthful
boccetta *f* small bottle
boccia *f* bud; decanter;
boccone *m* bit; mouthful
boia *m* executioner
bolgia *m* pocket; bag
bolla *f* bubble; blister
  bull (papal)
bollare seal; stamp
bolletta *f* bill (of health)
bollire boil
bollo *m* stamp
bomba *f* bomb
bonaccia *f* calm
bonaccio good-natured
bonificare improve
bontà *f* goodness   [ble
borbottare grunt; grum-
bordello *m* brothel
bordo *m* edge; board
bordone *m* pilgrim's staff
borea *m* north-wind
borghese   *m*   burgess;
borgo *m* borough [citizen
boria *f* vanity
borrico *m* ass
borsa *f* purse; pocket
borsaiuolo *m* pickpocket
borzacchino *m* buskin
boscaiuolo *m* woodman
boschett(in)o *m* grove
bosco *m* forest; wood
botte *f* tub; cab
bottega *f* shop
bozza *f* sketch; proof
bozzo *f* free-stone

145

braca *f* trousers
braccare search; scent
bracciale *m* brassard; armlet
braccialetto *m* bracelet
braccio *m* arm [chair
bracciuolo *m* arm of a
brachiere *m* truss
brama *f* longing, eager
bramare long for [ness
branca *f* claw
branchie *f & pl* gills
branco *m* herd; flock
brandire brandish
Brasile *m* Brazil
bravaccio *m* braggart
bravo brave; bravo!
bravura *f* bravery
breccia *f* breach
breve brief
brevetto *m* patent
breviario *m* breviary
brevità *f* brevity
brezza *f* breeze
briaco drunk
briacone *m* drunkard
bricco *m* ass
brigare seek; strive
brigata *f* brigade
briglia *f* bridle
brillante brilliant, bright
brindisi *m* toast
brio *m* vivacity
brioso lively; fiery
brivido *m* shivering
brocca *f* jug
broccolo *m* brocoli
brod(ett)o *m* broth
broncio *m* anger
brontolare grumble
bronzo *m* bronze
bruccio *m* cream-cheese
bruciare burn [nut
bruciata *f* toasted chest-
bruco *m* caterpillar
brulicare swarm [ish
brunetto brownish, dark-

brusco rude; blunt
bruscolo *f* straw
brutale brutal
bruto *m* brute
bruttura *f* dirtiness
bruzzaglia *f* mob
buaggine *f* foolishness
buca *f* hole; cave
bucare perforate
bucato *m* lye; wash
buccia *f* bark; peel
buccina *f* trumpet
buccinare trumpet
buccioso thick-skinned
buccolica *f* bucolic
bucherare bore
bucinamento *m* buzzing
bucinare buzz; whisper
budellame *m* entrails
budello, della *m & f*
bue *m* ox; beef [bowel
bufera *f* hurricane
buffa *f* child's play
buffalo *m* buffalo
bugiare bore
bugigatto, tolo *m* hole; hiding-place
bugna *f* bump; basket
bugno *m* bee-hive
buio *m* darkness
buio, ia dark; obscure
bulbo *m* bulb
bulboso, sa bulbous
bulicame *m* spring
bulicare boil; bubble
bulima *f* crowd
bulimo *m* hunger
bulino *m* graver [port
bulletta *f* ballot; pass-
bullettino *m* note; safe conduct [cord
buonaccordo *m* harpsi-
buonamente certainly
buonavoglia *m* volunteer
buondì *m* good day; good morning
buono, na good; proper;

alla buona simply; sincerely

buonpresso *m* bowsprit

burbero, ra *a & n* surly; grumbler

burchia, burchio *f & m* row-boat

burchiello *m* small boat

burello *m* woollen cloth

burla *f* joke

burlare joke [burlesque

burlesco, ca, burlevole

burletta *f* joke

burrasca *f* squall; storm

burrascoso, sa stormy

burro, butirro *m* butter

burrone *m* precipice

busca *f* quest; inquest

buscare cheat

busecchia, secchio, chione *f & m* bowels

bussa *f* grief

bussare strike

busse *fp* blows

bussola *f* compass

busta *f* case

busto *m* bust

buttare dart; throw

C

cacare evacuate

cacatoio *m* water-closet

cacazibetto *m* coxcomb; dandy [ies; grimaces

caccabaldole *fp* cajoler-

caccao *m* cocoa-nut [ing

caccia *f* hunting; shoot-

cacciaffanni entertaining

cacciagione *f* hunt; game

cacciapassere *m* scare-crow

cacciare expel; hum

cacciatoia *f* nail-driver

cacciatore, trice *m & f*

hunter

cacciavite *f* screw-driver

caccio *m* cheese

cacio *m* cheese

cacume *m* top; summit

cadauno each; every

cadavere, ro *m* corpse

cadaverico, ca cadaverous

cadente falling; decaying

cadenza *f* cadence

cadere fall; happen

cadetto *m* cadet; junior

cadevole old; fragile

cadimento *m* fall: fault

caducità *f* weakness; decay

caduco decaying

caduta *f* fall

caduto, ta fallen; ruin

caffè *m* coffee

caffettiera *m* coffee-pot

cagionevole sickly; weak

cagliare abate; coagulate

cagna *f* bitch [titute

cagnaccia *f* hussy; pros-

cagnaccio *m* big dog; bad

caimane *m* alligator

cala *f* hold (ship); slip; dock-yard [drone

calabrone *m* hornet;

calafatare calk

calamaio *m* inkstand

calamita *f* magnet

calamità *f* calamity

calamitare magnetize

calamitoso, sa calamitous

calandra *f* weevil

calandrella *f* lark

calappio *m* snare; trap

calare take down; go down [stonecutter

calastra *f* stonecutting;

calata *f* descent, fall

calca *f* crowd

calcagnare fly; run away

calcare tread upon;

crush [chalky
calcareo calcareous;
calcatura *f* pressure
calce *f* lime. chalk
calcestruzzo *p* cement
calcetto *m* sock; pump
calcina *f* lime
calcinare calcinate
calcio *m* heel: kick
calcistruzzo *m* cement
calcitrante recalcitrant
calcitrare kick
calcitroso kicking; recalcitrant
calcolare calculate
calcolatore *m* calculator; accountant [tion
calcolazione *f* calcula-
caldana *f* heat; pleurisy
caldanino *m* small stove
caldano *m* stove
caldaro *m* boiler [seller
caldarrostaio *m* chestnut-
caldeggiare protect
calderaio *m* brazier
calderone *m* boiler
calderuola *f* small caldron
caldezza *f* heat; warmth
caldo, da warm; *m* heat
calduccio lukewarm
calere signify
calessino *m* cab

calice *m* chalice
calido, da warm; hot
califfo *m* calif
caligine *f* obscurity
caliginoso obscure; dark
calla *f* opening; gap
calle *f* road; street
callido, da astute
calma *m* calmness
calmare calm; – si compose one's self
calmo, ma calm
calore *m* warmth
caloria *f* improvement;

manure
calorico *m* caloric
calorifico calorific
caloroso warm
calotta *f* cap
calpestare tread upon
calpestio *m* treading upon
calterire graze; raze
calunnia *f* calumny
calunniare calumniate
calunniatore, trice *m & f* calumniator
calunnioso. sa slanderous
calvare make become bald
calvario *m* calvary
calvezza *f* baldness
calvinista *m* calvinist
calvizie *f* baldness
calvo *m* bald man
calza *f* stocking
calzaiuolo *m* hosier
calzamento. turn *m & f* covering for the feet (boots; shoes etc.).
calzare *m* shoe
calzare put on one's shoes
calzetta *f* stocking
cambiamento *m* change
cambiare change; vary
cambiario, via change; exchange
cambio *m* change; change; in – instead of
cambista *m* money changer; banker [lia
camelea, camelia *f* camel-
camello *m* camel
camera *f* chamber; room
camerata *m* comrade
cameriera *f* chambermaid
cameriere *m* waiter
camerino *m* closet; bath-
camicia *f* shirt [room
camiciuola *f* undervest
camino *m* chimney(-piece)

148

cammello *m* camel
camminare walk
camminata *f* walk [ney
cammino *m* road; jour-
camoscio *m* chamois
campagna *f* country;
 campaign

campagnuolo *m* peasant
campana *f* bell
campanaio *m* bellringer
campanello *m* bell
campanile *m* steeple
campare save; live
campestre rural
Campidoglio *m* Capitol
campionario *m* book of
 samples   [ship
campionate *m* champion-
campione *m* champion;
 sample   [cemetery
campo *m* field – santo
camuso flat-nosed
canaglia *f* rabble
canale *m* canal
canapa *f* hemp
canapè *m* sofa
canapo *m* cable
cancrena *f* gangrene
candela *f* candle
candelabro *m* chandelier
candelliere *m* candlestick
candidato *m* candidate
candido white; candid
candito candied
cane *m* dog
canestro *m* basket
canfora *f* camphor
cangiare change; vary
canicola *f* dog-days
canile *m* dog-kennel
canino canine   [barrel
canna *f* reed; cane;
cannella *f* cinnamon
cannocchiale *m* spy-glass
cansare remove
cantabile ·cantabile

cantante *m* singer
cantare sing
cantina *f* cellar
canto *m* song; corner
cantonata *f* corner
cantone *m* angle; corner
cantoniere *m* road-sur-
 veyor; watchman
cantore *m* singer
cantuccio *m* biscuit
canuto grey-haired
canzone *f* song
canzonare jest; laugh at
canzoniere *m* song-book
caos *m* chaos
capace capable
capacità *f* capacity
capanna *f* cottage; bran
caparbio stubborn

capello *m* hair
capelluto hairy
capestro *m* cord
capezzale *m* pillow
capire understand
capitalista *m* capitalist
capitano *m* captain
capitello *m* capital
capitolare capitulate
capitolo *m* chapter
capitombolare tumble
capo *m*   head; chief;
 cape; – d'anno New-
 year's day; da – once
 more
capogiro *m* giddiness
capolavoro *m* master-
 piece
capovolgere turn upside
cappa *f* cloak; cape [down
cappella *f* chapel
cappellano *m* chaplain
cappelliera *f* hat-box
cappellinaio *m* hat-stand
cappello *m* hat
cappero *m* caper
cappio *m* knot

cappuccio *m* hood
capra *f* she-goat
capraio *m* goat-herd
capriccio *m* caprice
capriccioso capricious
caraffa *f* decanter
carato *m* carat
carattere *m* character
caratteristico character-
  istic
carbone *m* coal
carbonio *m* carbon
carbonico carbonic
carbonizzare carbonize
carcerare imprison
carcere *m* prison
carciofo *m* artichoke
cardare card
carrezza(re) caress
carica *f* load; office
caricare load; attack
caricatura *f* caricature
carie *f* caries
carino dear; darling
carità *f* charity
carmelitano *m* carmelite
carminio carmine
carnagione *f* carnation;
  complexion
carnale carnal; sensual
carne *f* flesh; meat
carreggiare cart; carry
carreggiata *f* cart-road
carretta *m* cart
carriera *f* run; career
carro *m* cart; waggon
carrozza *f* carriage; coach
carruba *f* carob
carrucola *f* pulley
carta *f* paper; deed;
  map; card; – sugante
  blotting paper; – mon-
  eta paper-money;
cartella *f* bill; portfolio
cartello(ne) *m* placard
cartiera *f* paper-mill

cartilagine *f* cartilage
cartoccio *m* cartouche;
  cup of paper
cartoleria *f* paper-trade
cartone *m* pasteboard
cartuccia *f* cartridge
casa *f* house; home
casale *m* hamlet
casalingo domestic
casata *m* family name
cascare fall
cascata *f* water-fall
cascina *f* dairy
casella *f* cell
caserma *m* barracks
caso *m* case; chance
casotto *m* watch-box
cassa *f* chest; box; coffin
cassare cancel
cassetta *f* casket; box
cassettone *m* chest of
  drawers
cassiere *m* cashier
castagna *f* chestnut
castagneto *m* grove of
  chestnut-trees
castagno *m* chestnut-tree
castello *m* castle
castigare chastise
castigo *m* punishment
castità *f* chastity
casto chaste; modest
castoro *m* beaver
catastrofe *f* catastrophe
catechismo *m* catechism
categorico categorical
catena *f* chain
catinella *f* basin
catramare, catrame *m* tar
cattedra *f* chair; pulpit
cattedrale *f* cathedral
cattivare captivate
cattivo wicked   [ism
cattolicismo *m* catholic-
cattolicità *f* catholicity
cattolico catholic

150

cattura *f* capture
causare, causa *f* cause
caustico caustic
cautela *f* caution
cauto cautious
cauzione *f* bail; security
cava *f* pit
cavadenti *m* dentist
cavalla *f* mare
cavallaro *m* muleteer
cavalleresco chivalrous
cavalleria *f* cavalry;
  gallantry   [school]
cavallerizza *f* riding-
cavalerizzo *m* riding-
  master
cavalletta *f* locust
cavalletto *m* easel
cavallo *m* horse
cavare dig; draw out
caverna *f* cavern; den
caviale *m* caviare
cavicchia *m* peg
cavità *f* cavity
cavo hollow
cavolfiore *m* cauliflower
cavolo *m* cabbage
cazzottare box
cece *m* pea
cedere cede; yield
cedola *f* schedule; bill
cedrare season with lemon
cedro *m* cedar
ceffata *f* box on the ear
ceffo *m* muzzle
ceffone *m* cuff; slap
celare hide
celebrare celebrate
celebre celebrated
celebrità *f* celebrity
celere speedy
celerità *f* speed
celeste celestial
celia *f*, celiare jest; joke
celibato *m* celibacy
celibe unmarried; bache-

cella *f* cell   [lor
cencio *m* rag; — so rag-
cenere *f* ash   [ged
cenerino ash-coloured
cenno *m* signal; nod
censo *m* census; tax
centigrado centigrade
centimetro *m* centimetre
centinaio *m* hundred
cento hundred
centrale central
centrifugo centrifugal
centro *m* centre
centuplo hundredfold
ceppo *m* trunk
cera *f* wax; air; mien
cerca *f* cercare search
cerchio *m* circle; hoop
cerco *m* circus
cereale cereal
cerebrale cerebral
cessare cease; leave
cesso *m* water-closet
cesta *f* basket
cetra *f* cithern
cetriuolo *m* cucumber
che which? what? that
checche whatever
cherica *f* tonsure
chericato *m* clergy
cherico *m* priest
chetare, cheto quiet
chi who
chiacchiera *f*; — re chat;
  prattle
chiamata *f* call; appeal
chiamare call; name
chiappare snatch; catch
chiara *f* white of egg
chiarire clear up
chiaro *m* clearness; light
chiaro clear; illustrious
chiaroscuro chiaroscuro
chiasso *m* great noise
chiave *f* key

chiavistello *m* bolt
chicca *f* sweetmeats
chicchera *f* cup
chicco *m* grain; seed
chiedere demand; ask
chiesa *f* church
chiglia *f* keel   [me
chilogramma *m* kilogram-
chilometro *m* kilometre
chimera *f* chimera
chimica *f* chemistry
chimico chemical; chem-
China *f* China   [ist
china *f* slope
chinachina *f* quinquina
chinare bend; incline
chincaglieria *f* hardware
chinina *f* quinine
chiocciola *f* snail; scala
a – winding staircase
chicdo *m* nail
chiostro *m* cloister
chiotto silent
chirurgo *m* surgeon
chitarra *f* guitar
chiudere enclose; shut up
chiusa *f* enclosure; fence
ciarla *f*; – re chat; talk
ciarlatano *m* mountebank
ciascheduno each
cibare feed
cibo *m* food; aliment
cicala *f* grasshopper
cicatrice *f* cicatrice
cicerone *m* guide
cicisbeo *m* lover; gallant
ciclista *m* cyclist
ciclo *m* cycle
cicogna *f* stork
cicoria *f* chicory
cicuta *f* hemlock
ciecità *f* blindness
cieco blind
cialo *m* heaven
ciera *f* mien; looks
cifra *f* cipher; figure
ciglio *m* eye-lashes

cignere gird; surround
cigno *m* swan
ciliegia *f* cherry
ciliegio *m* cherry-tree
cilindro *m* cylinder
cima *f* top; summit
cimentare risk
cimice *f* bug
cimitero *m* cemetery
cinabro *m* cinnabar
cingere gird; surround
cinghia *f* girth
cinghiale *m* wild boar
cinquantina *f* about fifty
cinque five
cinta *f* enclosure
cintura *f* girdle
ciò this; that
ciocca *f* bunch; tuft
cioccolata *f* chocolate
cioccolattiera *f* chocolate-
pot
ciocia *f* kind of sandal;
– re inhabitant of the
Campagna
cioè that is; namely
cioncare tipple
ciondolare sway; dangle
ciottolo *m* pebble
cipolla *f* onion
cipresso *m* cypress
circolo *m* circle
circoncidere circumcise
circoncisione *f* circum-
cision
circondare surround
circondario *m* district
circostanza *f* circum-
stance
circuito *m* circuit
cislonga *f* couch
cità *f* city
cittadinanza *f* citizenship
cittadino *m* citizen
ciuco *m* ass
ciurma *f* gang; rabble

152

civaia _f_ vegetable
civile civil; polite
civilizzare civilize
clamore _m_ clamour
clandestino clandestine
clarinetto _m_ clarinet
classe _f_ class
classico classic
clausola _f_ clause

clavicola _f_ collar-bone
clemente clement
clemenza _f_ clemency
clero _m_ clergy
cliente _m_ customer
clientela _f_ customers
clima _m_ climate
cloaca _f_ sink; sewer
cloro _m_ chlorine
cloroformio _m_ chloroform
coagulare coagulate
coalizione _f_ coalition
cocchiere _m_ coachman
cocchio _m_ carriage; coach
coccodrillo _m_ crocodile
cocomero _m_ water-melon
cocuzzo _m_ top; crown of
  the head
coda _f_ tail; train
codardo coward
codesto that
codice _m_ code
codino _m_ pigtail
coerente coherent
coevo, coetaneo contem-
cofano _m_ box   [porary
cogliere gather
cognato brother-in-law;
  related
cognizione _f_ knowledge
cognome _m_ family name
coiaio _m_ tanner
coincidenza _f_ coincidence
colà there
colaggiù down yonder
colare a fondo sink

colassù there above

colazione _f_ breakfast
colera _m_ cholera
colica _f_ colic
colla _f_ paste; glue
collaborare collaborate
colle _m_ hill
collega _m_ colleague
collegio _m_ college
collera _f_ anger
colletto _m_ collar; — ritto
  stand-up collar; — ro-
  vesciato double collar
collezione _f_ collection
collina _f_ hill
collisione _f_ collision
collo _m_ neck
collocare place

colmo full
colomba _f_ pigeon
colombaia _f_ pigeon-house
colonia _f_ colony
coloniale colonial
colonizarre _va_ colonize
colonna _f_ column
colorare colour
colore _m_ colour
colorito _m_ colouring
colossale colossal
Colosseo _m_ Coliseum
colpevole guilty
colpire strike; hit
colpo _m_ stroke; blow
coltellinaio _m_ cutler
coltello _m_ knife
coltivare cultivate [man
coltivatore _m_ husband-
colto caught; cultivated
coltre _f_ coverlet
coltrice _f_ featherbed
comandare command
comare _f_ gossip
combattere fight
combattimento _m_ fight
combinare combine
combinazione _f_ combina-
  tion; chance   [how?

come like; as; why?

comecchè though; how-ever [tary

comentario *m* commen-

cometa *f* comet

comico comical

cominciare begin

comino *m* cumin

comitato *m* committee

commedia *f* comedy

commediante *m* comedian

commemorare remember

commemorazione *f* com-memoration

commendare recommend

commerciare trade

commercio *m* commerce

commettere commit

commiato *m* leave

commozione *f* commotion

commuovere move; affect

commutare commute

comodino *m* night-table;

comodo convenient; *m*

comodità *f* convenience

compagnia *f* company

compagno equal ; *m* companion

comparabile comparable

comparare compare

comparativo comparative

comparazione *f* compari-

comparire appear [son

compressa *f* compress

comprimere (com)press

compromesso *m* com-promise

comunicare communicate

comunione communion

con with

conca *f* tub; shell

concavo concave; hollow

concedere grant

concentrare concentrate

concepire conceive

concernere concern

concertare concert

concerto *m* concert

concetto *m* idea; pun

concessione *f* concession

concezione *f* conception

conchiglia *f* shell

concia *f* tan; tannery

conciare adorn; tan

conciatore *m* tanner

conciliare conciliate

concilio *m* council

concime *m* manure

conciso concise

concittadino *m* citizen

conclave *m* conclave

concussione *f* extortion

condannare condemn

condensare condense

condimento *m* condiment

condire season; preserve

condiscendere condescend

condizionale conditional

condizione *f* condition

condoglianza *f* condolence

condolersi condole

condonare pardon

condotta *f* conduct

condottiere *m* leader

condurre conduct

confabulare chat

confarsi agree; suit

confederarsi confederate

confederazione *f* confed-eracy

conferenza *f* conference

conferire confer

confermare confirm

confessare confess

confess(at)ore *m* confes-sor

confessionario *m* confes-sional

confessione *f* confession

confetta *m* preserve

confettare preserve

confidare confide

confidente *m* confident

confidenza *f* confidence
confidenziale confidential
confinare, confine *m* confine; border
confiscare confiscate
conforme conform
confortabile comfort(able)
confortare comfort; strengthen
confrontare confront
confusione *f* confusion
confuso confused
confutare confute
congedare dismiss
congedo *m* leave
congestione *f* congestion
congiura *f* conspiracy
congiurare conspire
congruente congruous
coniare coin
conico conical
coniglio *m* rabbit
conio *m* die; coin
coniugale conjugal
connessione *f* connexion

conoscenza *f* knowledge; acquaintance
conoscere know   [seur
conoscitore *m* connois-
conquista *f* conquest; –re conquer; *m* – tore conqueror
consacrare consecrate
consanguineo consanguineous
conscio conscious
consecutivo consecutive
consegnare consign; deposit   [quently
per conseguente conse-
conseguenza *f* consequence
conseguire obtain; result
consenso *m* consent
consentire consent
conserva *f* save; conserve

conservare conserve
conservatorio *m* conservatory
considerabile considerable
considerare consider
consigliare advise
consigliere *m* counsellor
consiglio *m* counsel; council
console *m* consul
consolidare strengthen
consonante *f* consonant
consorte *m f* husband; wife
conspirare conspire
constare subsist
constatare ascertain
consueto accustomed
consuetudine *f* custom
consultare consult
consultazione *f* consultation   [complish
consumare consume; ac-
contagioso contagious
contaminare stain
contante cash
contare number
contatore *m* (gas-) meter
contatto *m* contact
conte *m* count
contemplare contemplate
contemporaneo contemporary
contendere dispute
contenere contain
contentare content
contento contented
contenuto *m* contents
continente *m* continent
contingente *m* contingent
continuare continue
continuazione *f* continua-
continuo continuous [tion
conto *m* account; story
contorno *m* outline

contra against   [gler
contrabbandiere *m* smug-
contrabbando *m* smug-
  gling   [ange
contraccambiare exch-
contracchiave *f* false key
contraccolpo *m* counter-
  blow
contrada *f* country
contraddire contradict
contradizione *f* contradiction
contraffare counterfeit
contrariare contradict
contrario contrary
contrarre contract [sign
contrassegnare counter-
contrastare contest
contrasto *m* contrast
contrattempo di—un-
  seasonably
contratto *m* contract
contravveleno *m* antidote
contravvenire infringe

contribuire contribute
contribuzione *f* contri-
contrito contrite [bution
contro against; opposite

controllare control [order
contrordine *m* counter-
controverso doubtful
contumacia *f.* contumacy
contumelioso injurious
contusione *f* contusion
convalescente convalescent   [cence
convalescenza *f* convales-
convegno *m* meeting
convenevole convenient;
  decent
convenire agree; become
convento *m* convent
convenzione *f* agreement
convergere converge
convincere convince
convitare invite
convocare convoke

156

convoglio *m* convoy; train
convulsione *f* convulsion
cooperare co-operate
coperchio *m* lid
coprire cover
coraggio *m* courage
coraggioso courageous
corallo *m* coral
corame *m* leather
corazza *f* cuirass; armour
corazzata *f* iron-clad
corazziere *m* cuirassier
corba *f,* **corbello** *m* basket
corbellare banter; jeer
corbezzola *f* arbute-berry
corbezzolo *m* strawberry-
  plant
corda *f* cord; rope
cordaio *m* rope-maker
cordame *m* cordage
cordiale (*m*) cordial
cordialità *f* cordiality
cordiglio *m* string
cordone *m* string; band
coreggia *f* strap
coricare lay down
cornice *f* cornice; frame
corno *m* horn [plenty
cornucopia *f* horn of
cornuto horned
corredare equip; adorn
corredo *m* equipment
correggere correct
corrente *f* current
correre run; flow
corretto correct
corrispondente *m* corres-
  pondent   [pondence
corrispondenza *f* corres-
corrispondere correspond
corroborare corroborate
corrodere corrode
corrompere corrupt
corrugare corrugate
corruttibile corruptible
corruzione *f* corruption
corsa *f* course; drive

corso *m* course
corte *f* court
corteggiare court
cortese courteous
cortesia *f* courtesy
cortezza *f* brevity
cortina *f* curtain
corto short; brief
corvo *m* raven
cosa *f* thing
coscia *f* thigh
coscienza *f* conscience
cosi so   [tan
cosmopolitano cosmopoli-
cospetto *m* aspect
cospirare conspire   [tor
cospiratore *m* conspira-
cospirazione *f* conspiracy
costa *f* hill; rib; coast;
costà there   [side
costante constant
costanza *f* constancy
costare cost   [tion
costellazione *f* constalla-
costernare confound
costernazione *f* consternation
costi here   [tion
costipazione *f* constipa-
costipare constipate
costituire constitute
costituzione *f* constitution
costo *m* expense; costs
costola *f* rib
costoletta *f* cutlet; chop
costoso expensive
costringere constrain
costruttore *m* construc-
  tor   [tion
costruzione *f* construc-
costume *m* & *f* custom
costumato well-bred
cotale such a one
cotanto so much
cote *f* whetstone
cotenna *f* rind

cotesto this; that
cotidiano daily

cotogna *f* quince
cotone *m* cotton
cottimo *m* job
cotto cooked; baked
cottura *f* cooking
covare brood; hatch
covile, covo *m* den
cranio *m* skull
crapulone *m* dissolute
creare create
creatore *m* creator
creatura *f* creature
creazione *f* creation
credente *m* believer
credenza *f* faith; credit;
  buffet
credere believe

credulo credulous
creduto believed
crema *f* cream
cremisi *m* crimson; grain
cren *m* wild raddish
creolo *m* creole
crepaccio *m* crevice; chap
crepare burst out; die
creputante crackling
crepitare crackle
crepolare crack
crepuscolo *m* twilight
crescente increasing
crescenza *f* growth
crescere grow
crescione *m* water-cress
cresciuto increased
cresima *f* chrism
cresimare confirm
crespa *f* frown; wrinkle
crespare frown; knit;
cresta *f* summit   [curl
criminale criminal
crimine *m* crime; mis-
  demeanour
criminoso criminal

crinale hairy
crine m hair   [hair
criniera f mane; horse-
crisalide f chrysalis
crise, crisi f crisis
crisma m confirmation
cristallino crystalline
cristallizzare crystallize
cristallo m crystal
cristeo, stere m. clyster;
  injection   [tianity
cristianesimo m Chris-
cristiano christian
Cristo m Christ
criterio m criterion
critica f censure
criticare criticise; cen-
  sure   [critic
criticatore m censor;
critico critic
crocchiare beat; chat
crocchio m circle; club
croce f cross; torment
crocefisso m crucifix
crociare crucify; torment
crociata f crusade
crociato crossed; tor-
  mented; n. torment
crocicchio m cross-road
crocifiggere crucify
crocifisso m crucified;
  n crucifix
croio, ia rough; harsh
crollare agitate
crollo shaking
cronico chronic
cronista m chronicler
cronologia f chronology
cronologico chronological
crosciare pour (rain)
croscio m bubbling
crosta f crust
crostare to cover
crucciamento, cruccio m
  passion
crucciare irritate
crucciato tormented

cruciare torment
crudele cruel
crudeltà f cruelty
crudetto crudish; sourish
crudezza cruelty
crudo crude
cruento horrible
cruna f eye (needle)
cubatura f cubing
cubico cubic
cubitale cubital
cubito p cubit
cubo m cube
cuccagna f feast
cuchiaia f drag
cucchiaiata f spoonful
cucchiaio spoon
cuccia f seat
cucina f kitchen
cucinare cook
cuciniere, ra m & f cook
cucire sew
cucito m sewing
cucitore m stitcher
cucitrice f seamstress
cucullato hooded
cucurbita f pumpkin
cugino, na m & f cousin
cui of whom
culata f backside
culla f cradle
cullamento m. rocking
cullare rock
culminare culminate
culmine m summit
culo bottom
culto m worship
cultore m farmer
cumulare cumulate
cumulativo cumulative
cumulo m heap
cuna f cradle
cuneo m wedge
cunicolo, culo m mine
cuoca f cook
cuocere cook

cuoco *m* cook
cupola dome *f*
cura *f* care
curabile curable
curadenti *m* tooth-pick
curante careful; caring
curare to cure
curiosità *f* curiosity
curioso curious
cursore *m* policeman
curva *f* curve
curvare curve
curvità *f* curvature
curvo bent
cuscino *m* cushion
cuspide *f* point
custode *m* guardian
custodia *f* custodian
custodia *f* custody
custodire keep
cutaneo cutaneous
cute *f* skin

D

da of; by; from; in; for; near; according to
dabbasso underneath
dabbene good
dacchè as; since
dado *m* uie; *pl* dice
daga *f* dagger
daina *f* doe
daino *m* deer
dalla of the
dama *f* lady
damigella *f* young lady
damigello *m* young man
damina *f* miss
damma *f* doe
damo *m* gallant
danaio *m* money
dannabile damnable
dannare condemn
dannato *m* reprobate

dannazione *f* sentence
danneggiare damage
danno *m* damage; injury
dante *m* curried deerskin
danza *f* dance
danzare dance
danzatore *m* & *f* dancer
dappié *ad* from below
dappoco lazy
dappoi from; after
dappoichè since
dardeggiare shoot
dardo *m* dart
dare give; grant; permit; produce; yield; show; tell
darsena *f* wet-dock
dassezzo finally
data *f* date
datare date
dativo dative
dato given
davanzale *m* frontal
davvantaggio more
davvero truly
daziare tax
daziere tax-collector
dazio tax
dea goddess
debaccare rage; rave
debellare conquer
debile weak; sickly
debito owed
debitore debtor
debolezza *f* weakness
debolmente weakly
debordare overflow
decadenza decay
decadere decline
decano *m* dean
decantare laud; decant
decapitare behead
decapitazione *f* beheading
decennale decennial
decennio ten years
decente decent
decenza *f* decency

decesso dead
decezione f deception
decidere decide
deciferare decipher
decima f tithe
decimale decimal

decimare tithe
decimo tenth
decisione f decision
decisivo decisive
declive steep
declivio slope
decollare behead
decomporre decompose

decorrere overflow
decorso m overflowing
decotto decoction
decremento, crescimento
  m decrease
decrescere decrease
decretare decree

dedica f dedication
dedicare dedicate
dedurre deduct; deduce
deduzione f consequence;
  deduction
deferenza f deference
deferire condescend
deficit m deficit
definire define
definitivo decisive
definizione f definition
deformare disfigure
deforme deformed
defunto deceased
degnità f dignity
degno worthy
degradare degrade
degustare taste

delfino m dolphin
deliberare deliberate
delicatezza f delicacy
delicato delicate
delineamento m outline
delinquente m delinquent
delirare rave

delirio m delirium; raving
delitto m crime
delizioso delicious
demente mad
demenza f madness
democratico democratic
democrazio f democracy
demolire demolish
demonio m demon
denaro m money
denegare deny
denigrare slander
denominare name
denominatore m denom-
denotare denote [inator
densità f density
denso dense
dentatura f set of teeth

dente m tooth

dentista m dentist
dentizione f dentition
dentro within
denudare strip; uncover
denunziare denounce
depilatorio m depilatory
deplorabile deplorable
deplorare deplore [lation
depopolazione f depopu-
deporre deposit; depose
deportare transport
depositare deposit
deposito m deposit
depravare deprave
depredare plunder
depressione f depression
deprimere depress
deputato m deputy
descrivere describe
descrizione f description
deserto m desert

desiderabile desirable
desiderio m desire; wish
designare design
desinare dine; dinner
desistere desist
desolare desolate

desso same
destare w ke; awake
destinare destine
destinatario *m* addressee
destinazione *f* destination
destino *m* destiny; fate
destituire depose
desto awake
destrezza *f* dexterity
destra *f* right hand
determinare determine
determinazione *f* determination
detestabile detestable
detestare detest
detettivo *m* detective
detonazione *f* detonation
detrarre deduct
devastare lay waste
deviare deviate
devoto devoted; devout
devozione *f* devotion
di *m* day
diabete *f* diabetes
diabetico diabetic
diaframma *m* diaphragm
diagnosi *f* diagnosis
diagonale diagonal
dialetto *m* dialect
dialogo *m* dialogue
diamante *m* diamond
diametro *m* diameter
diario *m* diary
diarrea *f* diarrhœa
dibattere debate
dibattimento *m* debate
dicembre *m* December
dicervellato crazy
dichiarare declare
dichiarazione *f* declaration
dieci ten [tion
dieta *f* diet
dietro behind
difendere defend
difesa *f* defence
difetto *m* defect

dilettoso defective
diffamare defame
differente different
differenza *f* difference
differire differ; postpone
difficile difficult
difficoltà *f* difficulty
diffidare distrust
diffidente diffident
diffidenza *f* distrust
difterite *f* diphtheria
difformità *f* deformity
diga *f* dike
digestione *f* digestion
digiunare fast
digiuno fasting
dignità *f* dignity
dilatare dilate
dilazione *f* delay
dilemma *m* dilemma
dilettante *m* amateur
dilettare delight
dilettevole delightful
diletto loved
diluire dilute
diluvio *m* flood
dimagrare grow lean
dimensione *f* dimension
dimenticare forget
dimentichevole forgetful
dimettere forgive
dimorare live; reside
dimostrare demonstrate
dimostrazione *f* demonstration
dinamite *f* dynamite
dinamo *m* dynamo
dinanzi before
dintorno arrear; *m* neigh-
Dio *m* God   [bourhood
dipartimento *m* department
dipendente depending
dipendenza *f* dependence
dipendere depend

diploma *m* diploma
diplomatico diplomatic
diretto direct
direttore *m* director
direzione *f* direction
dirimpetto opposite
diritto (*m*) right; straight
dirotto excessively
dirupare fall down
disagio *m* want
disapprendere unlearn
disapprovare disapprove

disarmamento *m* disarm-
ing
disarmare disarm
disastro *m* disaster
disastroso disastrous
disattento inattentive
discendere descent
discepolo *m* pupil
disciplina *f* discipline
disco *m* disk
discernere discern

discorso *m* speech
discreditare discredit
discrezione *f* discretion
discreto discreet
discussione *f* discussion
discutere discuss
disdetta *f* denial
disegnare draw [design
disegno *m* drawing;
diseredare disinherit
disertare destroy; desert
disfare undo; dissolve
disfatta *f* defeat
disfidare challenge

disgrazia *f* disgrace
disgraziato unfortunate
disgustare disgust
disgusto *m* disgust
disimparare forget
disinfettare disinfect
disobbedire disobey
disoccupato unoccupied
disonestà *f* dishonesty

disonorare dishonour
disordine *m* disorder
dispaccio *m* despatch
dispari odd; uneven
disparte, in − aside
dispendioso expensive
dispensa distribution;
larder [tribute
dispensare dispense; dis-
disperare despair
disperazione *f* despair
disperato desperate

dispetto *m* anger; con-
tempt [displeasure
dispiacere displease; *m*
dispiacevole unpleasant
disponsibile disposable
disporre dispose
disposizione *f* disposition
disprezzare despise
disputa *f*, −re dispute
dissolvere dissolve
dissomigliare differ
dissonanza *f* dissonance
dissuadere dissuade
distaccare separate
distante distant
distanza *f* distance
distare be distant
distesa *f* extent
distillare distil
distilleria *f* distillery
distinguere distinguish
distinzione *f* distinction
distrarre distract
distrazione *f* distraction
distribuire distribute
distribuzione *f* distribu-
distruggere destroy [tion
distruzione *f* destruction
disubbidire disobey
disturbo *m* **disturbare**
trouble
divertire divert
divezzare disaccustom
dividere divide

divietare forbid
divieto *m* prohibition
divinità *f* divinity
divino divine   [parting
divisa *f* device; uniform;
divisione *f* division
divorare devour   [divorce
divorziare, divorzio *m*
dizionario *m* dictionary
doccia *f* shower-bath
docile docile
documento *m* document
dogana *f* custom-house
doganiere *m* custom-house officer
dogma, domma *m* dogma
dolce sweet; *m* & *pl*
dolere grieve   [sweets
dolore *m* grief; pain;
doloso fraudulent

domanda *f* demand

domandare ask
domani to-morrow
domare subdue; break
domattina to-morrow; morning
donare give; − zione *f*
gift; − tore *m* giver
donde, d'onde, dondeche
whence; why
dondolare swing
dondolo *m* joke
donna *f* woman; wife;
lady; − esco womanlike
donnaiuolo *m* beau
donno kind; *m* master;
donnola *f* weazel   [lord
donnona *f* stout woman
dono *m* gift; present
donora *f* wedding outfit
donzella *f* young lady
donzello *m* young gentleman; servant
dopo after; − chè when
doppia *f* pistole (coin); flounce

doppiare increase; -mente
doubly: wickedly
doppio *m* double; − piezza *f* duplicity
doppione *m* doubloon
dorare gild; − tura *f*
dramma *f* drachma
drappare, peggiare drape;
− peria *f* drapery; − piere *m* draper
drappello *m* troop; band
drappo *m* cloth; coat
drizzare raise; erect
droga *f* drug; − gheria
f drug-trade; − ghiere
m druggist
dromedario *m* dromedary
druda *f* sweet-heart; concubine
drudo gallant; loving
clever; *m* lover
dualità *f* duality; − lismo
dubbiare doubt [*m* dualism
dubbiezza, bio, biositá *f*
& *m* doubt

due two
duecento, ducento, gento
two hundred
duellante *m* duellist
duellare fight a duel
duello *m* duel
duennale biennial
duetanti double
duetto *m* duet
dumo *m* thorn; bramble
duna *f* down; sand-hill
dunque then; so [*m* grief
duodecimo twelfth; duolo
duomo *m* dome
duplicare double
duplicità *f* duplicity
durabilità, rata *f* duration; − bile durable
duramente hard; harshly
durante, turo durable
durare endure

E

e, ed and
ebanista *m* cabinet-maker
ebano *m* ebony
ebbrezza, brietà, bria-
chezza *f* drunkenness;
— bro, brioso, briaco
drunk; mad
ebdomadario weekly
ebete weak; stupid
ebollimento, ebullizione
m & f ebullition
ebraico hebraic; — ismo
m hebraism
ebreo, ea *n* Hebrew
eccellente excellent; —
tissimo very excellent
eccellenza *f* excellency
eccellere excel
eccelso high; eminent
eccentricità eccentricity;
— trico eccentric; *n* ec-
eccepire except [centric
eccessività, eccesso *f &*
m excess; — vo, va ex-
cessive; — vamente ex-
cessively
eccetera *m* etcetera
eccètto except; but
eccettuare except; — tu-
ato excepted
eccettuazione, cezione *f*
exception
eccidio *m* destruction
eccitare excite; — tativo
exciting [ecclesiastic
ecclesia *f* church; — stico
eclisse *f* eclipse
ecco here is
edera *f* ivy
edificare edify; build
edificio, zoi *m* edifice
edile *m* edile

edito published
editore *m* editor
editto *m* edict
edizione *f* edition
adotto educated
educazione *f* education
aducare educate; — tivo,
va educative; — tore *n*
educator
edulo *m* comestible
effabile expressible
effemeride *f* ephemeris
effeminare effeminate
efferatezza *f* cruelty;
efferato cruel
effervescenza *f* efferves-
cence; — cente efferves-
cent
effetto *m* effect; — tivo
tuale effective
effettuare effect; — tua-
zione *f* effect
effigiare make; imagine
effimero ephemeral
efflorescenza *f* efflores-
efflusso *m* flux [cence
effluvio *m* effluvium
effrenato unbridled
efod *m* ephod
egestione *f* evacuation

egida aegis
egli, ei, e' he
egoisme *m* egotism;
— ista egotist
egregiamente egregious-
ly; — gio, a egregious
egritudine *f* illness
egro sick; infirm
eguagliare equalize;
— glianza, lità *f* equality
eguale equal
eh, ehi eh!
eiezione *f* eiection
elaborare elaborate; — zione *f* elaboration
elasticità elasticity

– tico elastic
elazione *f* pride
elce *f* holm-oak
elefante *m* elephant
elegante *a & n f* elegant; – za *f* elegance
eleggere elect; – ggibile eligible; – gibilità *f* eligibility
elegia *f* elegy; – giaco elegiac
elemento *m* element; – tare elementary
elemosina *f* alms; charity; – nare give alms;
elogio *m* eulogy
eloquente eloquent
eloquenza *f* eloquence
eludere elude

emancipare emancipate
emblema *m* emblem
embrione *m* embryo
emendare mend
emergenza *f* occurrence
emergere emerge
emerito retired
emetico *m* emetic
emettere emit
emigrare emigrate
emigrazione *f* emigration
eminente eminent
eminenza *f* eminence
emisfero *m* hemisphere
emolumento *m* emolument
emorraggia *f* haemorrhage
emorroide *f/pl* haemorrhoids
emozione *f* emotion
empiere fill
empio impious
emporio *m* emporium
enfasi *f* emphasis
enfiare swell
enfiatura *f* swelling
enimma *m* riddle; – tico enigmatic

enorme enormous
ente *m* being
entrambi both
entrare enter
entrata *f* entrance
entusiasmo enthusiasm
enumerare enumerate
enunciare enunciate
epico epic
epidemia *f* disease
epidemico epidemic
epifania *f* epiphany
epigramm *m* epigram
epilessia *f* epilepsy
epilettico epileptic
episcopato *m* episcopate
equipaggio *m* equipment; carriage; luggage; crew
equipaggiare equip
equivalente equivalent
equivoco equivocal
era *f* era, epoch [table
erba *f* herb; grass; vege-
erbaiuolo *m* greengrocer
erborizzare botanise
erede *m* heir; eredità inheritance; ereditare inherit
eremita *m* hermit
eresia *f* heresy
eretico heretic
eretto, erigere erect
ergastolo *m* prison
erica *f* heath
ermellino *m* ermine
ermetico hermetic
ernia *f* hérnia [heroic
eroe *m* hero; eroice
errato *m* error
erroneo erroneous
errore *m* error
erta all' – on one's guard
erto steep
erudito learned
esagerare exaggerate
esagerazione *f* exaggera-

165

tion
esalazione *f* exhalation
esaltare exalt
esaminare examine
esame *m* examination
esasperare exasperate
esattezza *f* exactness
esatto exact
esaudire grant; hear
esaurire exhaust
esca *f* bait; tinder
escavazione *f* excavation
esclamare exclaim
esecutare execute; esecutivo executive; esecuzione *f* execution
eseguire execute
esempigrazia for instance
esempio *m* example
esemplare exemplary; copy
esente exempt
esequie *f / pl* exequies
esercitare exercise
esercito *m* army
esercizio *m* exercise
esibire exhibit
esibizione *f* exhibition
esigere exact; demand
esiliare, esilo *m* exile
esimere free
esimio excellent
esistere exist
esperienza *f* experience; experiment [perience
esperimentare try; esesperto expert
espiare expiate
esplicare explain
esplodere explode
esplosione *f* explosion
esplorare explore
esploratore *m* explorer
esporre expose
esportare export
esportazione *f* exportation
esposizione *f* exhibition

espressione *f* expression
espresso express
esprimere express
espropriare expropriate
espulsione *f* expulsion
essenza *f* essence
essenziale essential
essere be; *m* being
est *m* oriente; east
estasi *f* ecstasy
estate *f* summer
estendere extend
estensione *f* extension
estenuare extenuate
esteriore exterior
esterno external
estero foreign (country)
estradizione *f* extradition
estraneo strange(r)
estraordinario extraordinary
estrarre extract [nary
estravagante extravagant
estremo extreme
estremità *f* extremity
estro *m* poetry
estrudere expel; – sione *f* expulsion
estuante boiling
esturbare drive out
esuberante exuberant; – za *f* exuberance
esule *m* exile
esultare exult; – tanza *f* exultation; – zione *f* exultation
esurire be hungry
età, etade *f* age; time
etera, etere *f & m* ether; air; sky; – reo, a ethereal
eterno eternal, – mente eternally; – nare eternize; – nità *f* eternity
eterogene heterogenous
euro *m* East wind; – peo European

evacuare evacuate;
– cuamento, zione m &
f evacuation
evadere escape
evaporare evaporate;
– zione f evaporation
evasione f evasion;
– sivo evasive
evento m event; – tuale
eventual; – tualità f
eventuality
evidente evident; – za f
evidence [f eviction
evincere evict; – zione
evirato emasculated;
– zione f emasculation
evitare avoid; escape
evo evocation
evocare evoke; – zione
f evocation
evoluzione f evolution
extempore directly [yet
eziandio to; also; even;

F

fabbrica f factory; fab
ric; – are manufacture
– tore m manufacturer
fabbricieria f fabric

fabbro m smith; author
faccenda f affair; busi-
ness; – diere m intri-
guer
facchino m porter; scoun-
drel
faccia f face; side
facciata f front; facade
face f torch
facente doing
facezia f jest; joke;
facilità f facility; – le
easy; – tare facilitate;
– lmente easily
facinoroso wicked
facitoio feasible

facitore m author
fagiano m pheasant
fagiuolo m kidney bean;
falcare bend
falcastro m sickle
falce f scythe; – cetto
sickle; – ciare mow;
– tore m mower
falegname m carpenter
falinbello m booby
fallace fallacious; – cia
f fallacy; – lante de-
ceiving; – lanza f de-
ceit
fallare be mistaken; fail
fallire err; fail; deceive;
– libile fallible; – libi-
lità f fallibility; – mento m error; faliure
fallo m fault
falsa f discord
falsare, sificare falsify;
– so, sa false; – samen-
te falsely; – sario m
forger; – – sificazione f
falsefication
falsetto m falsetto
falta f fault
fama f fame; – moso,
sa famous
fame f hunger; – lico
famishing
famigerato famous
famiglia f family
famigliare familiar;
servant; friend; – rità
f familiarity
famiglio m servant
fanale m lantern
fanatico fanatic; – tismo
m fanatism
fanciulla f girl; maid
fanciullaggine, lezza f
childishness
fanciullesco childish [ish
fanciullo m child; child-

fandonia *f* story
fanghiglia *f* mud [muddy
fango *m* mud; – so , sa
fantaccino *m* foot-soldier
fantasia *f* fancy; opinion
fantasima *f* phantom
fantasmagoria *f* phantas-
  magoria
fantasticaggine, **cheria** *f*
  fancy; whim.
fantasticare rave; fancy;
  – co fantastic [soldier
fante *m* servant; foot-
fanteria *f* infantry
fantesca   maid-servant
fardaggio *m* luggage
fardello *m* lead
fare   make; do; work
farfalla *f* butterfly
farina *f* flour
farmacia *f* pharmacy
farmacista *m* chemist
faro *m* light-house
farsa *f* farce
fascia *f* band; bandage;
  sotto – by book-post;
  under wrapper
fasciare bind
fasciatura *f* bandage
fastidiare annoy
fasto *m* pomp
fata *f* fairy
fatale fatal; **fato** *m* fate
fatica *f*, – care fatigue
fatto made; *m* fact

fattorino *m* shop-boy
fattura *f* doing; invoice
favoloso fabulous
favore *m* favour
favorevole favourable
favorito *m* favourite
fazzoletto *m* handkerchief
fabbre *f* fever
febrifugo febrifuge
febrile feverish
feccia *f* dregs
fecondare fertilise

fecondo fruitful
fede *f* faith
fedele faithful
fedeltà *f* fidelity
federa *f* pillow-case
fegato *m* liver
felce *f* fern
felice happy
feltro *m* felt
femmina *f* woman; fe-
  male
femminile feminine
fendere cleave
fenile *m* hay-loft
fenomeno *m* phenomenon
feretro *m* coffin, bier
feria *f* holiday
ferire strike
ferita *f* wound
fermo firm; – **in posta**
  to be left till called for
feroce ferocious
ferro *m* iron
ferrovia *f* railway
ferruginoso ferruginous
fertilità *f* fertility
fertile fertile
fervente, **fervido** fervent
fetta *f* slice

fiaccare break
fiaccola *f* torch
fiala *f* phial
fiamma *f* flame
fiammifero *m* match
fianco *m* flank; side
fiasco *m* bottle (packed
  in straw, 2.25 litre)
fiatare breathe; **fiato** *m*
fibbia *f* buckle [breath
fibra *f* fibre
ficcare fix; drive in
fico *m* fig; fig-tree
fidanzare betroth; engage
fidare confide
fidanza *f* confidence
fido faithful

168

fiducia *f* confidence
fiele *m* gall
fieno *m* hay
fiera *f* wild beast; fair
fiero ferocious; proud
fievole weak
fievolezza *f* weakness
figgere fix
figliastra *f* daughter-in-law
figliastro, *m* son-in-law
figlio, figliuolo *m* son
figura *f* figure; face
figurare represent
fila *f* file; row
filare spin
filatoio *m* spinning-wheel
filatore *m* spinner
filetto *m* small thread;
filiale filial   [fillet
filiera *f* wire-drawing-mill;
filigrana *f* filigrane
filo *m* thread
filologia *f* philology
filologo *m* philologer
filosofo *m* philosopher
filtrare, filtro *m* filter

filza *f* file; string
finanza finance
finale final
fine *f* end
finestra *f* window
fingere feign
finire finish
fino fine
finocchio *m* fennel
finora till now
finzione *f* fiction
fiocco *m* tuft
fioco hoarse
fioraia *f* flower-girl
fioraliso *m* blue-bottle
fiordaliso *m* lily
fiore *m* flower
fiorire bloom
firma *f* signature; − re
  sign
firmamento *m* firmament

fischiare whisthle; hiss
fischi(etto) *m* .whistle
fisica *f* physics
fisciù *m* handkerchief
fisionomia *f* physiognomy
fisso fixed; permanent
fissare fix
flotta *f* .fleet
fluido fluid
flutto *m* wave
fluttuare waver; fluctuate
foca *f* seal
focaccia *f* cake
fochista *f* fireman; stoker
foce *f* mouth
focolare *m* hearth
fodera *f* lining
foderare line
foglia *f* leaf   [paper
foglio *m* sheet; news-
fogna *f* sewer
folata *f* flock of birds;
  gust of wind
fondamento *m* foundation
fondare found
fondata *f* dregs
fondere melt; fonderia
  f foundry [background
fondo deep; *m* bottom;
fontana *f* fountain
forare bore

forbici *f/pl* scissors
foresta *f* forest
forestiere *m* stranger
forma *f* formare form
formaggio *m* cheese
formale formal
formalità *f* formality
formalizzarsi take amiss
formazione *f* formation
formento *m* wheat
formica *f* ant; − io *m*
  ant-hill
formidabile formidable
formula *f* formula
fornace *f* furnace

fornaio *m* baker
fornire furnish; forni-
tore *m* purveyor
forno *m* oven
foro *m* hole; forum
forse perhaps
forte strong   [force
fortezza *f* stronghold;
fortificare fortify   [tion
fortificazione *f* fortifica-
fortuna *f* fortune
fortunato happy; lucky
forza *f* force; strength;
forzare force   [power
forziere *m* safe
fosforo *m* phosphorus
fossa *f* grave
fosso *m* ditch
fotografare photograph
fotografia *f* photograph(y)
fotografico photographic
fotografo *m* photographer
fra among; *m* friar
fracassare break; smash
fragile fragile
fragola *f* strawberry
franco frank
frangere break   [stand
frantendere misunder-
fraternità *f* fraternity
fraterno fraternal
fratellastro *m* step-brother
frattanto meanwhile
frattura *f* fracture
frazione *f* fraction
freccia *f* arrow
freddo freddura *f* cold
freddare cool
fregare rub
fregata *f* frigate
fregiare adorn
fremere shiver
frenare refrain
frenatore *m* brakesman
freno *m* bridle; brake
frequentare frequent
frequente frequent

fresco fresh; cool
freschezza *f* coolness
fretta *f* hurry
frettoloso in a hurry
fricassea *f* fricassee
friggere fry
frigido cold
frizione *f* friction [band
froda *f* fraud; contra-
frodare defraud; smuggle
frollo tender
fronda *f* foliage [leaves
frondeggiare put forth
frontiera *f* frontier
fronte *f* forehead; front
frontone *m* gable
frottola *f* story; ballad
frugalità *f* frugality

frugale frugal
frugare search
fruire enjoy
frumento *m* wheat
frusta *f*; – re whip
frustrare frustrate
frutto *m* fruit; produce
fucile *m* gun; fucilare
fucina *f* forge   [shoot
fuga *f* flight
fugare route
fuggire fly; flee; – ga
f flight; – tivo fugitive;
– gifatica idle; idler;
– giasco *m* fugitive
fulgere shine; – gidezza
f shine; – gido shiny
fuliggine *f* dusk; soot;
– noso fuliginous
fulmine *m* thunderbolt;
lightning;
funerale, nebre, reo fu-
nerale   [fatal
funestare afflict; – to
fungaia *f* mushroom-bed;
– go *m* mushroom
fungosità *f* fungosity;
– so fungous; spongy
funzione *f* function

170

fuoco _m_ fire; love;
– chista _f_ firework-
maker; – coso fiery

fuora, ri outside; – fuorchè; – solamente ex-
cept; save

fuormisura ·excessively

fuoruscito _m_ exile; out-

furacchiare juggle [law

furare rob; – race, rante
robbing; – tore _m_ robber

furbo _m_ knave; cheat;
– beria _f_ cheating;
– besco knavish; crafty;
– betto _m_ little rogue

furente furious

furfantare cheat; – tag-
gi·a, teria _f_ cheating;

furia _f_ fury; – riare be
angry; – bondo, oso

furoncolo, runcolo _m_ boil

furore _m_ fury [–vo furtive

furto _m_ theft; stealth;
di – by stealth

fusello _m_ tree

fusione _f_ fusion; melting;
– sibile fusible; – so
melting; spindle

fustigare whip; – zione
_f_ whipping

fusto _m_ trunk [futility

futile futile; – lità _f_

futuro future

G

gabbadeo _m_ hypocrite

gabbare deceive; – men-
to _m_ deceit; – – tore _m_
cheat

gabbione _m_ gabion

gabbo _m_ joke

gabella _f_ custom-duty;
– liere, lotto _m_ custom-
house officer

gabinetto _m_ closet; office

gaggio _m_ pledge

gagliardo playful; strong;

gagno _m_ sheepfold; trap

gagnolare whine; – men-
to, lio _m_ howling

gaiezza _f_ joy; – io gay

gala _f_ gala

galante gallant; gay; _m_
spark; – mente ele-
gantly; – teggiare
court; – ria _f_ gallantry

galantuomo _m_ gentleman

galappio _m_ trap; cheat

galassia _f_ galaxy

galbano _m_ galbanum

galea, lera _f_ galley;
– leotto _m_ convict

galeone _m_ galleon

galeotta _f_ gailot

galetta _f_ butter-paste;
sea-biscuit

galla _f_ gall-nut

gallare float; revel

gallina _f_ hen; – naccio
_m_ turkey; – naio _m_
hen roost; – nella _f_
young hen; (astr.)
pleiades; – lione _m_
capon

gallo _m_ cock [lace

gallone _m_ lace; – nare

galloria _f_ joy

gallozza, lozzola, luzza,
_f_ gallnut; bubble

galoppare gallop; – pata,
po _f_ & _m_ gallop

galoscia _f_ galosh

galuppo _m_ rude man

galvanismo _m_ galvanism;
–nico galvanic; – nizzare
galvanize

gamba _f_ leg; centipede

gambale _m_ trunk; stem

gambero _m_ crawfish;
(astr.) cancer

gambetto *m* tripping up
gambo *m* stalk

gara *f* debate; emulation
garabullare cheat
garbare please; – **tezza**
f good looks; – **to**
well bred

garbo *m* good looks
garbuglio *m* confusion
gareggiare complete; –
tore *m* rival; – **gioso**
quarrelsome

garetto *m* ham   [mur
gargagliare gurgle; mur-
gargarismo *m* gargle
gargarizzare *m* gargle
gariglione *m* chime
garofano *m* pink
garrire chirp
garzone *m* boy; servant;
gas *m* gas   [waiter

gatto *m*, **gatta** *f* cat
gazza *f* magpie
gazzetta *f* gazette
gelare freeze
gelato *m* ice(-cream)
gemma *m* gem; bud
generale (*m*) general

generalizzare generalize
generare engender
generazione *f* generation
genero *m* gender

genero *m* son-in-law
generosità *f* generosity
generoso generous
genesi *f* genesis
gengiva *f* gum
genio *m* genius
genitori *m pl* parents
gente *f* people
genuino genuine
geografia *f* geography
geografo *m* geographer
geologia *f* geology
geometria *f* geometry
gerarchia *f* hierarchy

gerente *m* manager
germe *m* germ
germinare germinate
gesso *m*, **gessare** plaster
gesto *m* gesture
Gesù *m* Jesus
Gesuita *m* Jesuit
gettare cast; **getto** *m*
throw(ing), cast
ghiacciaia *f* ice-house;
ice-safe; glacier
ghiacciare freeze
già already; **giacchè** as;
giacca *f* jacket   [since•
giacere lie
giallo yellow
giammai never   [ese
Giapponese *m* Japan-
giardiniere *m* gardener
giardino *m* garden

gianastica *f* gymnastics
ginocchio *m* knee; –**ne**
kneeling
giocolatore *m* juggler
giocondo jocose; gay
giogo *m* yoke   [stone
gioia *f* joy; precious
gioiello *m* jewel

gioelliere *m* jeweller
gioioso joyous
giornalaio *m* news-vendor
giornale *m* journal
giornalista *m* journalist
giornaliero daily
giornata *f* day; day's
work; day's wages;
giorno *m* day   [journey
giovane *m* young man;
f young woman

giracapo *m* dizziness
girare move round
girasole *m* sunflower
giro *m* round; turn
gita *f* going; excursion
giù down   [coat
giubba *f* mane; waist-

giubbileo *m* jubilee
giubilare rejoice
giudeo *m* jew
giudicare judge
giudice *m* judge
giudicio *m* judgment;
 –so judicious
giumenta *f* mare
giunco *m* rush
giungere arrive; join
giunta *f* arrival; increase;
 meeting
giuocare play
giuoco *m* play
giuramento *m* oath
giurare swear
giurato *m* juryman
giure *m* law; right
giuridico juridical
Giuseppe *m* Joseph
giustificare justify
giustizia *f* justice; –re
giusto just [execute
gloria *f* glory; fame; *re*
 glorify; glorioso glorious
glutinoso glutinous
gobba *f* hump
gobbo *m* hunchback
goccia *f* drop
gocciolare drip
godere enjoy; rejoice
godimento *m* pleasure
goffo silly; rude
gola *f* throat
golfo *m* gulf
goloso gluttonous
gomito *m* elbow
gomitolo *m* ball; clue
gomma *m* gum; – **ara-
 bica** gum arabic; –
 elastica india-rubber;
 –to gummed
gonfiare swell; blow up
gonfio swollen
gonn(ella) *f* gown
gonorrea *f* gonorrhœa

gorga, gorgia *f* throat
governante *f* housekeeper
governare govern
govern(ament)o *m* gov-
 ernment
gradevole agreeable
gradino *m* step
gradire please; approve
grado *m* liking; degree
graffiare scratch
grafite *f* black-lead
gragnola *f* hail(storm)
gramatica *f* grammar;
 –le grammatical
gramma *m* gram
granaio *m* granary
granata *f* grenade
granato *m* garnet
grande great; –zza *f*
 greatness; – ggiare play
 the lord [hail
grandine *f*; grandinare
grandioso magnificent
granduca *m* grand-duke;
 –to *m* grand-duchy;
 –chessa *f* grand-duchess
granello *m* grain; nugget
granita *f* iced lemonade
grano *m* grain; – turco
 maize [grapes
grappolo *f* bunch of
grassatore *m* highway-
 man
grasso stout; fat
grato agreeable; grateful
gratitudine *f* gratitude
grattare scratch
grattino *m* razor
gratuito gratuitous
gravare grieve; burden
grave grave
gravido pregnant; panino
 – sandwich
gravità *f* gravity
grazia *f* grace; thanks
graziare absolve; pardon

173

grazioso graceful
Greco *m* Greek; north-
greggio raw   [east
grembiale *m* apron
grembio *m* lap
greppia *f* manger
greppina *f* couch
gretto stingy
gridare shout; call
grido *m* cry; fame
grossa *f* gross   [nancy
grossezza *f* size; preg-
grosso big
grossolano rough
grotta *f* grotto
groviera *f* gruyère
gru *f* crane
gruccia *f* crutch
grugnare grunt
gruppare group
guadagnare gain; win
guadagnato *m* gain; profit

guancia *f* cheek; – – ciale
m pillow; – lino *m*
cushion; – ta *f* buffet;

guardare look at; con-
sider; keep;

guardamento *m* aspect
guardatore *m* spectator;
guardian
guardia *f* guard
guardiano *m* guardian
guardingo prudent
guardo *m* glance; look
guarentire guarantee; –
tia, tigia *f* warranty
guari (non) little; nearly
guarire cure; heal; –
gione *f* cure
guarnacca *f* (night)gown

guarnire furnish; trim;
– gione, tura *f* trimming

guatare look at; spy;
– tura *f* glance

guazzabugliare embroil;
confuse; – glio *m* con-

fusion
guazzare shake; ford;
– toiò *m* ford; –zzo *m*
ford; –zoso muddy
guazzetto *m* ragout; sauce
guercio squinting
guerra *f* war; obstacle;
– reggiare fight; –
giante belligerent; –
reggiamento *m* fight;
– reggiatore, riere, ro
m warrior; – ricciola *f*
guerrilla
gufare laugh at
gufo *m* owl
guida *m* guide
guidare guide; lead
guiderdonare reward; –
done *m* reward; salary
guirminella *f* deceit
guisa *f* way; will
guitto dirty; paltry
guizzare stir; swim;
–zo *m* stirring; swimming
guizzo faded
guscio *m* pod
gustare try; approve;

H

The letter **h** is used
only to harden the sound
of the letters **c** and **g**
before the vowels **e** and
i. It is used also to distinguish the words **ho,
hai, ha, hanno** from **o,
ai, a, anno**.

I

The **I** is used instead of
the **J**.
iacinto *m* hyacinth; –
aspide *m* jasper

iattura *f* lost; disgrace
iberno wintery
ibrido hybrid
icnografia *f* ichnography;
-fico ichnographic
iconoclasta *m* iconoclast
Iddio *m* God
idea *f* idea; -le ideal; -
lismo *m* idealism; -
lista *m* idealist; -lità *f*
ideality; -are imagine
idem ditto
identicità *f* identity; -co
identical; -tity *f* identity
idolo *m* idol; - trare
worship idols; - tria
f idoltary
idoneo fit; suitable; -
neità *f* convenience
idra *f* hydra
idraulica *f* hydraulics;
-co hydraulic
idrofobia *f* hydrophobia
iena *f* hyena
ierarchia *f* hierarchy
ieri *m* yesterday
ier l'altro *m* day before
yesterday   [hygienic
igiene *f* hygiene; -nico
ignaro, ra ignorant
ignavia *f* cowardice; -
vo cowardly
igneo igneous; fiery; -
gnizione *f* ignition

ignoranza *f* ignorance;
-te, tello ignorant;
-rare ignore
ignoto unknown
ignudare undress; -do
ib come   [naked
il the
ilare gay; -rità *f* hilarity
illativo, va consequent;
-zione *f* consequence
illecebra *f* flattery
illecito unlawful; *m*

crime   [illegality
illegale illegal; - lità
illeggibile ineligible
illegittimità *f* illegitimacy;
-mo illegitimate
illeso safe
illetterato illiterate
illibatezza *f* integrity;
-to honest
illimitato unlimited
illuminazione *f* illumination; - re illuminate;
-to illuminated
illusione *f* illusion; -sore
m deceiver; -sorio il-
lusory
illustrazione *f* illustration
illuvione *f* flood
imbaccarsi get tipsy
imbacuccare disguise
imbaldanzire be proud
imbaldire grow bold [of
imballaggio *m* packing;
- lare pack; - latore
m packer
imbalordire stupefy
imbalsamare embalm;
-zione *f* embalming
imbarazzare embarrass;
-zo *m* embarrassment
imbarcare embark; -co
m embarking
imbardare flatter
imbarrare bar
imbasamento *m* basis
imbasceria *f* embassy
imbastardire deprave
imbastare saddle
imbastire baste
imbasto *m* pack-saddle
imbattersi meet by chance
imbatto *m* chance; im-
pediment
imbeccare teach
imbecile silly; stupid;
-lità *f* imbecility

imbelle weak; faint

imbellettare shave; paint (face)

imbellire beautify

imbendare bind

imberbe beardless

imberciare hit (mark)

imbevere imbibe

imbonire appease

imborsare pocket

imboscare lie in ambush; –ta *f* ambush

imboschire plant woods

imbottare decant; –toio *m* funnel

imbottigliare bottle

imbracciare embrace

imbragacciare stick in mud

imbrandire brandish

imbrattare soil; damage –to *m* dirt; hog's wash

imbriacare get tipsy; –cato, co tipsy; –mento, tura *m* & *f* drunkenness

imbrigare embroil

imbrigliare bridle

imbroccare aim at

imbroglio *m* confusion

imbrunire become dark

imbruttire grow ugly

imbuto *m* funnel

imitare imitate

imitazione *f* imtation

imitatore *m* imitator

immacolato immaculate

immaginabile imaginable

immaginare imagine

immaginazione *f* imagination

immagrire grow thin

immediato immediate

immemorabile immemor-

immenso immense [able

immergere submerge

immeritato undeserved

immobile immovable

immollare moisten

immorale immoral

immortale immortal

immortalità *f* immortality

immutabile invariable

impacc(hett)are pack up

impagabile invaluable

impagliare stuff

impallidire turn pale

impalpabile impalpable

imparare learn [rable

impareggiabile incompa-

impari odd

imparziale impartial

impegnare pledge

impellere push; impel

impenetrabile impenetrable

impensato unforeseen

imperatore *m* emperor

imperatrice *f* empress

impercettibile unperceivable [able

imperdonabile unpardon-

imperturbabile calm

impetuoso impetuous

impiagare wound

impiccare hang

impicciare trouble [point

impiegare employ; ap-

impiegato *m* official

impiego *m* office

impiombare lead; stop

implacabile implacable

implicare embroil

implorare implore

impolverare powder

impopolare unpopular

imporre order; impose

importare matter

importante important

importanza *f* importance

importazione *f* importation

importunare trouble

importuno troublesome

impossibile impossible
impostare post
impostore *m* impostor
impotente impotent [able
impraticabile impractic-
impreccare curse
imprendere undertake
impresa *f* enterprise
impressione *f* impression

imprestare lend
imprigionare imprison
imprimere stamp
improbabile improbable
improbo wicked
impronta *f* stamp
improprio improper
improvveduto unforeseen
inanimare encourage
inappetenza *f* want of
   appetite   [able
inapprezzabile inestim-
inargentare silver
inaspettato unexpected
inaudito unheard of
inaugurare inaugurate
inazione *f* inaction
incagliare strand
incalzare pursue
incandescente incandes-
   cent   [cence
incandescenza *f* incandes-
incantare enchant
incarcerare imprison
incaricare load; charge
incartare wrap up
incassare cash; enshrine
incatenacciare bolt
incatenare chain
incavare dig; hollow
incendiare set on fire

inchiesta *f* inquest
inchinare incline
inchino *m* bow
inchiodare nail
inchiostro *m* ink
inchiudere enclose

incominciare begin
incomodare trouble
incomparabile incompa-
   rable
inconsolabile inconsolable
incontestabile indisput-
   able
incontanente directly
incontrare meet
incontro against; **andare
   all'** – go to meet
incoraggiare encourage
incorniciare frame
incoronare crown
incorporare incorporate
incorrere incur
incorrigibile incorrigible
incredibile incredible
increspare knit; curl
incrinare split

indarno in vain
indebitarsi run into debt
indebolire weaken
indeciso irresolute
indefinibile undefinable
indennità *f* indemnity
indenizzare indemnify
independenza *f* independ-
   dence   [able
indescrivibile indescrib-
indi afterwards
Indiano *m* Indian
indicare indicate [guide
indicatore *m* advertiser;
indice *m* fore-finger; index
indicibile inexpressible
indietro backward
indifferenza *f* indifference
indigeno indigenous
indigente poor
indigestione *f* indigestion
indignarsi grow angry
indignazione *f* indigna-
   tion   [address
indispensabile indispen-
sable

177

indisporre indispose
indisposizione *f* indisposition
individuale individual
indizio *m* indication; sign
indolcire soften
indolente indolent
indorare gild
indovinare guess
indubitabile indubitable
indugiare, indugio *m* delay
indulgente indulgent
indulgenza *f* indulgence
indurare harden
indurre engage; induce
industria *f* industry
inebbriare inebriate
inedito unpublished
ineguale unequal
inerme unarmed

infallibile infallible
infallibilità *f* infallibility
infamare slander
infame infamous
infantile childish
infanzia *f* infancy
infarinare flour
infaticabile indefatigable
infatti indeed
inferiore inferior
inferire infer
infermeria *f* infirmary
infermiere *m* nurse
infermità *f* infirmity
infernale infernal
inferno *m* hell
iniettare infect
infezione *f* infection
infiammare inflame
infilare thread
infimo very low; lowest
infine at last
infingardo idle
infinità *f* infinity
infinito infinite
infino till

influente influent
influenza *f* influence
informare inform [tion
informazione *f* informa-
informe deformed
infortunio *m* misfortune
infoscato darkened
infossato buried; hollow
infrangere break
ingabbiare put in a cage
ingaggiare pawn; pledge
ingannare deceive
inganno *m* deceit [try
ingegnarsi exert oneself;
ingegnere *m* engineer
ingegno *m* genius; – so
ingenious
ingenuo ingenuous
ingessare plaster
inghiottire swallow
ingiallire get yellow
inginocchiarsi kneel
inginocchiatoio *m* kneel-
ing-stool
ingiù down; below
ingiungere enjoin; order
ingiuria *f* injury; – re
insult
ingoiare swallow
ingommare gum
ingrandire increase
ingrassare fatten
ingrato ungrateful
ingraziarsi ingratiate
ingrediente *m* ingredient
ingresso *m* entrance
ingrossare increase
ingrosso *m* wholesale
inguantarsi put on gloves
inibire inhibit
iniettare inject
iniziale initial
iniziare initiate
innamorarsi fall in love
innanzi before
innato innate

178

innegabile indisputable
innestare graft
inno *m* hymn
innocente innocent
innoncenza *f* innocence
innominato nameless
innovare innovate
innovazione *f* innovation

insalare salt
insalata *f* salad
insano insane
insaponare soap
insaziabile insatiable
inscrivere inscribe
inscrizione *f* inscription

insegna *f* flag; arms
insegnamento *m* teaching
insegnare teach
inseguire pursue
insensato foolish
inseparabile inseparable
inserire insert
insetticida, polvere
  insect-powder
insetto *m* insect
insidioso insidious

insieme together [cant
insignificante insignifi-
insino till

insonne sleepless
insonnia *f* sleeplessness
insopportabile unbearable
insorgere revolt
insozzare stain; soil

insperato unhoped for
inspirare inspire
installare instal
instancabile indefatigable
instantaneo instantaneous
instante *m* instant
instigare instigate
instruire instruct
instrumento *m* instru-
  ment   [sult
insultare, insulto *m* in-

insuperabile insuperable
insurrezione *f* insurrec-
intagliare engrave. [tion
intaglio *m* carving; cut
intanto in the mean time
intarlato worm-eaten
intarsio *m* inlaid work
intascare pocket
intatto entire

intendere hear; under-
  stand; wish; s' intende
  of course
intenerire soften
intensità *f* intensity

intensivo intense
intenzione *f* intention

intercettare intercept
interdire interdict
interessare interest
interesse *m* interest
interiore interior

intermezzo *m* interlude
interno internal
interminabile intermin-
intero entire   [able
interprete *m* interpreter
interporre interpose
interrogare interrogate

intervista *f* interview
intesa *f* intention; con-
intestino intestine [sent
intignato worm-eaten
intimare summon
intimidire intimidate

intimo intimate
intorno(a) round; about
intraducibile untranslat-
intralciare embroil [able
intraprendere undertake
intrapresa *f* enterprise
intrattabile intractable
intrattenere entertain
intrepido intrepid
intrigare, intrigo *m* intrigue   [tion

introduzione *f* introduc-
introdurre introduce
introito *m* entrance
intronizzare instal
intrudere intrude
intuizione *f* intuition
inudito unheard of
inumare bury
invadere invade
invalidare invalidate
invalido invalid
invano in vain
invariabile invariable
invasione *f* invasion
invecchiare grow old
invece instead of
inventare invent
inventivo inventive
inventore *m* inventor
inventario *m* inventory
invenzione *f* invention
inverisimile unlikely
inverniciare varnish
inverno *m* winter
invero truly
invertere upset; invert
investigare search
investire invest
invetrare glaze
invettiva *f* invective
inviare send
invidia *f* envy; – bile
  enviable; – re envy
invigorire strengthen
inviluppare wrap up
invincibile invincible
invio *m* sending
inviolabile inviolable
invisibile invisible
invitare invite
invito *m* invitation
invocare invoke
involgere wrap up
involto *m* parcel
involtare envelope
ipocrisia *f* hypocrisy
ipocrita *m* hypocrite

ipoteca *f* mortgage
ippodromo *m* hippodrome
ippopotamo *m* hippo-
ira *f* anger   [potamus
ire go
iri. iride *f* iris; rainbow
ironia *f* irony; – nico
  ironical
irradiare irradiate; – zione *f* irradiation [able
irragionevole unreason-
irrazionabile irrational
irreduttibile irreducible
irrefragabile irrefragable
irregolare irregular; –
  rità *f* irregularity
irreligione *f* irreligion;
  – so irreligious
irremediabile irremediable
irremissibile irremissible
irreparabile irreparable
irresistibile irresistible
  – bilmente irresistibly
irresoluto irresolute; – zione *f* irresolution
irretire embroil; net
irreverente irreverent;
  – za *f* irreverence
irrevocabile irrevocable
irricordevole oblivious
irriflessivo thoughtless
irrigare irrigate; – zione
  f irrigation.
irritabile irritable; – lità
  f irritability; – re provoke; irritate; – zi-
one *f* irritation
irritrosire grow stubborn
irriverente irreverent;
  – za *f* irriverence
irrorare water; besprin-
irrugginire rust   [kle
irrugiadare bedew
irruzione *f* irruption
irsuto, irto bristling;
  hideous
islamismo *p* islamism

180

isola *f* island; – no *a* insular

istantaneo instantaneous; – te instant; moment

isterismo *m* hysterics; – rico hysteric

istesso *m* the same

istigare instigate; – tore *m* instigator; – zione *f* instigation

istinto *m* instinct; – tivo instinctive

istituire institue

istmo *m* isthmus

istoria *f* history; story; – rico historic; – rietta *f* novel; – riografo *m* historian

istrice *m* porcupine

istruire instruct; teach; – zione *f* instruction; information

itterizia *f* jaundice

iugero *m* acre

iuniore junior

iussione *f* order

ivi there

izza *f* anger; wrath

J

The letter 'J' does not exist in Italian, and the words beginning with 'J' will be found under the letter 'I'

L

la the; her; it

là there; yonder; quà e là here and here

labbro *m* lip

labe *f* stain; – fatto stained   [byrinth

laberinto, birinto *m* labile decaying; slippery; – lità *f* decay

laboratorio *m* laboratory

lacca *f* haunch; lac

lacchè *m* lackey

laccio *m* snare; net

lacerare lacerate; – mento, zione *m & f* laceration; – ro lacerated

lacerto *m* forearm

laco, go *m* lake

lacuna *f* marsh; defect

laddove so that; where; whereas

laddovunque everywhere

ladino fluid

ladramente disagreably

ladreria *f* leprosy; stinginess

ladro, ne *m* thief; – neggiare rob

laggiù, giuso below

lagno, mento *m* affliction; – gnarsi complain

lagrima *f* tear; – bile, mevole, moso deplorable; – male lacrimal; – mare cry; bewail; – zione *f* weeping

lagume *m* marsh; pudlaguna *f* lagoon   [dle

lai *mpl* lamentations

laico lay

lama *f* plain; blade

lambire lick

lamentare lament

lamentevole lamentable

lamina sheet; laminare laminate

lampada *f* lamp

lampeggiare lighten

lampione *m* lantern

lampone *m* raspberry

lampreda *f* lamprey

181

lana _f_ wool
lanceita _f_ lancet; hand
lancia _f_ lance
lanciare throw; fling
lancio _m_ leap
languire languish
lanterna _f_ lantern
laonde therefore
lapidare stone
lapide _f_ tomb-stone
lapis _m_ lead-pencil
lappola _f_ trifle
lardellare lard
lardo _m_ lard; bacon
larghetto easy

larva _f_ phantom; mask;
  chrysalis   [mit
lasciapassare _m_ pass; per-
lasciare leave; let
lascito _m_ legacy
lascivio lascivious
lassare, lasso weary
lassù up there   [stone
lastra _f_ sheet; paving
lastricare pave
lastrico _m_ pavement
laterale lateral
latifondo _m_ landed
Latino Latin   [property
latitudine _f_ latitude;
lato _m_ side; wide

lavanda _f_ washing
lavandaia _f_ washer-wo-
lavare wash   [man
lavorare, lavoro _m_ work
leale loyal
lebbra _f_ leprosy
leccare lick; flatter
leccio _m_ holm-oak
lecito lawful
lega _f_ league; allay
legale lawful
legalizzare authenticate
legame _m_ tie; chain
legare bind; tie; be-
  queath
legge _f_ law

leggenda _f_ legend
leggere read
leggiadro graceful; ele-
leggibile legible   [gant
leggiero light
leggio _m_ desk
legione _f_ legion
legislativo legislative
legislazione _f_ legislation
legislatore _m_ legislator
legittimare legitimate
legittimo legitimate
legna _f_ wood
legnaiuolo _m_ carpenter
legname _m_ timber
legno _m_ wood; cab

legume _m_ vegetable
lena _f_ breath; strength
lente _f_ lens
lento slow
lentezza _f_ slowness
lenticchia _f_ lentil
lenzuolo _m_ sheet
leone _m_ lion
leonessa _f_ lioness
leopardo _m_ leopard
lesina _f_ avarice; miser
lessare boil
lesso _m_ boiled beef
letizia _f_ joy
lettera _f_ letter; – le li-
  teral; – rio literary;
  – to learned; – tura _f_
  literature
lettiera _f_ bedstead
letto _m_ bed
lettore _m_ reader
lettura _f_ reading
leva _f_ levy
levare raise; – si rise
lezzare lezzo _m_ stink
libbra _f_ pound
libeccio _m_ S. W. wind
libello _m_ libel
liberale liberal
liberare free; deliver
libero free

182

libertà *f* liberty
libro *m* book
libreria *f* library
licenza *f* liberty
licenziare discharge
licenzioso licentious
liceo *m* lyceum
lido *m* shore
lieto gay
lieve light
lignite *f* lignite
lila *m* lilac
lima *f* file; – re file
limbo *m* limb
limitare, limite *m* limit
linguaggio *m* language
lino *m* lint, flax
liquefare liquefy
liquido liquid
liquirizia *f* liquorice
liquore *m* liquor

lira *f* lyre; lira
lirico lyric
lisca *f* fish-bone
lisciare burnish; polish
liscio smooth; polished
lista *f* sash; list
litanie *f pl* litanies
lite *f* law-suit
litigare plead
litografia *f* lithography
litro *m* litre
liturgia *f* liturgy
livellare, livello *m* level
livido livid
livrea *f* livery
locale local
località *f* locality
locanda *f* inn
locandiere *m* inn-keeper
locare let
locomotiva *m* locomotive
logico logical
logorare wear out
logoro worn out
lolla *f* chaff

lombagine *f* lumbago
lombata *f* sirloin; loin
lombo *m* loin
lombrico *m* earth-worm
longitudine *f* longitude
lontananza *f* distance
lontano distant; far
lucciola *f* firefly; glow-
luce *f* light   [worm
lucertola *f* lizard
lucido bright; lucid
lucidare elucidate; – dezza *f* clearness; – dità *f*
lucidity; – do lucid;
ludificare deceive; – zi-
one *f* deceit
lue *f* infection; pest;
– venerea venereal dis-
ease
lui *m* him; it; he
lumaca *f* snail; – cone
m snail
lume *m* light; genius;
star; – metto *m* candle;
– minello *m* wick;
– minoso shining
lumiera *f* torch
luminaria *f*, illumina-
zione illumination
luna *f* moon; – re lunar;
– ria *f* moon-wort; – rio
m calendar; – tico *a*
whimsical; – to moon-
shaped; – zione *f* luna-
tion
lunetta *f* glass
lunga *f* strap; length of
time
lungo long; *m* length;
along; long time; – ge,
gi far; – gheria, ghezza
f length; – ghesso
along; near
luogo *m* place; motive
luogotenente *m* lieuten-
ant; – za *f* lieutenancy

lusinga *f* flattery; – **gare**
caress; – **ghevole, ghiero**
charming; – **tore** *m*
flatterer

lusso *m* luxury

lustrare lighten; illustrate; – **le** lustral;
– **tura** *f* mangling;
– **tro** *m* lustre

lustre *f* *pl* grimaces

lustrino *m* lustrine; tinsel

luteranismo *m* Lutheran-
ism; – **no** Lutheran

lutifigolo *m* potter

luto *m* mud; – **so, tu-
lento** muddy

lutta *f* wrestling; debate

lutto *m* lute; grief;
– **tuoso** painful; – **samente** painfully

M

ma but

macca *f* plenty; store

macchina *f* machine;
plot; – **le** machinal;
– **nista** *m* machinist;
– **re** plot; – **zione** *f* plot

macchione *m* thicket

macco *m* shambles

mace *f* mace

macellaio *m* butcher;
– **lare** kill; – **lo** *m*
shambles

macerare macerate; mor-
tify; – **mento, zione**
m & *f* maceration; – **ro**
macerated; maceration

maceratoia *m* retting-
pool

maceria *f* rubbish

machiavellismo *m* ma-
chiavelism

macigno *m* stone

macilento flabby; lank

macina *f* grinding-stone;
– **nare** grind; ruin;
– **toio** *m* oil-mill;
– **tura, zione** *f* grinding

macinello *m* grindstone

madia *f* kneading-trough;
hutch   [Virgin

madonna *f* lady; the

madornale great; – **lità**
f greatness

madre *f* mother; origin;
mould

madreperla *f* mother-of-
pearl

madreselva *f* honey-
suckle

madrevite *f* screw-nut;
female screw

madrigale *m* madrigal

madrigna *f* step-mother

madrina *f* god-mother

maestà *f* majesty; noble-
ness; – **tevole, toso**
majestic

maestra *f* mistress (school)

maestrale *m* north-west-
wind

maestrare teach; – **tran-
za** *f* workmen; – **tre-
vole** industrious; – **tra-
mento, tria** *m* & *f* art;
skill; – **tro** *m* teacher;
professor;   director;

maga *f* sorceress

magagna *f* defect; – **gnare** vitiate; spoil

magari please God

magazzino *m* magazine;
– **niere** *m* warehouse-
keeper

maggengo of May

maggio *m* May; greater

maggiore of age; greater;
m elder son; superior;
– **renne** of age; – **ri**

184

m pl ancestors; – **rità** *f*
majority [magical
magia *f* sorcery; – **co**
magione *f* house
magisterio, stero *m* skill;
mastership; – **trale, tre-**
vole magisterial
magistrato *m* magistrate;
– **tura** *f* magistracy
maglia *f* witchcraft;
mail; link
magnetizzare magnetize
magnificare magnify;
praise
magnificente magnificent
mai ever; **non** – never
maiolica *f* majolica
malagevole difficult
malandare ruin one's self
malandrino *m* highway-
man
malaticcio sickly
malaria *f* malaria
malattia *f* sickness; illness
malcontento discontented
male *m* evil; sickness;
–**di testa** headache;
–**di mare** sea-sickness
maledetto cursed
maledire curse
maleficio *m* witchcraft
malevole malevolent
malfatto *m* misdeed;
–**re** *m* malefactor
malgrado in spite of
malia *f* witchcraft
malignità *f* malignity
maligno wicked; *m* devil
malo bad
malora *f* ruin
malore *m* illness; disease
malsano unwholesome
malvagio wicked
malvisto hated
malvolentieri against
once's will
malvolere *m* hatred

mamma *f* mamma;
breast [nipple
mammella *f* breast;
mammola *f* violet
manata *f* handful
mancare fail; want
mancanza *f* defect
manchevole defective
mancia *f* tip
mancino left-handed
manco defective, left;
m fault
mandare send; inform
mandato *m* order
mandarino *m* mandarin
mandibola *f* jaw
mandorla *f* almond [cake
mandorlato *m* almond-
mandorlo *m* almond-tree
mandolino *m* mandolin
mandra *f* flock; herd
maneggiare manage
maneggevole manageable
mania *f* mania; – **co**
maniac
manica *f* sleeve
manico *m* handle
maniera *f* manner [ture
manifattura *f* manufac-
manifestare manifest
manifestazione *f* manifestation
manitesto *m* manifest
maniglia *f* bracelet
maniglio *m* handle
mano *f* hand [script
manoscritto *m* manu-
manovale *m* labourer
manovella *f* crank
manovra *f*; – **re** man-
mansueto mild [œuvre
mantello *m* cloak
mantenere maintain
manuale manual
manubrio *m* handle;
mappa(mondo) map (of
the world)

maraviglia *f* marvel;
wonder; a – admirably; – rsi wonder
maraviglioso wonderful
marca *f* mark; – re mark
marchesa *f* marchioness
marchese *m* marquis
marcia *f* march; pus
marciapiede *m* footway
marciare march
marea *f* tide
maremma *f* marsh
margherita *f* pearl; daisy
margine *m* margin; border   [shore
marina *f* navy; marine;
marinaio *m* sailor
marinare pickle
maritale marital
maritare marry
martello *m* hammer
martíre *m* martyr
martirio *m* martyrdom
marzapane *m* marzipan
marzolino *m* march-cheese
mascella *f* jaw
maschera *f*; – re mask
mascherata *f* masquerade
maschile manly
maschio male
mascolino masculine
masnada *f* gang; troop
massa *f* mass
massaio *m* steward
massima *f* maxim
massimo greatest
masso *m* rock
massone *m* free-mason
masticare chew
mastice *m* mastic
matassa *f* hank; heap
matematica *f* mathematics
materassa *f* mattress
materia *f* matter; substance; – le material;

– lista *m* materialist
materno maternal
maternità *f* maternity
matita *f* pencil
matrigna *f* step-mother
matrimonio *m* marriage
matrina *f* god-mother
matrona *f* matron
mattana *f* ill-humour
mattina *f* morning
mattinata *f* forenoon
matto mad
mattonare pave with bricks
mattone *m* brick
maturare ripen
maturo ripe
meccanica *f* mechanics
meccanico mechanic
meccanismo *m* mechanism
medaglia *f* medal
medaglione *m* medallion
medesimo same; self
media *f* mean; average
mediante by means of
mediano, medio middle
mediatore *m* mediator
medicamento *m*, medicina *f* medicine
medico *m* physician
mediocre indifferent
mediocrità *f* mediocrity
meditare meditate
meditazione *f* meditation
meglio better
mela *f* apple
melo *m* apple-tree
melagrana *f* pomegranate
melassa *f* treacle
mele *m* honey
mellone *m* melon
melodia *f* melody
melodioso melodious
membro *m* limb; member
mendace lying; liar
mendicante *m* beggar

186

mendicare beg
meno less; al – at least
menomo very small; least
mensa f table
mensuale monthly
mentale mental
menta f mint
mente f mind; a – by
heart
mentire lie; mentitore
mento m chin [m liar
menzognero lying; false
mercante m merchant
mercant(eggi)are trade;
haggle
mercantile mercantile
mercanzia f goods
mercato m market
merce f goods [pity
mercè, mercede f reward;
merceria f hosiery
merciaio m mercer
mercurio m mercury
merenda f luncheon
meretrice f prostitute
meridiano meridian
meridionale southern
meriggiare lie down
(sleep) in the shade
meriggio m midday
meritare deserve; merit
merito m merit

mescolanza f mixture
mescolare mingle
messa f mass; stake
messaggiere m messenger
messaggio m message

mestare mingle; stir
mestiere m business;
mestola f ladle [trade
metà f half
metallo m metal
metropoli f metropolis;
– tano metropolitan
mettere put; place
mezzana f procuress;
flagstone

mezzanino m entresol
mezzano middle
mezzanotte f midnight
mezzo half; m half;
middle; mean; – busto
m half-bust; – di noon;
– giorno noon; south
mezzombra f mezzotinto
miagolare mew
mica (non) not at all

miele m honey
mietere reap
mietitore m reaper
mietitrice f mowing-
machine
migliaio m thousand
miglio m mile
migliorare improve
miglioramento m im-
provement
milionario m millionaire
milione m million
militare military
milizia f militia
millantarsi boast
mille thousand
millepiedi m millipede
milligrammo m milligram
millimetro m millimetre
milza f spleen
mimico mimic
mina f mine; – re mine
minaccia f threat; – re
threaten
minatore m miner
miniera f mine
minimo very little; least
ministero m ministry
ministro m minister
minoranza f minority
minore smaller; younger;
under age; minor
minorità f minority
minuetto m minuet
minugia f intestine
minuscolo minuscule
minuta f minute

minuto (*m*) minute; **al -**
minuzia *f* trifle [by retail
mio my; mine
miope short-sighted
miopia *f* short-sightedness
mira *f* aim
mirabile wonderful
miracolo *m* miracle; **- so**
  miraculous
mirare look at; aim
miscellanea *f* miscellany
mischia *f* fight; **- re** mix
misconoscere mistake
miscuglio *m* mixture
miserabile miserable
miseria *f* misery
misericordia *f* mercy
misericordioso merciful
misfatto *m* crime
missionario *m* missionary
missione *f* mission
misterio *m* mystery; **- so**
  mysterious
mobiliare furnish
mobilitare mobilise
moccio *m* mucus
moccolo *m* bit of candle
moda *f* fashion
modellare mould
modello *m* model
moderare moderate
moderazione *f* modera-
moderno modern   [tion
modestia *f* modesty
modesto modest
modico moderate
modificare modify
modista *f* milliner
modo *m* manner; mood;
  di - che soft hat
modulo *m* module; form
mole *f* mass; large build-
molestare molest   [ing
molesto troublesome
molla *f* spring; *pl* nip-
  pers

molle tender; moist
mollezza *f* softness
moltiplicare multiply
moltitudine *f* multitude
molto much; very
momento *m* moment
momentaneo momentary
monaca *f* nun
monaco *m* monk
monarca *m* monarch
monarchia *f* monarchy
monastero *m* monastery
moncare maim
monco maimed
mondare cleanse
mondano wordly
mondo *m* world
monello *m* cheast; rogue
moneta *f* coin; **- re** coin
monna *f* mistress; ape
monocolo one-eyed; mo-
  nocle
monopolio *m* monopoly
monogramma *m* mono-
  gram
monologo *m* monologue
monotono monotonous
Monsignore *m* my Lord
montagna *f* mountain
montagnoso mountainous
montare ascend; amount
montanaro *m* mountain-
Moresco Moorish
morfina *f* morphine
moribondo dying
morire die
mormorare murmur ;
  grumble   [tree
moro *m* moor; mulberry-
moroso morose
morsello *m* morsel
morso bitten; *m* bit
mortaio *m* mortar
mortale mortal
mortalità *f* mortality
morte *f* death

188

morto, ta dead; – *m* corpse; – **torio** *m* funeral; – **tuario** funereal

morviglione *m* small pox; measles *pl.*

mosaico mosaic

mosca *f* fly; – **cieca** blindman's buff

moscada *f* nutmeg

moscadello *m* muscatel

moscaiuola *f* larder

moscardino *m* sparrow-hawk; fop

moscato musky

moscherino, schino *m* mosquito; gnat

moschea *f* mosque

moschettare shoot; – **teria** *f* volley; – **tiere** *m* musketeer; – **to** *m* musket

moscio flabby; soft

moscione *m* mosquito; drunkard

Mosè *pm* Moses

mostarda *f* mustard

mosto *m* must; new wine

mostra *f* review; trial; face; – **trare** demonstrate

mostro *m* monster; prodigy; – **sità** *f* monstrosity; – **truoso** monstrous

mota *f* mud; mire; – **toso** muddy [cause

motivare *m* motive; **moto** *m* movement; – **tore** *m* mover

mottetto *m* anthem

motto *m* pun; motto

movenza *f* movement; – **vere** move; – **vibile** changeable; – **vimento** *m* movement; moving; – **vitore** *m* motor

mozione *f* motion

muco *m* mucus; – **sità** *f* mucosity; – **so** mucous

muda *f* moulting; – **dare** change

muffa *f* mouldiness; – **fare** grow musty or **muffetto** *m* fop [mouldy

mugghiare, gire bellow; – **gito** *m* bellowing

mughetto *m* lily of the valley [gull

mugnaio *m* miller; sea

mugnere suck; milk

mugolare grunt; yelp

mula *f* mule; slipper; – **laggine** *f* obstinacy

mulacchia *f* crow; jackdaw

mulattiere *m* muleteer; – **latto** *m* mulatto

muliebre feminine

mulinare dream

mulinaro *m* miller

mulinello *m* handmill

mulo *m* mule

multa *f* fine; – **re** fine

multiforme multiform

multiplicare multiply; – **zione** *f* multiplication; – **tore** *m* multiplicator

multitudine *f* multitude

mummia *f* mummy; – **mificare** mummify

munerare reward; remunerate; – **zione** *f* reward

municipale municipal; – **lità** *f* municipality; – **pio** *m* town council

munificenza *f* munificence; – **fico** liberal

munire provide; – **zione** *f* ammunition; stores

munto milked [ade

muovere move; persu-

muraglia *f* wall; – **rale** mural; – **rata** *f* tower;

– **ratore** *m* mason;
– **rare** build; wall
musica *f* music; – **cale**
musical
musoliera *f* muzzle
musone scorning
mussolina *f* muslin

mutare change; – **bile,**
tevole changeable; – **lità**
f mutability; – **mento**
m change
mutande *fpl* drawings
mutilare mutilate; – **zi-**
one *f* mutilation
muto dumb; mute; *n*
dumb person; **mutismo**
m dumbness
mutuare lend money;
– **tuante, tuatario** *m* bor-
rower; – **tuazione** *j*reciprocity; – **tuo** mu-
tual; – **tuamente** mu-
tually

N

nabissare make a noise;
destroy; bluster; – **so**
m abyss; hell
nappo *m* glass; cup;
fountain
narciso *m* narcissus
narcotico narcotic
nari, narici *fpl* nostrils
narrare relate; – **tiva,**
zione *f* narration;
tore *m* relater
nasale nasal
nascere be born; set;
proceed; – **cimento, ta**
f & m birth; extrac-
tion; descent; – **cituro**
future
nascondere abscond;
hide; – **diglio** *m* hiding-
place; – **samente** se-

cretly
nasello *m* haddock
naso *m* nose; **nasuto**
big-nosed
nastro *m* ribbon
natalizio *m* birthday
natale native; Christmas
natività *f* nativity
nativo native
natura *f* nature; natural;
– **lista** *m* naturalist;
– **lizzare** naturalise
naufragare be wrecked
naufragio *m* wreck
nausea *f* nausea; – **bondo**
nauseous; – **re** give
nausea
nauta *m* mariner
nautico nautical
navale naval
navigare sail; navigate
navicella *f* boat
nè nor; ne of it; of them
nebbia *f* fog; mist; cloud
nebbioso cloudy; misty
necessario necessary
necessità *f* necessity
nefando infamous
nefasto unlucky
negare deny; disown
negativo negative
negazione *f* negation
negligente negligent
negligenza *f* negligence
negoziante *m* merchant
negoziare negotiate
negoziatore *m* negotiator
negoziazione *f* negotia-
negozio *m* trade   [tion
negro *m* negro; black
neonato *m* new-born
nerbo *m* nerve
nerbuto nervous
nero black
nerastro blackish
nervo *m* nerve; – **so**

190

nervous
nescienza *f* ignorance
nespola *f* medlar
nespolo *m* medlar tree
nessuno no; none
nettare clean; scour
netto clean; pure; net
Nettuno Neptune
neutrale, neutro neutral
neutralità *f* neutrality
nevata *f* snow-fall
nevicare snow
neve *f* snow

nidificare nestle
niente nothing
nientedimeno nevertheless; however
Nilo *m* Nile
ninfa *f* nymph
ninnolo *m* trifle
nipote *m* nephew; grand-
nissuno none   [son
no no; not
nobile noble
nobilizzare ennoble
nobiltà *f* nobility
nocca *f* knuckle
nocchio *m* knot
nocciolo *m* stone; pip
nocciuola *f* filbert; hazel-
nut   [tree
noce *f* walnut; walnut
noia *f* tediousness; – **re**
noioso tedious   [annoy
noleggiare freight
nolo *m* freighting; rent
nomade wandering
nome *m* name; fame
nomina *f* nomination;
fame
nominale nominal
nominare nominate
nominatamente namely
non not
non che not only
noncurante careless

nondimeno nevertheless
nonna *f* grand-mother
nonno *m* grand-father
nono ninth
nonostante nevertheless
nonsenso *m* nonsense
norte *m* North
norma *f* rule; – **le** normal
nosco with us
nostalgia ; home-sickness
nostrale of our country
nostro our(s)   [notable
nota *f* note; – **bile**
notaio *m* notary
notare note; swim
notevole remarkable
notificare notify
notizia *f* news; notice
novanta ninety
novella *f* story; news
novello new; young
novembre *m* November
nulla nothing, – **di** don't
mention it; – **dimeno**
nevertheless
nullo null; void
numerare number
numeratore *m* numerator
numero *m* number
numeroso numerous
numisma *f* medal
nunziare announce
nuocere hurt; harm
nuora *f* daughter-in-law
nuotare swim
nuova *f* news; notice
nuovo new
nutatore *m* swimmer
nutrimento *m* food;
nourishment
nutritivo nutritive
nutrire feed; nourish
nuvola *f* cloud
nuvoloso cloudy
nuziale nuptial

191

O

o, od or
oasi *f* oasis
obbedienza *f* obedience;
– dire obey; – dient
obeying
obbiettare object; –
biezione *f* objection;
– biettivo objective; – to
m cause; object
obbioso suspicious
obblazione *f* oblation
obbliare forget
obbligare oblige; bind;
– gante obliging; –
obbliquare slant; de-
cline; – quità *f* obli-
quity; – quo oblique
obbrobrio *m* dishonour;
shame; – so shameful
obbumbrare darken; –
zione *f* darkness
obelisco *m* obelisk
oberato *m* indebted
obesità *f* obesity
obice, obizzo *m* mortar
obito *m* death
obliterare obliterate;
cancel
oblungo oblong
occasionare cause; occa-
sion; – nale occasional;
– sione *f* occasion;
cause; – so *m* chance
occhialaio *m* spectacle-
maker; – le, letto *m*
spectacles; telescope
occhiare eye; ogle; –
chiazzurro blue eyed
occhiello *m* buttonhole;
eyelet [will; bud
occhio *m* eye; sight;
occidente *m* west; –

tale occidental; western
occidere kill; – ditore *m*
killer; – sione *f* killing;
death
occipite *m* occiput
occorrenza *f* occurrence;
need; – rere happen;
occur; be necessary
occultare conceal; hide;
– to hidden
occupare occupy; pos-
sess; seize; – mento,
zione *m & f* occupation;
abode
oceano *m* ocean; – nico
oceanic
ocra *f* ochre
oculare ocular
oculatezza *f* care; – to
prudent; sharp
odorare smell
odorato *m* smelling
odore *m* smell; scent
offendere offend; hurt
offrire offer
oftalmia *f* ophthalmia
oggetto *m* object
oggi to-day
osliaro *m* oil merchant
ogni every
olio *m* oil
oliva *f* olive
oliveto *m* olive-yard
olivo *m* olive-tree
olmo *m* elm-tree
olocausto *m* holocaust
oltraccio moreover
oltraggiare offend
oltre beyond; further
oltremodo extraordinarily
omaggio *m* homage
omai now
ombelico *m* navel
ombra *f* shade; shadow
ombreggiare shadow

ombrello *m* umbrella
ombrellino *m* sunshade
ombroso shady; shy
omelia *f* homily
omeopatia *f* homœopathy
omero *m* shoulder
omettere omit
omicidio *m* man-slaughter
ommissione *f* omission
omnibus *m* omnibus
omogeneo homogeneous
omonimo homonymous
onda *f* wave; sea; billow
onde where; therefore;
onorabile, onorevole honourable
onore *m* honour
onorare honour
onorario *m* honorary
onta *f* shame; injury
onoso shameful; bash-
ontano *m* alder-tree [ful
opaco opaque
opalo *m* opal
opera, opra *f* work;
 opera; deed   [do
operare work; make;
operaio *m* workman
operatore *m* operator
operazione *f* operation
opificio *m* studio
opimo abundant; rich
opinare opine; vote
opinante *m* voter
opinione *f* opinion
oppio *m* opium
opporre oppose
opportunità *f* opportunity
opportuno seasonable
opposito opposite
opposizione *f* opposition
opprimere oppress
oppure that is; or
opulento wealthy
ora *f* hour; time; now;
 che –? what time is it?
oracolo *m* oracle

oragano *m* hurricane
orafo *m* goldsmith
oratore *m* orator
oratorio *m* oratory
orbe *f* orb; universe
orbene well done
orbita *f* orbit; rut
orchestra *f* orchestra
orcio *m* jug; pitcher
ordegno *m* engine; tool
ordinare order; ordain
ordinario ordinary
ordine *m* order
ordire warp; plot
ordo dirty
orrechiare listen
orezza *f* breeze
orfano *m* orphan
orfanotrofio *m* orphanage
organizzare organize
organo *m* organ
organista *m* organist
orgoglio *m* pride; – so
orientale oriental [proud
oriente *m* orient; east
orifizio *m* opening
originale, originario orig-
origine *f* origin   [inal
orina *f* urine; – le *m*
 urinal); – re urinate
orizzonte *m* horizon
orrizontale horizontal
orlare hem; border
orlo *m* edge; hem
ormai now
ornamento *m* ornament
ornare adorn
orno *m* ash-tree
oro gold
orologio *m* clock
orrendo, orribile horrible
orzo *m* barley
osare dare
oscenità *f* obscenity
osceno obscene
oscillare oscillate; vacil-

osculare kiss [late
oscurare darken; defame
oscurità *f* obscurity
oscuro dark; vile
ospedale, ospitale *m*
hospital
ospitabile hospitable
ospite *m* guest; host
ospizio *m* hospice; asylum
ossame *m* bones
ossequio *m* reverence
osservare observe [tory
osservatorio *m* observa-
osservatore *m* observer
osservazione *f* observa-
ossesso obsessed [tion
ossidare oxidize
ossigeno *m* oxygen
osso *m* bone; stone (of
fruit)
ostacolo *m* obstacle
ostare oppose; resist
oste *m* host; guest
ostensorio *m* ostensory
ostentare display; boast
osteria *f* inn
ostessa *f* hostess
ostilità *f* hostility
ostile hostile
ostinarsi be obstinate ·
ostinato obstinate
ostrica *f* oyster
ostruire obstruct
ottarda *f* bustard
ottanta eighty
ottava *f* octave
ottavo eighth
ottenere obtain
ottica *f* optic
ottico optic; optician
ottimo best; perfect
otto eight
ottone *m* brass
ottuplo eightfold
otturare stop up; dam
ottuso stupid; obtuse

ovvio obvious
ovvolo *m* mushroom
ozio *m* leisure; idleness

P

pacca *f* stroke; wound
pacchebotto *m* steamer;
- chetto *m* steamer;
pace *f* peace; quietness;
- ciere, cificatore *m*
peace-maker; - fico
pacific; - cificare pacify;
appease; reconcile
padella *f* frying-pan;
knee-pan
padiglione *m* pavilion;
tent
padre *m* father; - drino
m god-father
padrone *m* master; coxs-
wain; patron; - na *f*
mistress
paesaggio *m* landscape
paesano, na *a & n* pea-
sant
paesante, sista *m* land-
scape-painter [scape
paesi *m* country; land-
paffuto plumb; fat
paga *f* salary; wages
paganesimo *m* paganism;
- no pagan
pagare pay; punish; -
bile payable; -ghero
m promissory note; -
gamento *m* payment
paggio *m* page
pagina *f* page
paglia *f* straw; - gliaio
m straw-rick; - glieri-
ccio *m* straw-mattress
- gliuola *f* gold dust
pagnotta *f* small loaf

pago satisfied; *m* pay- [ment

pagoda *f* pagoda

pagonazzo violet

paio *m* pair; brace

paiuolo *m* boiler; kettle

pala *f* shovel; spade

paletta *f* shovel

paletto *m* bolt

palio *m* cloak; canopy

palla *f* ball; bullet; bow

palleggiare play tennis

pallido pale; pallid

pallidezza *f* paleness

pallini *m pl* shot; small shot [ball

pallone *m* balloon; foot-

pallore *m* paleness

palma *f* palm; palm-tree

palmeto *m* palm-tree-grove [branch

palpitazione *f* palpitation

palude *f* marsh; **paludoso** marshy

panattiera *f* bread-basket

panca *f* bench

panchetta *f* little bench

pancia *f* paunch; belly

panciotto *m* waistcoat

pancone *m* bench

pane *m* bread; loaf

panegirico *m* panegyric

panforte *m* gingerbread

pania *f* bird-lime

panico panic

paniera *f* basket; – **io** *m* basket-maker

panino gravido sandwich

panna *f* cream

panno *m* cloth

panneggiare drape

pantofola *f* slipper

pantomima *f* pantomime

papa *m* pope; – **le** papa

papavero *m* poppy

papiro *m* papyrus

pappa *f* pap

pappare eat to excess

parabola *f* parable; parabola; – **no** bragger

paracadute *m* parachute

paracolpi *m* buffer

paradiso *m* paradise

paradosso paradox(ical)

parafrasi *f* paraphrase

parafulmine *m* lightning-conductor

parafuoco *m* fire-screen

paraggio *m* country shore [comparison

paragone *m* touch-stone;

paragonare compare

paragrafo *m* paragraph

paralisi *f* paralysis

paralitico paralytic

parallelo parallel

paralume *m* lampshade; screen [apparel

paramento *m* sacerdotal

parapetto *m* parapet

parare adorn; dress

parata *f* parade; show

parasito *m* parasite

paravento *m* screen

parco sober; *m* park

parecchi several

parecchio equal; like

pareggiare compare

parénte *m* kinsman

parentella *f* affinity; relationship

parentesi *f* parenthesis

parere appear; *m* opinion

parete *f* wall

pargolo *m* little child

pari like; equal

parità *f* equality

parroco *m* parson

parrucca *f* wig [dresser

parrucchiere *m* hair-

parte *f* part; country; party; **da** – aside

partecipare partake

partenza *f* departure

particolare particular; private

parziale partial

parzialità *f* partiality

pascere, pascolare graze

paseolo *m* pasture

Pasqua *f* Easter

pasquinata *f* satire

passabile tolerable

passaporto *m* passport

passare pass

passata *f* passage

passatempo *m* pastime

passato (*m*) past

passeggiare walk

passione *f* passion

passivo passive [passage

passo faded; *m* step;

pasta *f* paste; dough

pasteggiare board

pasticcio *m* pie

pasto *m* food; meal

pastore *m* shepherd

pastoso soft; sweet

patire suffer

patimento *m* suffering

patria *f* native country

patriarca *m* patriarch

patrigno *m* step-father

patrimonio *m* patrimony

patriota *f* patriot

patrono *m* patron

patteggiare agree

pattinare, pattino *m* skate

pattuglia *f* patrol

pattume *m* sweepings

paura *f* fear

pauroso timorous

pausa *f*; – re pause

paventare fear

pavimento *m* pavement

pavone *m* peacock

pavoneggiarsi boast

paziente patient

pazienza *f* patience

pazzia *f* madness

pazzo mad; fool

pecca *f* fault

peccare. peccato *m* sin

peccatore *m* sinner

pecchia *f* bee

peccia *f* paunch

pece *f* pitch

pecora *f* sheep

pecorino *m* lamb; cheese

peculiare peculiar

pecunia *f* money

pedaggio *m* toll

pedagogia *f* pedagogy

pedalare bike

pedale *m* pedal; trunk

pedante *m* pedant

pedata *f* track; kick

pedestre pedestrian

pedina *f* pawn

pedone *m* pedestrian

peggio worse [worse

peggiorare make (grow)

pegno *m* pawn

pellegrino *m* stranger;

pelo *m* hair; split; – so hairy

pena *f* punishment; pain; care; penal; – re suffer

pendaglio *m* belt [ful

pendente hanging; doubt-

pendenza *f* declivity

pendere hang; incline

pendice, pendio *m* slope

penetrare penetrate

penetrazione *f* penetration

penisola *f* peninsula

penitente penitent

penitenza *f* penitence

penitenziario *m* penitentiary

penna *f* feather; pen

pennacchio *m* plume

pennello *m* pencil; brush

pennino *m* steel-pen

pennone *m* pennon

pentimento *m* repentance
pentola *f* pot; – io *m*
penuria *f* penury [potter
penzolare dangle
pepe *m* pepper
pera *f* pear
percepire perceive
percezione *f* perception
perchè because
percorrere peruse
percuotere strike
perdere lose; ruin
perdita *f* loss
perditore *m* loser
perdonare, perdono *m*
  pardon
perdonabile pardonable
peregrinare wander
perfetto perfect
perfeziohare perfect
perfezione *f* perfection
perfidia *f* perfidy
perfido perfidious
perforare perforate
pergamena *f* parchment
pergamo *m* pulpit
perire perish
perito experienced
perizia *f* skill
perla *f* pearl
perlustrare explore
permanente permanent
permesso permitted; *m*
  permit; permission
permettere permit
pernice *f* partridge
pernicioso pernicious
pernio *m* pivot
pernottare pass the night
pero *m* pear-tree
però therefore; – chè
pbecause [cular
perpendicolare perpendi-
perpetrare perpetrate
perpetuare perpetuate
perpetuo perpetual
 erplesso perplexed

197

perquisizione *f* perquisi-
  tion [tion
persecuzione *f* persecu-
perseguire pursue; per-
  secute [ance
perseveranza *f* persever-
perseverare persevere
persuadere persuade
persusione *f* persuasion
pertanto however
pertica *f* pole
pertinace obstinate
perturbare disturb
pervenire arrive
perverso perverse; de-
pesanto heavy [praved
pesantezza *f* weight
pesare weigh
pesca *f* peach
pesca *f* fishing
pescaia *f* dike, sluice
pescare fish
pescatore *m* fisherman
pesce *m* fish
pescheria *f* fish-market
peschiera *f* fish-pond
pesciaiuolo *m* fishmonger
pesco *m* peach-tree
peso *m* weight
pessimo very bad; worst
petardo *m* petard
petizione *f* petition
peto *m* fart
petrolio *m* petroleum
pettegola *f* chatter-box;
  – re chatter
pettinare comb
pettine *m* comb
pettino *m* shirt-front
petto *m* breast; – rale
  pectoral
petulante arrogant
pezza *f* piece; strip
pezzato speckled
pezzo *m* piece; bit
pezzuola *f* handkerchief
piacere please; *m* plea-

piaga *f* wound   [sure
piaggia *f* strand; declivity   [lament
piagnere, piangere weep;
pialla *f*, - re plane
pianella *f* slipper; tile
pianerottolo *m* landing-
pianeta *m* planet [place
pianista *m* pianist
pianto *m* lament; weep-
pianura *f* plain   [ing
piataforma *f* platform
piatto flat; *m* dish
piattola *f* cockroach
piazza *f* place; market
picchiare strike; knock
picchio *m* stroke; wood-
  pecker
picchiotto *m* knocker
piccino small (boy)
piccolo little; small
piccone *m* pick-axe
pidocchio *m* louse
pie, piede *m* foot; a –
  on foot
piedestallo *m* pedestal
piega *m* fold; – re fold;
  bend; incline; yield
pieghevole flexible
piena *f* flood; throng
pieno full
pieta *f* grief; sorrow
pietà *f* pity; piety; love
pigliare take; receive
pignatta *f* pot; kettle
pignone *m* dike   [gage
pignorare pawn; mort-
pigolare pip; chirp
pigrizia *f* laziness
pigro idle
pilone *m* pilaster
pilota *m* pilot
pina *f* pine-apple
pineto *m* pine-grove
pingere paint
pingue fat

piovere rain
piovoso rainy
piovigginare drizzle
pipa *f* pipe; – re smoke
pipistrello *m* bat
pira *f* wood-pile
piramide *f* pyramid
pirata *m* pirate
piroscafo *m* steamer
piscia *f* urine; – re
  urinate; – toio *m* urinal
piscina *f* fish-pond
pisello *m* green pea
pispigliare whisper
pisside *f* pyx   [nut
pistacchio *m* pistachio-
pistagna *f* furbelow;
pistillo *m* pistil [flounce
pistola *f* pistol
pistone *m* piston
  itale *m* urinal
pitocare beg
pitocco *m* beggar
pittore *m* painter
pittoresco picturesque
pittura *f* painting; picture
più more; al – at most;
  per lo – mostly; i –
  most (men)
piuma *f* feather
piuolo *m* stake; peg
piuttosto rather
piva *f* bagpipe
pizzicagnolo *m* pork-
  butcher   [prick
pizzicare itch; pinch;
pizzo *m* pointed beard
placare appease
placido placid
plagio *m* plagiarism
plagiario *m* plagiarist
plasmare model
plastica *f* plastico plastic
platano *m* platane
platea *f* pit (theatre)

198

platino *m* platina
platonico platonic
plausibile plausible
plauso *m* applause
plebaglia *f* mob
plebe *f* common people
pluviale rainy
pneumatico pneumatic
pneumonia *f* pneumonia
po', poco little
podere *m* estate; power
podestà *f* power; bailiff
poema *m* poem
poesia *f* poetry
poeta *m* poet
poetico poetical
poggia *f* prop
poggio *m* hill [as; when
poi afterwards; – chè
polare polar
poledro *m* colt; foal
polemico polemical
polenta *f* polenta
poligono *m* polygon
polipo *m* polypus
polire polish
politica *f* politics
politico political; politician
polizia *f* police
polizza *f* note; bill
pollice *m* thumb
polmone *m* lung
polmonare pulmonary
polo *m* pole
polpa *f* pulp
polpaccio *m* calf (leg)
polsetto *m* bracelet
polsino *m* cuff
polso *m* pulse
poltiglia *m* mire
poltrona *f* easy-chair
pomello *m* knob
pomeridiano afternoon
pomice *f* pumice-stone
pomo *m* apple

pompa *f* pump
ponce *m* punch
ponderare weigh
pondi *f m pl* dysentry
ponente *m* West
ponte *m* bridge; deck
pontefice *m* pontiff; –
cale pontificial
pontone *m* pontoon
popolaccio *m* mob [late
popolare popular; popu-
popolazione *f* population
popolo *m* people; nation
popoloso populous
popone *m* melon
poppa *f* breast
poppare suck
porgere offer; present
poro *m* pore; – so porous
porpora *f* purple
perre place; put
porro *m* leek; wart
porta *f* door; – bandiera
ensign-bearer; – bile
portable; – fogli port-
folio; – lettere postman;
– ta range; tonnage;
course; – tore bearer
portare bring; carry
portiera *f* door-curtain;
coach-door
portiere *m* door-keeper
portico *m* portico [riage
porto *m* harbour; car-
portolano *m* pilot; door-
portone *m* gate [keeper
porzione *f* portion
posa *f* pause
posare place; stand
posata *f* rest; cover
poscia afterwards
poscritto *m* postcript
posdomani after to-
morrow
positivo positive
posizione *f* position

possedere possess
possessione *f* possession
possente powerful
possibilità *f* possibility
possibile possible
posta *f* post; ambush; stake; – **le** postal; **a** – expressly
posteri *m pl* posterity
posteriore (*m*) posterior
posterità *f* posterity
posticcio sham; false
posticipare delay
postino *m* postman
posto *m* place; situation
postremo last
potente powerful
potenza *f* power
potere be able; *m* power
povero poor
povertà *f* poverty
pozza(nghera) *f* puddle
pozzetta *f* dimple
pozzo *m* well   [dinner
pranzare dine; **pranzo** *m*
practica *f* practice; – **bile** practicable; – **re** practise
practico practical
precedere precede
precedenza *f* precedence
precetto *m* precept; – **re** preceptor; tutor
precidere remove; shorten
precipitare precipitate
precipizio *m* precipice
precisamente precisely
precisione *f* precision
preciso precise
precoce precocious
precogitare premeditate
preconio *m* praise
precursore *m* precursor
predestinare predestinate
predellino *m* step
predellone *m* bench

predica *f* sermon; – **re** preach; – **tore** *m* preacher   [beloved
prediletto   preferred;
predilezione *f* preference
predire foretell
predominare prevail
prefazione *f* preface
preferire prefer
prefetto *m* prefect
prefiggere prefix
pregare pray; entreat
preghiera *f* prayer
pregiaro value; praise
pregio *m* value; repute
pregiudizio *m* prejudice
pregno pregnant
premere urge; press
premiare, premio reward; prize
preminente pre-eminent
premunire   forewarn;
preoccupare preoccupy
preparare prepare   [tion
preparazione *f* prepara-
preponderare preponder-
preporre prefer   [ate
prepostero preposterous
prerogativa *f* prerogative
presa *f* taking; prize;
presciutto *m* ham
prescrivere prescribe
prescrizione *f* prescrip-tion
presentare offer; present
presentazione *f* presenta-
presente present   [tion
presenza *f* presence
presentire foresee; **pre-sentimento** *m* foresight; presentiment
preservare preserve
presidente *m* president
presidio *m* garrison
pressa *f* crowd; press;

200

– re urge; –. nte urgent
pressione *f* pressure
prestidigitatore *m* juggler
prestito *m* loan
presto quick; sudden
presumere presume
presupponere presuppose
prete *m* priest
pretendere claim; pretend
pretendente pretender
pretensione *f* pretension
preterire omit; neglect
preterito past
pretesto *m* pretext
previo previous
previsione *f* foresight
prezioso precious
prezzare value; esteem
prezzo *m* price
prezzemolo *m* parsley
prezzolare pay; hire
pria before
priego *m* prayer
prigione *f* prison
prigioniero *m* prisoner
prima before
primario principal
primavera *f* spring
prim(ier)o first; former
primogenito *m* first-born
prince, principe *m* prince
priorità *f* priority
pristino old; former
privare deprive
privazione *f* privation
privato private; *m* water-closet
privilegio *m* privilege
pro *m* advantage; for
probabile probable
procedere proceed
procella *f* storm
processione *f* procession
processo *m* law-suit; progress [clamation
proclama(zione) *f* pro-proclamare proclaim

procrastinare delay
procreare procreate
prode brave
prodigalità *f* prodigality
prodigo prodigal
prodigio *m* prodigy; – so prodigious
proditore *m* traitor
prodotto *m* product
produrre produce; create
produrre produce
produzione *f* production
profanare, profano pro-proferire utter [fane
professare profess
professione *f* profession
profeta *m* prophet; – re prophesy
profezia *f* prophecy
proffilo *m* profile [profit
profittare, profitto *m*
profondare dig; sink
profondità *f* depth
profondo deep [perfume
profumare, profumo *m*
profusione *f* profusion
progettare, progetto *m* project
programma *m* programme
progredire, progresso *m* progress
proibire prohibit
proibizione *f* prohibition
proiettile *m* projectile
prole *f* offspring
prominente prominent
promontorio *m* promontory
pronostico *m* prognostic
pronto quick; ready
pronunziare pronounce
pronunzia(zione) *f* pro-nunciation
propagare propagate
propensione *f* propensity
propinquo near
propizio favourable

201

proporre propose
proporzione *f* proportion
proposito *m* purpose
proposizione *f* proposition
proprietà *f* property; −
rio *m* proprietor; owner
proprio *m* proper
propulsare repel
propulsore *m* propeller
prora *f* prow; bow
prorogare prorogue
prorompere burst; rush
out
prosa *f* prose; − ico prosaic
prosperare prosper
prosperità *f* prosperity
prospettiva *f* perspective
prospetto *m* prospect
prossimità *f* proximity
prossimo nearest
prosternare prostrate
prostituta *f* prostitute
proteggere protect
protestante protestant
protesta(zione) *f* protes-
tation   [protest
protestare, protesto *m*
protettore *m* protector
protezione *f* protection
protrarre protract; draw
prova *f* proof; experi-
provare prove   [ment
provenire proceed
provenienza *f* origin
proverbio *m* proverb
proverbiale proverbial
provincia *f* province; −
le provincial
provocare provoke
provocazione *f* provoca-
provvedere provide [tion
provvisione *f* provision
provvisorio temporary
provvisto supplied; ready
pudico modest; cha.te
pudino *m* pudding

puerilità *f* puerility
puerile puerile
puerizia *f* childhood
puerperio *m* lying in
pugna *f* fight; − re
fight; − le *m* dagger;
− lare stab   [writing
pugno *m* fist; hand-
pulce *f* flea
pulcella *f* maid
Pulcinella *m* Punch
pulcino *m* chicken
puledro *m* colt; foal
puleggia *f* pulley
pulire polish; clean
pullulare swarm; spring
pulpito *m* pulpit
pulsazione *f* pulsation
pungere prick; sting
puntata *f* stab
punteggiare punctuate
puntualità *f* punctuality
puntuale punctual
pupilla *f* ward; pupil
purchè provided; if
pure also; however
purezza, rità *f* purity
purga *f* purge; − re purge;
− tivo purgative; −
torio *m* purgatory
purgatura *f* rubbish; dirt
purificare purify; − zione
f purification
puritano *m* puritan; −
nismo *m* puritanism
puro pure; clean; −
ramente purely
pusillità *f* smallness; vileness; − lo low
pustola *f* pustule
putativo supposed
putidezza *f* stink; − tire
stink; − tente, tido
stinking
putredine *f* rottenness;
− tredinoso, trido rotten

202

putrefare, tridire putrefy;
– fazione. tridità. tri-

puttella ƒ young girl;
– tello, tino, to m young
boy

puzza zo m pus; stench;
– zare stink; – zolente
stinking

Q

quà here; hither; – e là
here and there; di –
this way

quaderno m sheet of
paper; writing book;

quadra ƒ dial
quadragesima ƒ Lent
quadrangolare quadran-
gular; – lo m quadrangle
quadrante m quadrant
quadrare quadrate; agree;
– to square

quaggiù giuso here below
quaglia ƒ quail   [late
quagliarsi curdle; coagu-
qualche some; any;
whatever; whoever; –
duno somebody; – cosa
ƒ something

quale who; whoever;
which; that
qualifica, zione ƒ qualification; – re qualify
qualità ƒ quality
qualmente how; like; as

qualora when; whenever
qualsisia, qualunque who-
quando when   [ever
quandochè when(ever)

quandunque whenever
quantità ƒ quantity
quanto how much; how
many; – a me as for

me; – prima as soon
as possible

quantochè though
quantunque so much;
some; though

quaranta forty; – tesimo
fortieth; – tinà ƒ
quarantine
quarantigia ƒ guarantee
quare why   [days
quaresima ƒ Lent; forty
quarta quart; quarter
quarterone m quarter
(moon)
quartiere m quarter;
quarto fourth [descent
quasi almost
quassù above
quattordici fourteen

quattro four

quetare appease; calm
qui here; – dentro herein
quietanza ƒ acquittance
quinci herefrom; after
quindi therefore; hereby
quindici fifteen
quindicesimo fifteenth
quintale m hundred-
weight
quinta decima ƒ full moon
quitare acquit
quinto fifth

quintuplo fivefold
quiproquo m blunder
quivi there; then
quota ƒ quota; share
quotidiano daily
quoto m order

R

rabacchio, m baby;
child; boy
rabbia ƒ rage; fury;
– bioso mad; furious

rabbonacciare lull; calm
rabbonire quiet; reconcile
rabbrenciare repair
rabbruscarsi darken; – mento *m* darkening
rabbuffare dishevel; disorder; fight; darken; – fo *m* rebuff; reprimand

raccapricciare frighten; terrify; – ciamento *m* fright; terror
raccartocciare twist
raccattare recover; redeem

raccenciare mend; patch
raccendere rekindle
raccennare beckon
raccertare assure
raccettare lodge; house – tore *m* lodger; – to *m* lodging; shelter
racchettare console
racchetta *f* racket
raccogliere gather
raccolta *f* drop; collection
raccomandare recommend
raccommandazione *f* recommendation [mend
raccomodare repair;
raccontare relate; tell
racconto *m* relation: tale

raccorciare shorten;
raccordare reconcile;

raddensare condense
raddirizzare redress
raddolcire soften; sweeten
raddoppiare redouble
raddormentarsi fall asleep
radere shave [again
radiotelegrafia *m* wireless telegraphy
radio *m* beam; ray
radioso beaming
radunanza *f* heap
radunare assemble

rafano *m* horse-radish
raffermare confirm; ratify
raffica *f* squall
raffilare sharpen; clip
raffinare refine
raffineria *f* refinery
rafforzare reinforce; fortify [cold
raffreddare cool; catch
raffreddore *m* cold
raffrenare refrain
ragazza *f* young girl
ragazzo *m* boy
raggelare congeal
raggiare beam; radiate

ragguardevole remarkable
ragia *f* resin; snare
ragionare reason; argue
ragione *f* reason; right; rate; firm; – vole reasonable

ragno(lo) *m* spider
rallegrare divert; rejoice
rallentare slacken; rerama *f* branch [lease
ramaccia *f* sled
ramancina *f* reprimand
rame *m* copper
ramaio *m* coppersmith
ramerino *m* rosemary
ramificare ramify
rammaricarsi grieve
rammarico *m* grief
rammassare heap up
rammendare mend
rammentare remind
ramo *m* branch; bough
rauolaccio *m* radish
rampicare climb
rampollo *m* spring; shoot
rana, *f* ranocchio *m* frog
rancido rancid
rancore *m* grudge;
rapido rapid
rapina *f* rapine
rapire rob; ravish

rapparare learn again
rapparire reappear
rappellare recall
rappezzare mend
rapportare relate; refer
rapporto *m* relation
rappresentare represent
rappresentazione *f* representation
raschiare rasp; scrape
rasciugare dry up

rasentare graze; touch
raso *m* satin
rasoio *m* razor
raspa *f*; – re rasp; grater
rassegna *f* review; sum-
rassegnare resign [mary
rassembrare resemble;
 gather [teach
rasserenare clear up;
rassettare mend; settle
rassicurare encourage
rassomiglianza *f* resem-
 blance
rassomigliare resemble
rastione *m* brush
rastrello *m* rake
rata *f* portion; share
ratificare ratify
rattaccare reunite
rattaconare new-sole
rattenere detain; stop
ratto quick; ready; *m*
 rape; robbery; rat
rattoppare mend; patch
rattristare afflict; grieve
rauco hoarse
raucedine *f* hoarseness
ravanello *m* radish
ravvedimento *m* repen-
ravvedersi repent [tance
ravviare arrange; guide
ravvisare advise; inform
ravviure frighten
ravvivare revive
ravvolgere envelope; turn
razionale rational

razione *f* ration
razza *f* race; spoke
razzo *m* ray; spoke;
 fusee
razzolare scratch; file
re *m* king; – ale royal;
 – ame *m* realm
reale real; – mente really
realità *f* reality
realizzare realise
reato *m* crime; sin
reazione *f* reaction
rebbio *m* prong [liver
recapitare address; de-
recapito *m* address
recere vomit
recesso *m* retreat; recess
recidiva *f* relapse
recinte *m* enclosure
recipiente *m* recipient
reciprocità *f* reciprocity
reciproco reciprocal
recita *f* representation;
 – re recite; perform
redazione *f* redaction
redentore *m* redeemer
redenzione *f* redemption
redimere redeem
redine *f* rein
regalare give; present
regale royal
regalo *m* present
regata *f* regatta [last
reggero rule; oppose;
reggia *f* royal palace
reggimento *m* regiment
regicida *m* regicide
regina *f* queen; regio
regione *f* region [royal
registrare registro *m*
 register
regnare reign
regno *m* kingdom; reign
regola *f* rule; law; order
regolare regulate; regular
regolarità *f* regularity
regolizia *f* liquorice
regola *f* rule; law

regolo *m* ruler
reietto waste; rejected
reintegrare reintegrate
reiterare reiterate
relativo relative
relazione *f* relation
remo *m* oar
remoto distant
rena *f* sand; gravel
rendere give back; render;
  yield; – si surrender
rendita *f* rent; revenue
rene *m* kidney; *pl* loins
renischio *m* sand
renitente obstinate
renna *f* rein-deer
renoso sandy
reo guilty; wicked
reparare repair

repellere repel; repulse
repente sudden
repertorio *m* repertory
replica *f*. – re reply;
  retort
reprimere repress; check
reputare esteem
reputazione *f* reputation
requiare rest; – quie
  requiem   [sary
requisito required; neces-
resa *f* surrender [cree
rescritto *m* rescript; de-
residenza *f* residence
residente resident
resina *f* resin
resistenza *f* resistence
resistere resist; last
respignere repulse
respirare breathe; exhale
respirazione *f* breathing
respiro *m* breath; pause
responsa *f* answer; –
  bile responsible; –
  bilità *f* responsibility
resta *f* repose; delay;
fish-bone; – re remain;
– nte residue; re-

mainder
restaurare repair; correct
resto *m* rest; del –
  besides   [train
restringere restrict; res-
restrizione *f* restriction
resultare, resultato *m*
  result

retaggio *m* inheritance.
rete *f* net; snare
reticenza *f* reticence
reticolla *f* mantle
retina *f* retina
retribuire reward
retro behind; afterwards
retroattivo retroactive
retrogradare retrograde
retroguardia *f* rear-guard
retta *f* duration; resis-
  tance; dar – consent
rettangolo *m* rectangle
rettificare rectify
rettile *m* reptile
rettilineo rectilinear
retto right; straight
rettore *m* rector
rialzare raise
riamicare reconcile
riandare examine; search
riassumere sum up
riavere recover
ribalzare rebound
ribasso *m* abatement;
  discount
ribellione *f* rebellion
ribelle rebel   [berry
ribes *m* currant; goose-
riboccare overflow
ribrezzare tremble;

  shiver   [ing
ribrezzo *m* fright; shiver-
ributtare disgust; re-
ricacciare repulse [pulse
ricaggimente *m* relapse
ricalcitrare be reluctant
ricamare embroider

ricamo *m* embroidery
ricambiare reward; barter   [reward
ricambio *m* exchange;
ricapito *m* remittance;
– lare recapitulate
ricattare redeem
ricavare gain; profit by
riccio *m* curl; curly ;
hedgehog   [richly
ricco rich; – camente
richiamare claim; call
back   [complaint
richiamo *m* reclamation;
richiedere ask; require
richiesta *f* demand;
petition
ricino castor-oil plant
ricogliere gather; reap
ricompense *f* – re reward;
compensate
riconciliare reconcile
riconcio seasoned
ricondire provide
riconoscenza *f* gratitude
ricondito hidden
riconfermare ratify
riconoscente grateful
riconoscere recognise
ricordare remind
ricordo *m* remembrance
ricorrente periodical
ricorrere have recourse
ricorso *m* refuge
ricoverarsi take refuge
ricreare divert; recreate
ricreazione *f* recreation
ricucire mend; sew again
ricuperare recover
ricusare refuse; challenge
ridda *f* country dance
ridere laugh; shine
ridicolo ridiculous
ridire repeat; blame
rividere subdivide
ridondare overflow

ridotto *m* retreat; club
ridurre reduce
riduzione *f* reduction
riempiere fill; fill again
riescire succeed
rifare do again; repair
riferire refer; ascribe
rifinire cease: get tired
rifiutare refuse; renounce
riflessione *f* reflexion
rigattiere *m* broker
rigenerare regenerate
rigentilire beautify
rigetto *m* waste; refuse
rigido rigid   [roam
rigirare turn round;
rignare neigh; grunt
rigoglio *m* pride
riguardare look at; conriguardato prudente [cern
riguardo *m* look; regard
rilevante notable   [up
rilevare lift up; – si get
rilievo *m* remnant; importance; relief
rilucere shine; glitter
riluttante reluctant
rima *f* – re rhyme
rimandare restore; rerimanere remain [pudiate
rimanente remaining; remainder
rimarcabile remarkable
rimbalzare rebound;
jump
rimbastire rebuild; baste
rimbellire beautify
rimborsare reimburse
rimbrottare reprimand
rimediare, rimedio *m*
remedy
rimembranza *f* memory
rimembrare remind; remember
rimessione confidence;
pardon
rimettere replace; remit

207

rimodernare modernize
rimounare whirl
rimondare cleanse
rimonta f remount
rimovere remove; dis-
rimpetto opposite [suade
rimpiagnere lament
rimpiazzare replace
rimproverare, rimprovero
 m reproach; blame
rimunerare remunerate
rimuovere remove
rinascimento m revival;
 renaissance [dearer
rincarare grow (make)
rincontra, alla go to meet
rincontrare meet
rincontro m meeting
rincrescere be sorry for
rinculare recoil; withdraw [blame
rinfacciare reproach;
rinfrescare refresh; renew
rinfresco m refreshment
rinfuso confused; mixed
ringhiare growl; neigh;
 snarl
ringhiera f pulpit; hust-
 ings [again
ringiovanire grow young
ringraziamento m thanks
ringraziare thank

rinomato celebrated
rintoppare meet; mend
rintoppo m meeting
rintrecciare interweave
rintracciare trace; search
rintuzzare resist; abate;
 blunt
rinunciare renounce
rinvenire recover one's
 self; meet; found
rinviare send back
riparare repair
riparabile reparable
ripartire share; divide
ripentirsi repent

ripercuotere repercuss
ripetere repeat
ripetio m dispute
ripiego m expedient;
ripieno full [refuge
ripienezza f fullness
ripiguare retake
riportare report; win
riposare. riposo m rest;
riposto hidden [repose
riprendere recover; reprimand
riprensibile reprehensible
riprensione f reprimand
ripresa f repetition;
 reprimand
ripresentare represent
riprodurre reproduce
riprova f proof; evidence
riprovare reprove
ripudiare repudiate
ripugnare repulse; resist
ripulsa f repulse
riputare repute; attribute
riputazione f reputation
risaia f rice-field
risaltare rebound; excel
risalto m projection
risarcire repair; compensate
risata f derision; scorn
riscaldare warm
riscaldamento m heating;
riscattare redeem [anger
rischiarare explain
rischiare risk
rischio m risk; danger;
 − so dangerous
risciacquare wash; rinse
riscontare discount;
 abate [pare
riscontrare meet; com-
riscontro m meeting;
 comparison; − d' aria
 draught
riscorrimento m running

208

riscossa *f* recovery
riscuotere shake; redeem
risecare cut
riseccare dry up
risedere reside
risegnare resign [tion
risegna(zione) *f* resigna-
risicare, risico *m* risk
risma *f* ream; faction
riso *m* laughing; rice
risolare resole
risolvere resolve; dissolve
risoluzione *f* resolution; dissolution
risoluto resolute
risomiguare resemble
risonare resound [tion
risorgimento *m* resurrec-
risparmiare spare; save
risparmio *m* savings
rispettare respect; honour
rispettabile respectable
rispetto *m* respect
rispettoso respectful
rispianato smooth; *m*
rispondere answer [plain
risposare remarry
risposta *m* answer
rissa *f*, – re fight; dispute
ritardo *m* delay
ritaglio *m* shred
ritegno *m* obstacle
ritenuto reserved
ritenere retain; keep
ritirata *f* retreat; W.C.
ritirarsi withdraw; retire
ritiro *m* retirement
ritmo *m* rhythm
rito *m* rite
ritoccare revise; vex
ritornare, ritorno *m* return
ritrarre retire; paint a portrait
ritrattare retract [painter
ritrattista *m* portrait-
ritratta *f* retreat

ritrato *m* portrait
ritrosa *f* bird-net; snare
ritroso obstinate
ritto right; straight
rituale *m* ritual
riunire unite; reconcile
riuscire succeed; happen
riuscita *f* success
riva *f* shore; bank
rivale *m* rival
rivelare reveal
rivelazione *f* revelation
rivendere sell again
rivendicare revenge;
rivenire return [claim
riverenza *f* reverence
riverire revere; respect
riversare upset
rivertere return
rivertire convert
rivestire dress again;
riviera *f* river [clothe
rivista *f* review
rivoltella *f* revolver
rivoltoso rebel
rivoluzione *f* revolution
rizzare erect
roba *f* goods; gown
robaccia *f* trash; slut
robusto strong; sturdy
rocaggine *f* hoarseness
rocca *f* stronghold; rock
roccia *f* rock; dress
rogna *f* scab
rognone *m* kidney
rogo *m* wood pile
romaiuolo *m* ladle
romantico romantic
romanza *f* romance
romanzo *m* novel
romba *f* sling [turbot
rombo *m* hum; rhomb;
rombare resound; buzz
romitaggio *m* hermitage
romito solitary; *m* hermit
romore *m* noise; rumour
rompere break; interrupt

rompicollo *m* precipice;
ruin

rompinoci *m* nut-cracker

roncare weed

ronchio *m* block

ronda *f* round

ronzare buzz; ramble

rosa *f* rose

rosaio *m* rose-bush

roseto *m* rose-field

rosario *m* rosary

rotaia *f* rut; track

rotare rotate

rotella *f* knee-pan; wheel

rotolare roll

rotondo round [rupture

rotta *f.* rout; defeat;

rotto broken; tired

rottura *f* rupture; gap

rovente red-hot

rovesciare overthrow;
spill [reverse

rovescio *m* wrong side;

roveto *m* thorn-hedge

rovina *f*; – re ruin

rovo *m* briar; thorn

rozza *f* jade

rozzo rough; rude

rubare steal; rob

rubacello *m* topaz

rubicondo ruddy

rubino *m* ruby

rugginoso rusty

ruggine *f* rust; grudge

ruggire roar

rugiada *f* dew; comfort

rullo *m* roller

rullare roll

rum *m* rum

rumore *m* noise; rumour

ruolo *m* roll: list

ruota, rota *f* wheel; rota

ruoteggio *m* road

rupe *f* rock; – pinoso
rocky

ruspare wind [snoring

russare snore; – so *m*

rusticaggine *f* rusticity

rutilare shine; glitter

ruttare belch; vomit

ruvido rough; rugged;
– damente roughly

ruzzare jest

ruzzola *f* small; wheel;
spinning-top

ruzzolone *m* large stone

ruzzoloni rolling

S

Sabato, sabbato *m* Sab-
bath; Saturday

sabbia *f* sand; gravel;
– bioso sandy [hole

sabordo *m* (mar.) port-

sacca *f* sack; bag

saccardo *m* errand boy;

saccheggiare ransack;
destroy; – tore *m* plun-
derer

sacco *m* sack; ransack-
ing; – coccia *f* pocket;

sacerdote *m* priest; – tale
priestly; – tessa *f* priest-
ess; – zio *m* priesthood

sacramento *m* sacrament;
oath; – tale sacra-
mental; – tare conse-
crate; swear

sacrare consecrate; – rio
m sanctuary

sacro, cra sacred; – santo
holy

sadduceo sadducee

saetta *f* arrow; thunderbolt; lancet; – tamento
m shooting; – tore *m*
bowman

saggezza *f* wisdom; pru-
dence; – gio *a* wise

saggiare try; taste; –
tore *m* assayer

saggina *f* maize

saggitario *m* bowman

210

sagliente striking
sago *m* sago
sagola *f* sounding line
sagoma *f* counterpoise
sagra *f* dedication
sagrestano *m* sexton;
– tia *f* sacristy
sagro coronation; con-
secration
saio *m* robe; cassock
saime *m* pork; fat
sala *m* hall; dining-room
salace salacious; salty
salagione *f* salt provisions
salamandra *f* salamander
salame *m* salt meat;
salt-pork [bow
salamelecche *m* profound
salamoia *f* brine; pickle
salamone *m* salmon
salare salt; – to *m* bacon
salariare pay; – rio *m*
salassare let blood [salary
salcigno twisted; uneven

sound; solid; *n* bal-
ance; – damente firmly
sale *m* salt; wit
salgemma *m* mineral salt
saliare splendid; sump-
saliera *f* salt-cellar [tuous
salificare salt; – zione
f salting; – gno; no salt
salire go up; – toio *m*
ladder
saliscendi *m* latch-key
saliva *f* spittle; – re
salivate
salma *f* weight; ton
salmone *m* salmon
salnitro *m* nitre; salt-
petre; – trato nitrous
salsedine *f* saltness; –
sugginoso salted
salsiccia *f* sausage; –
ciaio *m* sausage maker;
–ciuolo *m* slice of sausage

salso salted; sharp
salsume *m* salting; salt-
meat [bol
saltabeccare jump; gam-
saltamartino *m* fop
saltambarco *m* jacket
saltamindosso *m* short
jacket; scanty dress
saltare jump; dance;
– tore jumper;
saltuariamente from time
to time
salubre wholesome
salume salted meat or
fish; – miere *m* pork-
butcher [salute
salutare wholesome;
saluto *m* salutation;
salute
salute *f* health; salute
salva *f* volley; proof
salvadanaio *m* money-box
salvaggina *f* game
salvaguardia *f* safeguard
salvare save; – dore, tore
m, saviour; – mento *m*
salvation; – torio *m*
asylum ·
salvietta *f* napkin; towel
salvigia *f* asylum; refuge
salvo safe; excepted
salvocondotto *m* safe-
conduct
sanare cure; heal; be
cured; – bile curable
sancire decree
sandalo *m* sandalwood;
sandal
sangue *m* blood; race;
– guifero bloody;
– nario bloodthirsty; –
noso sanguine; con-
sanguineous; – nità *f*
consanguinity
sanguigno sanguine;
bloody
sanguinaccio *m* black

pudding

sanguinario sanguinary; cruel   [sucker

sanguisuga *f* leech; blood

santificare sanctify; canonize; – **ceturo** *m* hypocrite; – **monia** *f* sanctity

santo holy; saint; *m* church; – **toccheria** *f* hypocrisy; – **tocchio** *m* hypocrite

santoccio *m* simpleton

santolo, la *m & f* godfather; mother   [relic

santuario *m* sanctuary;

sanzionare sanction; – **zione** *f* sanction; confirmation

sapere know; understand; – **amente** know by heart; learning; knowledge; – **vole** learned; wise

sapienza *f* wisdom; school; – **temente** wisely

sapone *m* soap; – **naceo** soapy; – **naio** soap-boiler

saporare relish; – **re** *m* savour; taste; – **roso** savoury; agreeable

sarchiare weed; – **mento** *m* weeding

sarcofago *m* sarcophagus

sarda *f* cornelian

sardella, dina *f* pilchard

sardonico sardonic

sargano *m* woollen-cloth

sargia *f* serge

sarpare weigh anchor

sarrocchino *m* pilgrim

sartiame *m* cordage;

sarto *m* tailor   [shrouds

sassaiuola *f* stone; fight

212

Satan, tana *m* Satan; – **nico** satanical

satellite *m* satellite; policeman   [satirical

satira *f* satire; – **tirico**

satiro *m* satyr; satirical poet   [bail

satisdazione *f* security;

satisfare satisfy

saviezza *f* wisdom

savina *f* sabine

savore *m* savour; – **rare** savour; – **roso** savoury

savorra *f* ballast; cargo

saziare satiate; satisfy; – **zietà** *f* satiety

sbaccellare husk; shell

sbadataggine *f* inattention; – **to** inattentive

sbadigliare yawn ; – **mento** *m* yawning

sbagliare be mistaken; – **glio** *m* mistake; blunder

sbaldeggiare grow bold; – **dore** *m* courage

sballare unpack; brag

sbalordire astonish; confound; – **mento** *m* astonishment

sbalzare throw; leap

sbandare scatter; disband   [exile

sbandire exile; – **to** *m*

sbaragliare rout; disperse; – **mento, glio** *f* rout; disorder

sbarazzare clear; rid

sbarbagliare scatter

sbarra *f* bar; barrier; – **re** bar; barricade; unbar; – **ro** *m* barrier obstacle

sbassare lower; abate

sbatsare unsaddle

sbattagliare ring (bells)

sbattere shake; torment; – **timento** *m* agitation

sbattezzare change reli-

gion   [agitation
sbattito *m* confusion;
sbavagliare unmask
sbeffare laugh at; ridicule
sbellicarsi burst out
sbendare unveil; relax
sbevazzare sip; drink;
  – **mento** *m* sipping
sbezzicare peck
sbiancare whiten; – **cato**
  pale
sbiecare slope; – **co, sco**
  aslant; crooked
sbietolare be moved
sbigottire frighten ;
  terrify; – **mento** fright
sbilenco crooked; bandy-
  legged
sbirbato cheated; deceived
sbirciare ogle
sbirro *m* policeman;
  bailiff
sboccare overflow; break
  off the neck(of a bottle);
  – **co** mouth (of river)
sboccato improper; wild;
  – **tamente** indecently
sbocciare open; expand
sbocconcellare nibble
sbombardare bombard
sbombettare tipple
sbordellare be lewd; –
  mento *m* lewd life
sborsare disburse; –
  mento, so *m* disburse-
  ment   [insult
sbottonare unbutton;
sbrattare cleanse; clear
sbrigare dispatch; hasten
sbrigliare unbridle; untie
sbrogliare unravel; clear
sbruffare besprinkle
sbruttare cleanse
sbucchiare skin; peel
scacchi *m pl* chess; – **era**
  f chess-board
sacco *m* square; – **matto**

check-mate
scaglia *f* scale; – **re** throw
scagnardo ugly
scala *f* staircase; ladder
scalciare kick   [pan
scaldaletto *m* warming-
scaldare warm; excite
scampagnata *f* excursion
  into the country
scampanare chime
scampare save; deliver
scampol(ett)o *m* remnant
  (of cloth)
scandalo *m* scandal
scandalezzare scandalize
scannare cut the throat
scanno *m* bench
scansare avoid; escape
scapigliare dishevel
scapolo *m* bachelor
scappare escape

scappellari salute
scarabocchiare scribble
scarabocchio *m* scribbling
scarafaggio *m* scarab
scaramuccia *f* skirmish
scarlattina *f* scarlet fever
scarlattino scarlet
scarmo *m* thole-pin
scarno emaciated
scarpa *f* shoe; slope
scarpino *m* light shoe
scarpione *m* scorpion
scarsella *f* purse
scarso scarce
scartabellare peruse
scartare discard; reject
scassare unpack
scastagnare flinch
scatola *f* box; case
scattare get loose; pass
  (time)
scaturire spring; spout
  out
scavare excavate; dig
scavo *m* excavation;
  hollow

scegliere choose
scellerato wicked
scena *f* scene
scendere descend; invade
scenico scenic; theatrical
scesa *f* descent; declivity
scettico sceptic
scettro *m* sceptre
scettrato crowned
sceverare sever; divide
scheda *f* schedule; bill
schermire fence; defend
scherno *m* scorn; mockery
scherzare, scherzo *m* jest
schiacciare squash; crush
schiaffo *m* box on the ear
schiamazzare brawl; jest
schiantare split; rend
schiarire clear up; explain
schiatta *f* race; breed
schiavo *m* slave
schiccherare scribble

schiena *f* back; chine
schiera *f* troop; gang
schietto frank; candid
schifare shun; loathe
schifltà *f* modesty

schifo *m* disgust; boat
schifoso disgusting
schioppo *m* gun; musket
schiudere open; uncork

schiuma *f*, – re foam
scialacquare lavish;
sciallo *m* shawl [waste
scialuppa *f* shallop;
launch
sciamare, sciame *m*
swarm
sciampagna *m* cham-
pagne
sciarpa *f* scarf
sciatica *f* sciatica
sciattare botch
sciente learned; – mente
knowingly

scilinguare stammer;
to stammering
sciliva *f* spittle; saliva
scimunitaggine *f* stupi-
dity; blunder
scindere separate; loosen
scintilla spark; – lare
sparkle
sciocco stupid; fool
sciogliere untie; absolve;
– tore *m* deliverer
sciolezza *f* boasting
scioltezza *f* nimbleness
sciolto nimble; liquid
sciolvere breakfast
scionata, scione *f* squall;
whirlwind
sciorinare air; publish
sciorre untie; absolve
scipa *m* goose; blockhead
scipare waste; miscarry;
– tore *m* spendthrift
scipidezza *f* insipidity;
trifle
sciringa *f* syringe; – re
syringe; inject
scirocco *m* sirocco
sciroppo *m* syrup
scisma *m* schism; dis-
sension; – tico *m* schis-
matic
scissione *f* scission; cleft
sciugare wipe; dry;
– toio *m* towel [sume
sciupare squander; con-
sciupinio *m* squandering
scivolare rebound
sclamare exclaim; cry
out; – zione *f* exclama-
scoccolare pick off [tion
scodare crop; – to crop-
scodella *f* porringer [ped
scofacciare crush; flatten
scoffina *f* rasp; grater
scoglio *m* sand-bank;
reef; – gliera *f* shoal
scoiare flay; skin

214

scoiatto *m* squirrel
scolare *m* scholar
scolare drain; trickle
scolaresca *f* scholar
scolastico scholastic
scolatoio *m* sewer; strainer
scolatura *f* residue
scolazione *f* gonorrhœa
scommettere separate; embroil; bet
scommiatare dismiss; — si to take leave
scommuovere move; revolt
scomodare trouble
scompagnare separate; uncouple
scomparire disappear
scompartire distribute
scompigliare confound; disturb; — mento *m* confusion; disturbance
scomunica, zione *f* excommunication; — re excommunicate
scomuzzolo not at all
sconcare put; draw out
sconcertare disturb; disconcert
sconcezza *f* disorder; indecency
sconciare damage; —cio out of order; unbecoming; ndecent
sconcorde discordant; — dia *f* discord
scondere conceal
sconfacevole indecorous
sconferma *f* confirmation; — re confirm   [own
sconfessare deny; disconfidare mistrust; — danza *f* mistrust
sconfiggere rout; disturb
sconfondere confound
sconnettere separate; be

incoherent; — ssione *f* incoherence
scontraffatto deformed
scontramento *m* meeting; — re meet with; encounter;
scontro *m* meeting
sconturbare confound; — bo *m* confusion
scoperchiare uncover
sconoscere be ungrateful; — scente ungrateful; low; — temente inconsiderately; — sciuto ubknown; low
sconquasso *m* destruction; — sare destroy
sconsacrare profane
sconsenso *m* approval
sconsentire refuse; dissent; — mento *m* refusal
sconsideratezza *f* inconsideration; — to inconsiderate
sconsigliare dissuade; — tezza *f* imprudence
sconsolare afflict; dishearten   •
scontare discount; expiate; — to *m* discount
scontentare discontent; — mento, tezza *m & f* discontent
scontinuare discontinue
scoppiare burst; come forth; — mento, tura *m & f* explosion; noise
scoppiettare crackle; explode   [cover
scoprire discover; unscoraggiare, gire discourage; — si lose courage
scorare discourage
scorcare get up; to rise
scorciare shorten;

215

abridge; — **toia** *f* cross-road

scordare disagree; forget

scoreggiare whip; fart; — **ta** *f* whip

scorgere discover; guide; — **gimento** *m* discovery

scoria dross; scum

scornacchiare banter; laugh at; — **mento** *m* joke

scorno *m* insult; affront

scorta *f* escort

scortare shorten; escort

scortecciare peel

scortese discourteous; impolite; — **sia** *f* rudeness

scorticare peel; flay

scorto *m* bark

scorto prudent

scorza *f* rind; cuticle

scorzone *m* churl; serpent

scoscendere lop; split

scosciare disjoint; — **scio** *m* precipice [— **re** shake

scossa *f* toss; squall;

scostare remove; drive away; — **mento** *m* removal

scostumatezza *m* dissoluteness; indecency

scotennato *m* fat (pig)

scottare burn; scald;

scotto *m* share; Scot

scovare start; find out

scozzare shuffle (cards)

scozzonare break (horse); — **tore** *m* horsebreaker

scranna *f* folding stool; chair [tumacious

scredente infidel; con-

screditare discredit

scremento *m* excrement

scremenzia *m* quinsy

screpolare split; burst

216

screscere decrease

scriato slender; weak

scriba writer; copyist

scricchiare clash; crackle

scriccio *m* wren

scrigno *m* jewel-box; — **gnuto** concave; con-

scrima *f* fencing [vex

scrimaglia *f* defence

scrinare dishevel

scritta *f* writing; inscription

scritto written; erased; *m* writing; — **toio** *m* writing-desk; inkstand; — **tore** *m* writer; author; — **tura** *f* writing; scripture

scrivacchiare scribble

scrivere write; — **zione** *f* writing

scrollare shake; toss

scrosciare split; boil

scrupoleggiare have scruples; — **lo, sità** *m & f* scruple; — **so** scrupulous

scrutare tinare scrutinize; ballot; — **tinio** *m* ballot

scucire unstitch; undo

scudare shield; — **do** *m* shield; scutcheon

scuderia *f* stable; stud; — **diere** *m* equerry

scudisciare whip; — **scio** *m* switch; rod

scuffia *f* coif; head-dress;

— **ra** *f* milliner

scuffiare swallow; devour

scultore *m* carver; engraver; — **tura** *f* sculpture

scumarola *f* skimmer

scuola *f* school

scusa *f* excuse; pretext; — **bile** excusable

scusare excuse; justify

scusso deprived; shaken
scutica *f* whip
sdegnare despise; decay;
– **si** get angry; – **gno**
m disdain; anger
sdicevole improper
sdilacciare untie; unlace
sdilinquire faint; – **mento**
m fainting
sdormentare wake; – **si**
sdossare unload [awaken
sdottorare take away
degree of doctor
sdraiarsi stretch one's
self; lie down
sdurare quiet
se if; whether
sé one's self; himself;
herself; itself; them-
selves
sebbene though
secante *f* secant
secca, gna *f* sand-bank;
shallow [some person
seccafistole *m* trouble-
seccaggine *f* drought; im-
portunity
seccare dry up; bother;
waste; – **ticcia** *f* dry
wood; – **to** dry; barren
secchia *f* pail; bucket;
– **ta** *f* pailful
seccia *f* stubble [*m* drought
secco dry; flabby; thin;
secedere part; – **cessione**
f defection; insurrection
secesso *m* retirement
seco with one's self
secolare profane; secular;
– **rizzare** secularize
secolo *m* century; help
secondare help; second
secondario secondary;
accessory
secreto *m* secret; con-
fidant
secrezione *f* secretion;
– **torio** secretary

sedizione *f* sedition;
tumult; – **so** seditious
sedurre seduce; corrupt;
– **cimento** *m* seduction;
– **duttore** *m* seducer
sega *f* saw; – **are** saw; *f*
reap; – **tura** *f* sawing;
saw-dust
segale *m* rye
segaligno dry; lean
segavene *m* leech
seggetta *f* sedan-chair
segmento *m* segment
segnacolo *m* register;
signet
segnalare signalize; – **to**
illustrious; – **tamente** re-
markably
segnale *m* description;
token; signal
segnare note; sign; bless;
bleed; – **si** cross one's
self; be surprised; – **to**
signed; marked; – **ta-
mente** expressly; – **tore**
m indicator; – **gno** *m*
seal; signal; mark
sego *m* tallow; suet
segregare separate; –
mento *m* separation
segreta *f* secret place;
secret prayer; – **rio, ro**
m secretary; – **to** *m*
secret; confident;
– **tamente** secretly
seguace, guitatore fol-
lowing; follower
seguitare follow; torment; – **mento** *m* fol-
lowing; pursuing; – **to**
m suite; issue; – **to**
part; reputed
sei six
selce, selice *f* paving-
stone; *f* – **ciare** pave;
– **to, liciato** *m* pave-

ment; – **cioso** stony
sella *f* saddle; chair;
– **laio** *m* saddler; – **re**
saddle

sembiante alike; resem-
bling; face; counten-
ance; – **brare** look;
appear

seme *m* seed; origin
sementa, za *f* seed;
origin; sowing; – **re**
sow; – **tore** *m* sower
semestre *m* space of six
months: – **trale** half-
yearly
semi half; – **addottorato**
simple; – **cerchio, cir-
colo** *m* semi-circle; –
circolare semi-circular;
– **croma** *f* semi-quaver;
– **deo, dio** *m* demi-god;
everlasting; – **nare** perpetuate
semplice simple; pure;
– **mente** simply; – **cista**
m herbalist; botanical
garden; – **cità** *f* simpli-
city; candour
sempre ever; always;
– **che** so often as; **mai** –
for ever
sena *f* senna
senapa, pe *f* mustard-
seed; mustard: – **pismo**
m mustard-plaster
senario of six
senato *m* senate; – **tore**
m senator   [senility
senile senile; – **lità** *f*
seniore senior; older
senno *m* sense; wisdom;
a mio – at my pleasure;
da - **in** earnest; **con-**
wisely
seno *m* bosom; intellect
se non if not; but

sensale *m* broker; agent;
– **seria** *f* brokerage
sensatezza *f* sense; prudence
sensazione *f* sensation
sensibile *f* sensible; per-
ceptible; – **lità, tività** *f*
sensibility; – **tivo** sensitive; scrupulous
senso *m* sense; feeling;
– **suale** sensual; – **lità**
f sensuality
sentarsi sit down
sentente feeling; hearing
sentenza *f* sentence;
maxim; – **zialmente**
sententiously; – **ziare**
judge; sentence; –
ziato *m* convict; – **zia-
tore** *m* judge   [way
sentiere, o *m* path; bye-
sentimento *m* feeling;
judgment; – **tale** senti-
mental
senza without; **senz'-
altro** – without doubt;
– **che** besides; more-
over; – **più** without any
thing else
senziente sensible
sepa *f* snake
separare separate; remove; – **tamente** sep-
arately; – **mento, zione**
m & f separation
sera *f* evening; night;
– **le** evening   [seraphic
serafino *m* seraph; – **fico**
serbanza *f* keeping; care
serbare keep; reserve;
delay; – **toio** *m* reservoir; – **tore** *m* deposi-
sere *m* sire; master [tary
serenare quieten; bright-
en; – **no** serene
serenata *f* serenade
sergente *m* sergeant;

218

bailiff
sergoncello *m* sorrel
serico silk
serie *f* series
serietà *f* seriousness; − **rio** serious; − **riamente, riosamente** seriously
sermento *m* vine-shoot
sermocinare, nare, neggiare preach; − **natore** *m* preacher; − **ne** *m* sermon; speech; salmon
serpe, pente *f & m* snake;
serpegiare wind [serpent
serpentare plague; bore
serpere meander; creep
serpetta *f* adder
serpillo *m* wild thyme
serra *f* mountain; dike; crowd [closure
serraglio *m* seraglio; en-
serrare lock up; conceal; press; − **to** strained; close; − **tamente** tightly; briefly; − **tura** *f* lock
serto *m* garland
serva, vente *f* maid servant [vitude
servaggio *m* slavery ; ser-
servare keep; hold; − **tore** *m* keeper
servente *m* servant; lover
servire serve; wait on; − **dore, tore, vo** servant; valet; foot-man; − **gio. zio** *m* service; business; use; − **vile** servile
sesamo *m* sesame
sessagono sexagonal
sessanta *m* sixty; − **tesimo** sixtieth; − **tina** *f* threescore
sessione *f* session
sesso *m* sex; − **suale** sexual
sessola *f* scoop

sesta *f* compass; sixth; − **tante** *m* sextant
sesterzio *m* sesterce
sestile *m* sextile
sesto sixth; sixthly; *m* order; compass
sestodecimo sixteenth
settanta seventy; − **tesimo** seventieth
sette seven
setteggiare revolt
settentrione *m* north; − **nale** northern
settimana *f* week; − **le** weekly; − **nalmente** weekly
settina *f* seven
setto split; divided
settuplo septuple
severita *f* severity; − **ro** severe; − **ramente** severely; − **sevizia** *f* ill usage [verely
sevo *m* tallow; suet
sezione *f* section
sezzaio, sezzo *m* last; da sezzo late; too late
sfaccendato idle; unoccupied
sfanfanare waste; ruin
sfardellare unfold
sfare undo; destroy
sfarinare grind; pulverize
sfarzo *m* pomp; magnificence; − **so** pompous
sfasciare unswathe; pull down (walls)
sfastidiare pacify
sfatare scorn; disdain
sfatto undone; destroyed
sfavillare sparkle; glitter; − **mento** *m* shine
sferza *f* whip; discipline; − **re** scourge; imitate; − **ta** *f* whipping
sfessatura *f* slit
sfetteggiare cut in slices
sfiatare breathe; toil;

– to out of breath

sfibbiare unbutton

sfibrare enervate; – mento *m* enervation

sfidare challenge; mistrust; – da, damento *f* & *m* challenge; defiance; – tore *m* challenger

sfiduciato mistrust

sfigurare disfigure

sfilacciare unravel

sfilare file off; – ta *f* wiredrawing-iron; – to confused

sfingardaggine *f* idleness

sfinge *f* sphinx

sfinire finish; perfect; – mento *m* swoon

sfioccare unravel

sfiondare sling

sfocato cooled; cold

sfoderare unsheathe

sfogare evaporate; suppurate; – toio *m* airhole; tap; – mento *m* evaporation; relief

sfogliare strip of leaves; extenuate; – glia *f* metal sheet; spangle

sfogliazzo *m* diary

sfogo *m* evaporation; exhaling

sforacchiare drill

sformare disfigure; – to deformed; strange; – zione *f* deformity

sfortuna *f* misfortune; – to, tevole unfortunate

sfortunare make unhappy

sforzare constrain; ravish; – si endeavour; – to violent; unjust

sfracassare demolish

sfrattare dismiss; go away; – to *m* expulsion; flight

sfregare rub; – mento *m* rubbng; – toio *m* duster; scrubbing brush

sfregiare undress; slap

sfregio *m* undressing; insult

sfrenare unbridle; – si live dissolutely; – mento, tezza *m* & *f* licentiousness; – to dissolute

sfriggolare fry

sfrontarsi make bold; – taggine, tezza *f* boldness; – to bold

sfuggevole perishable; – lezza *f* rapidity

sfuggire·fly from; avoid; – mento *m* flight; – to fugitive [colours

sfumatura *f* gradation of

sgabello, lino *m* stool

sgagliardare weaken

sgallinare fuddle; banquet [get tired

sgangherare disorder; dislocate

sgannare undeceive

sgaraffare deceive

sgarare rire surpaes; vanquish

sgargarizzare gargle; – zo *m* gargling

sgarrare be mistaken

sgavazzare guttle; riot

sgelare thaw

sghembo oblique; tortuous; *m* obliquity

sghermire get loose; let go [throat

sgherro *m* bully; cutsghiacciare thaw

sghignare laugh at; deride; – gnazzare burst out laughing; – mento, ta *m* & *f* burst of laughter

sgocciolare distill; drop; – **toio** *m* gutter; – **tura, lo** *f & m* dripping

sgombinare, gominare jumble

sgomentare frighten; – **si** be frightened; – **mento** *m* fright, – **tevole** frightful

sgorgare overflow; chat

sgovernare govern; treat badly [swallow (insult)

sgozzare cut throat of;

sgradire disagree; disgust; – **devole** disagreeable

sgraffiare scratch; etch

sgraffignare steal

sgranare shell out

sgravare unburden; relieve; – **mento, vio** *m* relief

sgravidare be delivered; lie in; – **danza** *f* lying-in

sgraziato clumsy; unfortunate

sgretolare break; hash

sgretolio *m* fermentation

sgricchiolare crackle

sgridare scold; – **tore** *m* grumbler

sguardare look at; consider; – **ta** *f* glance; – **tore** *m* looker-on

sguarnire. guernire strip

sgufare jeer

sguinzagliare set (dogs) on; provoke

sguisciare swim; shell

siamese *m* Siamese

sibarita sybaritic; sybarite

sibilare, billare whistle; incite; – **tore** *m* whistler; – **lio, lo** *m* whistle

sicario *m* hired assassin

sicché so; also; thus; therefore

siocità *f* dryness; drought

siccome as; so; as soon as; owing

siclo *m* cycle

sicomoro *m* sycamore

sicumera *f* pomp; ceremony

sicuranza *f* security; boldness; – **rare** assure; secure; – **rezza. rità, curtà** security; – **ro** assured; firm

sido *m* great cold

sidro *m* cider

siepaglia *f* thicket

siepare enclose with a hedge; – **pe** *f* hedge;

sigillare seal; confirm; – **latamente** exactly; – **lo** *m* seal

signifero *m* ensign; standard-bearer

significamento *f* signification; notice; – **cantemente, cativamente** significantly; – **care** signify; give notice; – **cativo** significative

signora *f* lady; mistress; madam; – **rina** *f* miss

signore *m* Lord; God; sir; mister [govern

signoreggiare domineer;

signoria government; lordship; – **rilità** *f* lordship; – **rilmente** lordly

sillaba *f* syllable; – **re** pronounce

sillogismo *m* syllogism;

simpatia sympathy; – **tico** sympathetic; – **tizzare** sympathize

simplificare simplify; – **zione** *f* simplification

simposio *m* symposium

simulacro *m* image; likeness

simulare simulate; dissemble; – **mento, zione** *m & f* feint; dissimulation

simultaneità *f* simultaneity; – **neo** simultaneous; – **neamente** simultaneously

sinagoga *f* synagogue

sincerare justify; – **zione** *f* justification

sincerità *f* sincerity; candour; – **ro** sincere; – **ramente** sincerely

– **gizzare** argue

silvano sylvan

silvestro, tre wood

simboleggiare symbolize; – **leità, lità** *f* analogy; – **lo** *m* symbol; creed

simigliante alike; same; – **temente** in the same way; – **za, litudine** *f* comparison; – **gliare** resemble; imitate

similare similar; – **le** alike; same; – **milmente** similarly

simmetria *f* symmetry; – **trico** symmetric

singolare, gulare singular; only; – **rità** *f* singularity; – **lo** each

singulto *m* sob; sigh

sinistra *f* left; left hand; **da** – on the left hand; – **tro** left; sinister

sino till; until; **as** far as; **sin adesso** till now; hitherto; – **a che** till; until; **sin dove ?** how far? – **sin qui** hither

sinonimia *f* synonymy; – **mico, mo** synonymous; –**mo** *m* synonym

sintassi syntax

sintesi *f* synthesis; – **tico** synthetical

sintomatico symptomatic; – **mo** *m* symptom

siroccbia *f* sister

sirte *f* quicksands

sisimbrio *m* watercress

sistema *m* system; – **re** regulate; classify; – **tico** systematical

sistro *m* timbrel

sitare stink

sitibondo thirsty; covetous; – **re** be thirsty

sito situated; *m* site; stink

situamento *m* situation; – **zione** *f* situation

slacciare untie; unfold

slanciamento, cio *m* spring; – **re** throw; dart

slargamento *m* widening; – **re** widen

slegamento *m* loosening; – **re** loosen

slitta *f* sledge

slogamento, tura *m & f* dislocation; – **re** dislocate

slungare lengthen; remove [depreciate

smaccare crush; vilify;

smacchiare break cover

smagamento *m* astonishment; – **re** be astonished; mislead; – **smago** *m* fright; error

smagramento, grimento *f* growing thin; – **grare, grire** grow thin

smaliziato sharp; cunning

smallare peel

smaltare enamel; pave; – **mento, tura** *m & f* enamelling

smanceria *f* affection;
– **cinato, roso** affected

smania *f & m* fury;
frenzy; – **re** get furious;
rave; – **niante, nioso**
furious; frantic

smaniglia *f & m* bracelet

smantellare dismantle

smanziere *m* beau; dandy

smargiassare bully

smarrire mislay; – **si**
lose one's way

smascherare unmask

smembrare dismember

smenomare diminish

smentire belie

smeraldo *m* emerald

smerare clean; polish

smerciare sell; deliver;
– **cio** *m* sale; delivery

smerdare soil

smerigliare polish with
emery; – **glio** *m* emery

smeriglione *m* swivel

smerlo *m* merlin

smettere leave

smezzamento *m* parting

smillanta *m* bully; – **re**
bully

smilzo delicate; feeble

sminchionare jeer

sminuire lessen; – **mento**
m diminution

sminuzzare hash; detail

sminuzzolare hash; explain

smodamento *m* disorder;
– **dato** immoderate

smoderamento, ezza *m*
& f excess; immoderation

smogliato bachelor

smovitura *f* movement;
commotion

smozzicare maim

smozzicatura maiming

smugghiare bellow; roar

smugnere dry up; wither

smunire restore

smuovere move; excite

smurare demolish

smussare blunt

snaturare alter; – **tezza**
f cruelty; – **to** cruel

snebbiare clear up

snellezza *f* agility

soave sweet; gentle;
– **mente** *ad* sweetly;
gently; – **vità** *f* sweetness

sobbalzare tremble

sobbarcare conquer; – **si**
submit

sobbollire boil gently

sobborgo *m* suburb

sobbornare suborn

sobillare seduce; – **mento**
m seduction

soccorrere help; agree;
– **vole** helpful; – **rimento, so** *m* help;
– **ritore** *m* helper

sociabile sociable; – **ciale**
a social; sociable;
– **lismo** *m* socialism;
– **lista** *m* socialist; – **lità**
f sociability

società *f* society

socio *m* comrade; partner

soda *f* soda

sodale *m* comrade; companion; – **lizio** *m* company; fraternity

sodare consolidate; bail

soddisfacente, cevole
satisfactory; – **mente**
satisfactorily; – **cimento, zione** *m & f* satisfaction; – **fare** satisfy

sodezza *f* solidity; constancy; – **do** constant;
intrepid; *f* guarantee

sodomia *f* sodomy

sofà *m* sofa

sofferenza *f* suffering;

patience; – **revole** bearable; – **rire** suffer
soffermare stop
soffermata *f* pause; stop
soffiare blow; excite; move; *m* breath; – **il naso** blow one's nose
sofficcare conceal; hide
soffice soft
soffornato vaulted
soffraganeo suffragan
soffratta *f* want; penury
soffreddo coldish
soffriggere fry; – **fritto** *m* fricassee
soffrire suffer

soggettare subject; subdue; – **bile** subject; – **gezione** *f* subjection; – **getto** *m* subject; object
sogghignare smile; – **gno** *m* smile
soggiacere surrender; – **cimento** *m* subjection; submission
soggiogare subdue; surpass; – **mento, zione** *m & f* subjection
sorgolo *m* gorget; double chin
soglia *f* threshold; sole (fish) [hold
soglio *m* throne; thressogliola *f* sole (fish)
sognare dream; imagine; – **tore** *m* dreamer; – **gno** *m* dream; revery
soia *f* flattery; – **re** wheedle
solaio *m* floor; wainscot
solamente only
solare solar; – **zio** sunny; southern; *m* sunny place
solata *f* sun-stroke; sunshine

soldare recruit
soldato *m* soldier; – **tesca** *f* soldiery; – **tesco** soldierly
soldo *m* sou; pay; war
sole *m* sun; year
solecchio *m* parasol; canopy
solecismo *m* solecism
solenne solemn; – **neggiare, nizzare** solennize; – **mente** solemnly – **nità** *f* solennity; – **zione** *f* solemnization
solere be accustomed to
solerte careful; vigilant; – **zia** *f* care; vigilance
soletta *f* sole(stocking)
soletto alone
solfa *f* gamut; music
solfatara sulphur mine
solfato *m* sulphate
solfo *f* sulphur; brimstone; – **nello** *m* match; – **rico** sulphuric
solimato *m* sublimate
solingo alone; solitary
solio *m* throne
solitario, ria solitary
solito; usual; accustomed; *m* habit; **al** – usually
solitudine *f* solitude
solivago solitary
sollazzare amuse; entertain: – **lazzo** *m* amusement; sport
sollecitare solicit; urge; incite; – **tore** *m* suitor;
sollievo *m* ease; comfort
sollo soft; flabby
solo alone; only
solstizio *m* solstice
soltanto only; but; solely; – **che** provided
solubile soluble; separable; – **lità** *f* solubility

224

solvere dissolve; freet
– **vibile** solvent; – **lità**
f solvency
soma *f* load; burden;
– **ro. miere** *m* pack-
horse; beast of burden
somiglianza *f* likeness;
resemblance; – **gliare**
compare; resemble
somma *f* sum; summit;
result; in – in short
sommaco *m* morocco
leather [amount to
sommare sum up;
sommario summary
sommergere submerge;
sink; – **gibile** submer-
sible; – **gimento, sione**
m & f submersion
sommessione. missione *f*
submission; obedience;
– **sivo** submissive
somministrare supply;
administer; – **tore** *m*
purveyor; – **zione** *f*
supply; provision
sommità *f* summit
sommo, ma supreme; *m*
summit; – **mamente**

sonare, suonare ring;
play (instrument); **suono**
m sound
sonettare make sonnets;
– **netto** *m* sonnet
sonnacchiare, necchiare
doze; slumber
sonnambulismo *m* som-
nambulism; – **lo, la** *n*
somnambulist
sonno *m* slumber; rest;
– **lente, lo** to sleepy
sonorità *f* sonorousness;
– **ro** sonorous
sontuosità *f* sumptuous-
ness; – **so** sumptuous
soperchiamento *m* superabundance   [ceed
soperchiare surpass; ex-

sopercheria *f* cheat;
insult; – **chio** super-
fluity; superabundantly
sopire quiet; quench;
– **pore** *m* lethargy;
– **rifero, fico roso** sopo-
rific
soppalco *m* ceiling
soppanare line; trim;

soppressa *f* press; – **re**
mangle; press; – **pres-
sione** *f* oppression; sup
pression; – **primere** oppress; abolish
soppressata *f* sausage
sopra on; above; be-
yond; about; towards
soprabbondante. devole
superabundant; – **dan-
za** *f* superabundance;
– **dantemente, devol-
mente** superabundantly
soprabbuono very good
sopraccapo *m* superintendent; director
sopraccaricare overload;
– **co** *m* overload
sopraccarta *f* envelope
sopracchiedere ask too
much for
sopracchiusa *f* cover
sopracciglio *m* eye-brow
sopracinghia *f* surcingle
sopracciò *m* superintendent; director
sopraccomperare overpay
sopraccoperta *f* counter-
pane; envelope
sopraccorrere rush upon
sopraggirare turn round
sopraggiugnere super-
vene; surprise; – **giunto**
caught; surprised; *m*
addition
sopraggravare overload
soppraintendenza *f* super-
intendance
soprallodare praise ex-

sopralzare lift [cessively
sopramabile most amiable
soprammattone *m* brick-
  wall   [excessively
soprammisura extremely;
soprammodo inordinately
soprammontare grow;
  surpass
sopranimo passionately;
  with animosity
soprannaturale supernatural; – **lmente** supernaturally
sopransegna *f* regimentals
soprantendente, ditore *m*
  superintendent
soprappeso *m* overload
soprappigliare seize upon;
  take too much
soprappiù *m* surplus;
  addition; **di** – into the
  bargain; besides
soprapporre add; load;
  – **ponimento, sizione** *m*
  & *f* superposition
soprapprendere surprise;
  – **dimento** *m* surprise
soprapprofondo very deep
soprarrivare supervene
soprascritta, scrizione *f*
  inscription ; epitaph
soprascrivere superscribe
soprasoldo *m* extra-pay
soprassegnale *m* description; – – **gnare** make a
  mark; – **gno** *m* mark;
  sign
soprassello *m* surplus
soprasseminare sow again
soprassalare salt too
  much   [much
soprassapere know too
soprassedenza *f* suspension; delay; – **dere**
  suspend
sopravvedere supervise
sopravvenire supervene

sopravvento *m* windward
sopravvesta, te *f* sleeve-
  less coat; pretext
sopravvincere surpass
sopravvivenza *f* reversion;
  – **vere** out-live; survive
soprecedente superabundant; – **za** *f* superabundance   [lent
sopreccellente most excel-
sopreminente most high;
  sublime   [tend
soprintendere superin-
soprosso *m* splint; trouble
soprumano supernatural
soprusare misuse; abuse;
  – **so** *m* misuse; injury
soqquadrare overthrow;
  – **dro** *m* ruin; confusion
sorare cast (hawks)
sorbetto *m* sherbet; ice-
  cream; – **tiera** *f* ice-
  mould
sordaggine, dezza *f* deaf-
  nes ; – **do** deaf; – **do-
  muto** *m* deaf and dumb;
  – **dità** *f* deafness
sordido sordid
sorella *f* sister; nun
sorgente *m* spring; origin;
sornacchiare cough and
  spit; – **chio** *m* fit of
  coughing
sornuotare float
soro low; dark; *m* booby
sorpassare surpass; excel
sorprendere astonish; deceive; – **dente** surpris-
  ing; – **presa** *f* surprise;
sorradere graze   [deceit
sorreggere prop; bear
  up; – **si** stop
sorridere smile; – **dente-
  mente** smilingly; – **riso**
  m smile
sorsaltare start up

sorsara, sorseggiare sip
sorta *f* sort; manner
sorte *f* fate; hazard; luck
sortiere, tilego *m* sorcery;
– legio *m* witch-craft
sortire go out; draw lots
sorvenire supervene
sorvivere survive
sorvolare excel; float;
– lante surpassing;
floating
soscrittore *m* subscriber;
– vere subscribe; –
scrizione *f* subscription
sospendere hang; defer;
– dimento, sione *f* sus-
pense; suspension; –
sorio *m* truss; – peso
suspended; irresolute
sospettare, picare mis-
trust; suspect; – petto,
toso suspicious; *m* sus-
picion; mistrust; – ta-
mente, tosamente sus-
piciously
sospirare sigh; long for;
– tore *m* lover; – spiro
m sigh; minim rest
sossopra upside down
sostegno *m* prop; pro-
tection
sostenenza *f* toleration;
aliment; – nere sustain;
tolerate; last; – tore *m*
protector
sostentare prop; nourish;
– mento, zione, *m & f*
sustenance, support
sostentatore *m* protector

sostenutezza *f* gravity;
– to sustained; detained
sostituire substitute; –
tuto *m* substitute
sostituzione *f* substitution
sottacqua under water
sottacqueo subaqueous
sottana *f* cassock; petti-

coat   [stealth
sottecchi secretly; by
sotterfugio *m* subterfuge
sotterra under ground
sotterraneo subterraneous
sottomettere submit; –
messione, missione *f*
submission; subjection
sottomurata *f* foundation
sottordinare subordinate;
– ordinato subordinate;
subaltern
sottoscritta, scrizione *f*
subscription; – tore *m*
subscriber; – vere sub-
scribe
sottosopra upside down
sottosquadro *m* cavity
sottoterra under ground
sottovoce low voiced
sottraimento, zione *m &*
f subtraction; – trarre
substract; deceive
sovente frequently
soverchiare exceed; fall;
sovero *m* cork   [sink
sovra on; upon
sovrabbondanza *f* super-
abundance
sovradescritto aforesaid
sovraggrande very great
sovrapossente almighty
sovrapiù *m* excess
sovrasaltare throb
sovrastamento *m* super-
iority; – stante *m* superintendent
sovreccellente most excellent
sovrempiere fill up
sovresso over; on; upon
sovroffesa *f* offence
sovrumano supernatural
sovvenenza, nimento *f &*
m help; – nevole help-
ful; – nire. aid; relieve;
– nitore, ventore *m* benefactor; – venzione *f*

help; subsidy
sovversione *f* subversion
sozio *m* comrade
sozzare soil; corrupt;
− **zo** profligate; dirty
spaccare divide; cleave
spaccamonti *m* bully
spacciare sell; abbreviate; kill; − **bile** sale-
able
spada *f* sword; sword-
fish; **a** − **tratta** entirely
spaderno *m* fishing - line
spadina *f* hunting-knife
spadone *m* back-sword
spadulare drain
spagnolata *f* bragging

spalla *m* shoulder; top
spalletta *f* epaulet
spalliera *f* back (seat);
espalier
spampanare thin out
(vines) [*f* ostentation
spampanare brag; − **ta**
spandere shed; pour
spanditoio *m* drying-room
spanna *f* span; hand
spannare baffle; sweep
spantanare drain a march
spantare be frightened
sparagnare save; pardon;
− **gno** *m* frugality
sparalembo *m* apron
sparare forget; disfigure

sparecchiare take away;
swallow; clear
spareggio *m* disparity
spargere spill; shed;
spartamente separately
spartatamente apart
spartire divide; assess;
− **bile** divisible; − **mento,**
to *m* & *f* division
sparutello, to weak;
meagre [hawk
sparviere, ro *m* sparrow-

228

spasima, mo, spasmo *f* &
m convulsion; spasm;
− **smodico** spasmodic
spassarsi enjoy one's self
spasseggiare walk; take
a walk; − **gio** *m* walk
spassevole diverting
spasso *m* pastime
spatola *f* spatula
spatriare exile
spauracchio *m* scare-
crow; terror
spavalderia *f* impudence;
sauciness; − **do** bold;
impudent
spavenio *m* spavin
spaventacchio *m* bugbear
spaventare frighten; fear;
− **tevole, toso** fearful
spavento *m* fright; alarm
spaziare extend; stretch
spazieggare distance; −
zievole spacious
spaziosità *f* width; − **so**
wide; spacious
spazzacamino *m* chimney-
sweeper [**ade** *m* idler
spazzacampagne, contr-
spazzamento *m* sweeping;
− **zare** sweep; dust
spazzino *m* sweeper;
floor-scrubber
spazzo *m* pavement
spazzola *f* brush; − **re**
brush
specchiare look in a glass;
look at; examine; −
chio *m* looking-glass
speculare observe; speculate; meditate; trans-
parent [cavern
speculo *m* looking-glass;
spedale *m* hospital
spedarsi get tired; − **da-**
tura *f* fatigue; weariness [venient

spediente opportune; con-
spedire send; hasten;
– tezza *f* quickness;
– tivo expeditious
spegnere extinguish; des-
troy
spelda, spelta *f* spelt
spellare skin; – mento *m*
flaying
spelonca *f* cave; den
speme *f* hope; expecta-
tion
spendente lavish; – dere
spend; employ; *m*
spendthrift [*m* plume
spennachiare pick; – chio
speranza *f* hope; confi-
dence; – rare hope
sperdere lavish; dissi-
pate; – si die; faint

sperimentale experiment-
tal; – tare try; experi-
ment; – to experienced;
skilful; – to *m* experi-
ment
sperma *m* sperm; seed
spermaceti *m* spermaceti
spernere despise; scorn
sperone *m* spur
sperso scattered
sperticato long-legged;
exaggerated
sperto expert; skilful
spesa *f* expense; cost
spessamente frequently;
often [frequent
spesso thick; hard;
spesseggiare, sicare reiterate; repeat
spetrare soften; calm;
free
spettacolo *m* spectacle
spettatore *m* spectator
speziale special; – lità *f*
speciality; – lmente es-
pecially
spezie *f* species

spiacenza, cevolezza *f*
dislike [region
spiaggia *f* beach; coast;
spianare level; explain
spiantare level; eradi-
cate; raze; – to ruined;
miserable [– tore *m* spy
spiare spy; seek out;
spiattellare speak freely
spiccare detach; unhook;
distinguish one's self
spiccatamente brilliantly
spicchio *m* clove
spicciare spring; spout;
pronounce clearly; urge
spiedo *m* boar spear; spit
spiegare unfold; explain;
– bile explicable
spiegazzare fumble
spietatezza *f* cruelty;
inhumanity; – to *a*
inhuman; cruel
spietrare soften
spigolare glean; – tore *m*
gleaner; – tura *f* glean-
ing
spigolo *m* lavender
spigoso full of ears
spilla *f* pin [wool
spillaccherare cleanse
spillare tap; pour; dis-
til; sponge [gimlet
spillo *m* pin; sting;
spilorceria *f* avarice;
greediness [awl
spina *f* thorn; fish-bone
spinace *m* spinach
spinetta *f* trimming
spinosità *f* prickliness;
difficulty; – so thorny;
difficult
spinta *f* shock; thrust;
spiritale vital; spiritual
spiritare possessed by the
devil; be frightened
spirito, spirto *m* spirit;
breath; wit
spiritosità *f* spirituality;

– so spirituous; – tuale spiritual

spiro *m* breath; spirit

spiumacciare shake; – ta *f* slap

splebeire ennoble

splendente splendid; – mente, didamente splendidly; – dere shine; sparkle

spoglia *f* spoil; pod; cast off; – re spoil; strip naked; – toio *m* place for undressing; – tore *m* plunderer

spogliazza *f* flagging; furniture; spoil; – to half naked

spoglio *m* spoil; furniture

spollonare sweep; cleanse; – tura *f* cleansing

spolverare dust; search; – tura *f* dusting; – rizzare pulverize

sponda *f* bank; shore

spongiosso fungous

sponimento *m* exposition; explanation

sponsale nuptual; – zio *m* wedding

spontaneità *f* spontaneity; – neo spontaneous

spontone *m* pontoon

spopolare depopulate; – zione *f* depopulation

spoppare wean

sporre expose; explain

spossare debilitate

spossedere, sessare, spodestare dispossess

spostare change; remove

sprecare squander; waste

spregiare despise; disdain [judiced

spregiudicare be unpre-

spregnare bring forth

spremere squeeze out

sprezzare despise; disdain; – sprezzo *m* contempt; scorn

sprillare squeeze out

sprimacciare make a bed

sprimere express; state

sprizzare spring; irrigate

sprocco *m* shoot; sprig

sprofondare sink; dig; ruin [differ

sprolungare prolong;

sproporzionale disproportioned; – lità, ne *f* disproportion

spropositaggine, to *f* & *m* blunder; – tare act or speak foolishly

sprotetto unprotected

sprunare prune

spruneggio, neggiolo *m* dwarf holly [rain

spruzzaglia *f* drizzling

spugna *f* sponge

spurare, purgare purge; cleanse

spurgo *m* purge; spit

spurio, ria spurious; bastard

sputacchiare sputter; – chiera *f* spittoon; – tare spit

spuzzare stink

squaccherare, querare squirt; bungle; – chera *f* squirt [manifest

squadernare peruse;

squadra *f* square; squadron; – re quarter

squadronare marshal; – ne *m* squadron; troop

squalidezza *f* paleness; – lido squalid; wan

squalo *m* shark

squama, squamma *f* scale (fish); mail; – moso scaly

squarciare lacerate; rend

230

squarcione *m* boaster
squarquoio disgusting
squartare quater; brave;
  – toio *m* butcher's knife
squassare shake; agitate;
  – mento, so *m* shaking;
  shock
squilla *f* splinter; bell;
  – re ring; resound
squinanza *f* quincy
squisitezza *f* excellence;
  – to exquisite; excellent
squittinare ballot
squittire bark; yelp
sradicare eradicate
sragionevole unreason-
  able   [orderly
sregolato irregular; dis-
sreverente irreverent; –
  temente irreverently;
stabile firm; durable;
  – lire establish; ap-
  point; – mento *m* es-
  tablishment; – lità *f*
  stability; – bilmente
  firmly; constantly
stadera *f* steelyard
stadico *m* hostage; sheriff
stadio *m* stadium
staffilare whip
staggire seize; arrest
staggio *m* stick; sojourn;
  hostage   [mitigate
stagionare ripen; season;
stagione *f* season
stagliare hack; compute;
  – to distinctly; quickly
stagnare stanch; tin;
  stagnate; – ta *f* tin-ware
stagno *m* pond; marsh;
staio *m* bushel   [tin
stalattite *f* stalactite
stalla *f* stable; stall;
  rest; – tico *m* dung;
  – liere *m* ostler   [tion
stallo *m* house: habita-
stamane, mattina this

morning   [bow
stambecchino *m* archer;
stambecco *m* wild goat
stamberga *m* garret
stamburare beat the
  drum   [thread
stame *m* carded wool;
stampa *f* printing; press;
  print; kind; stamp;
  – re print; bore; – to
  printed; engraved; –
  tore *m* printer; coiner;
  – tura *f* printing
stampanare tear
stampella *f* crutch
stanare break cover
stancare tire; – si be
  tired; grow faint; –
  chezza *f* weariness; –
  chevole tiresome; – co
  fatigued
stanga *f* bar; row of
  pegs; – re bar   [night
stanotte to-night; this
stante being; *m* moment;
  since; afterwards; dur-
  ing
stanziale permanent
stare be situated; live;
  stop; stand; cost;
  last; go; work; bail;
  produce; become; sig-
  nify; come sta? how
  are you?
starnazzare shake; beat
starnutare, tire sneeze;
  – mento, to *m* sneezing
statista *m* politician;
  minister; – tico political
statistica *f* statistics
stato *m* rank; quality
statua *f* statue; – ria
  statuary
statuire ordain; enact
statura *f* stature; posture
statuto *m* statute
staza *f* gauge; – re
  gauge; – tore *m* gauger

stazione *f* dwelling; railway station; **– nale, rio** stationary

stazzo *m* rag; **– nare** fumble [knife; cue

stecca *f* splinter; paper-

steccadente *m* tooth-pick

steccheggiare switch

stecco *m* thorn; straw; tooth-pick

stecconato *m* palisade; **– ne** *m* paling

stefano *m* paunch

stella *f* star; fate; **– lante, lato, lifera** scintallating

steniare decamp

stendere spread; display; **– dimento, sione** *m & f* extension; extent

stenebrare illuminate

stenografia *f* stenography; **– nografo** *m* stenographer

stentare want; labour; vex; **– stento** *m* toil; suffering; **a** – with dufficulty

stentoreo stentorian

stenuare extenuate ; emaciate; **– tivo** extenuating; **– ione** *f* extenuation

steppi, steppe *f* steppe

sterco *m* dung; excrement

stereoscopia *f* stereoscopy; **– po** *m* stereoscope

stereotipare stereotype

sterile sterile; **– lità** *f* sterility; **– lire** sterilize

sterlino *m* sterling

sterminare exterminate; desolate; **– nio, ione** *m & f* extermination; desolation

sternuto *m* sneezing; **– nutare** sneeze

sterpare, extirpate; – mento *m* extirpation

stidione *m* spit

stigare excite; instigate

stige *f* styx

stigma *m* mark; seal

stile *m* style; way

stilettare stab; **– ta** *f* stab; **– to** *m* stiletto

stilla *f* drop; tear; **– re** distil; drizzle; **– tore** *m* distiller; **– ione, leria** *f* distillation; distillery [brocation

stillicidio *m* (med.) em-

stima *f* esteem; regard; **– bile** estimable; –

stimolare stimulate; provoke; **– lante, lativo** stimulating

stinco *m* shin-bone

stinguere extinguish; kill

stipendiare hire; **– dio** *m* stipend [maker

stipettaio *m* cabinet-

stipite *m* stalk; stake

stipito *m* pier

stipula *f* thatch; stubble

stipulare stipulate; **– zione** *f* stipulation

stirare stretch; strain

stirpare extirpate

stirpe *f* stock [peevish

stitico costive; stingy;

stivalarsi put on one's boots; **– to** booted; **– le** *m* boot; fool

stivare heap up; stow

stizza *f* anger; wrath; **– zarsi** be angry; **– zire** provoke

stoccata *f* thrust; pass; **– cheggiare** thrust

stoccofisso *m* salt codfish

stoffa *f* stuff

stoffo *m* stock; quantity

232

stoggio m flattery
stogliere dissuade
stoico f stoic; stoical
stola f stole
stolidezza. dità f stupidity; foolishness
stoppia f stubble; stubble-field
stoppinare light with a candle; – **no** m wick; rush-light   [dislocate
storcere twist; untwist
stordire stun; astound
storia f history; story; – **rico** historical; historian; – **re** illustrate
storione m sturgeon
stormo m troop; storm
stornare turn aside; dissuade
stornello m starling
storpiare, stroppiare maim; cripple
stracaro very dear
stracca f weariness
straccaggine f disgust; languor   [harness
straccale m breeching;
straccare tire; vex; – **chezza** f weariness; anger
stracciafoglio m scraper
stracciare scrape; tear
straccicalare chat
straccuocere overdo; – **cotto** overdone   [fied
stracontento very satis-
strada f road; street;
strafalciare run; neglect
strafficare sell; make; dispatch
strafigurare disfigure
straforare bore; – **ro** m boring
strage f slaughter
stragrande gigantic
stralciare prune; finish

233

strale m arrow; disgrace
stralignare degenerate
stralunare look every way
stralunato squinting
s'.amazzare knock down; faint.
strambellare break; tear to pieces
strambo crooked; bandy
strame m bay or straw; litter; lair
strampalato extravagant; – **teria** f extravagance
stranare alienate; sell
strangolare strangle; suffocate; – **mento** m strangulation
strangosciare grieve
stranio strange; foreign
strano strange; rare
straordinarietà f strangeness; – **rio** extraordin-
straparlare slander   [ary
strapazzare despise; disdain
strapuntino m counterpoint; – **to** m bolster
straricchire become wealthy; – **ricco** wealthy
strar.are overflow; – **mento** m overflowing
strascicare nare draw along; – **strascico** m drawing along; train of a gown
strasciconi dragging
stratagemma m stratagem
strategia f strategy; – **gico** strategic
stravalicare pass beyond
stravasare extravasate
stravero most true
stravestire disguise; – **mento** m disguise
straviziare feast; banquet
stravolgere twist violently

straziare provoke; tear; squander; – io *m* injury; slaughter

stregua *f* share

stremare cut; diminish

stremo extreme

stremenzire debilitate; extenuate [need

stremità *f* extremity;

strenna *f* new year's gift

strenuità *f* courage; strenuousness; – nuo courageous; gallant

strepere, pitare re-ound

strepito *m* noise

stretta *f* squeezing; distress; defile; – tezza *f* straightnes ; – to narrow; squeezed; *m* strait

strettoia *f* bandage

stridere cry; scream; crackle; – dente, dulo noisy; sharp

strigare rid; disentangle

striglia *f* curry comb; – re curry

strignere confine; bind

strillare shriek; – lo *m* shrieking

strimpellare play badly (instrument); – mento, tura *m & f* discordance

stringa *f* tag; lace

strippare eat too much

striscia *f* scarf; serpent; – re crawl; glide

strofinaccio *m* duster; dish-cloth; – nare rub; – mento, nio *m* rubbing; friction

strologo *m* astrologer

strombazzare bettare proclaim; trumpet

stromento *m* instrument; deed

stroncare cut off

stronzare maim; retrench

stropicciare rub; scour

strozza *f* throat; windstrozzare throttle [pipe

strozziere *m* falconer

strozzule *m* throat; gullet

strumentare compose music; – tale instrumental]; – to *m* instrument [– pro *m* rape

strupare force; violate;

struttura *f* structure; disposition

struzione *f* destruction

struzzo, zolo *m* ostrich

stuccare plaster with stucco; sicken

stucchevolare annoy; disgust; – chevole tedious

studente student; – diare study; – dio *m* study; school-room; diligence;

stuolo *m* troop; crowd

stuonare be out of tune

stupefare stupefy; astonish; stupefarsi be astonished; – zione *f* stupefaction

stupendo admirable; splendid; – diamente splendidly

stupire be astonished; – mento *m* astonishment; – pore *m* stupor; amazement

stuprare rape; violate

sturare uncork

sturbare disturb; – bo *m* disturbance

su concerning; on; over; near; su e giù up and down; su! su! cheer up!

subalternare subalternate; – no subaltern

subastare auction; – zione *f* auction

subbia *f* chisel

subbietto, subbietto *m*
subject
subbissare overthrow;
destroy; **– so** *m* ruin;
wonder
subcutaneo subcutaneous
subdividere subdivide
subillare suborn
subiugare subjugate
subiuntivo *m* subjunctive
sublimare exalt
sublime sublime; **– mità**
f sublimity
subodorare smell; foresee
subordinare subordinate;

– zione *f* subordination;
– to subordinate
subornare bribe
succedere succeed; happen; **– dimento** *m* event;
success; **– tore, cessore**
m successor
successibile successible;
– sione *f* succession;
success; **– vo** succes-
sive; **– so** *m* success;
event
succhiare suck
succhiellare drill; bore
succhio *m* juice; sap
succiare suck
succiasangue *f* leech
succinto succinct; tucked
up; **– tamente** suc-
cinctly
sudacchiare perspire
sudare sweat; perspire
sudario *m* winding-sheet
suddetto *m* aforesaid;
above mentioned
suddiacono *m* sub-deacon
suddito *m* subject
suddividere subdivide;
– sione *f* subdivision

sudiceria *f* dirtiness;
– cio nasty; dirty
sudore *m* sweat; toil

sufficente, ciente sufficient; **– mente** suffi-
ciently; **– ficienza** *f*
sufficiency
suffragio *m* vote; suffrage
sufolare whistle; hiss
sufolo *m* whistle
sugare suck; blot;
– gente blotting
suggellare seal; print
suggere suck
suggerire suggest; **–**
mento, gestione *m* &
f suggestion; **– tore** *m*
prompter
suggestivo deceitful
suggettare subject; constrain   [tree
sughero *m* cork; cork-
sugna *f* grease; hog's
lard; **– gnoso** greasy;
fat
sugo *m* juice; sap
suo his; her; its; **suoi**
their
suocera *f* mother-in-law;
– ro *m* father-in-law
suola *f* sole; hoof
suolo *m* ground; hoof
suono *m* sound; song
suora *f* sister; nun
superare surpass; surmount; **– bile** conquer-
able
superbia *f* pride; haughtiness; **– bo** proud;
haughty
supercilio *m* eye-brow
superficiale superficial
superfluità *f* superfluity;
– fluo superfluous
superiorità *f* superiority;
– riore *a* & *n* superior;
– rmente masterly
superlativo superlative;
– vamente superlatively
supernale supernal; di-

vine; – **nalmente** supernaturally

suppedaneo m floor

suppellettile f pl furniture; chattels [deceive

supplantare supplant;

supplementario supplementary; – **plente** substitute; – **plire** supply; substitute; – **plemento, plimento** m supplement

supporre suppose; substitute; – **sizione** f supposition; – **posto** supposed; supposition

suppregare supplicate

supprimere suppress; conceal; – **pressione** suppression

supremazia f supremacy; – **mo** supreme; – **mamente** supremely

sur on; upon; over

surgere come out; begin

surretizio surreptitious

surto elevated; ready

suscettibile, tivo susceptible; – **lità** f susceptibility

suscitare revive; excite

susina f plum; – **no** m plum-tree [interruption

suspensione f suspension;

suspicace suspicious; – **care** suspect; doubt; – **pizione** f suspicion

sussecutivo, guente, quente subsequent; –. **guentemente** subsequently

sussiego m seriousness; gravity

sussistenza f subsistence; – **tere** subsist

sussulto m surprise; start

susta f pack-cord; spring

sustantivo m substantive

sustanza f substance; – **ziale** substantial

sustentazione f sustenance

sustituire substitute; – **zione** f substitution

svagolare wander

svaligiare strip; rob

svampare evaporate

svanire evaporate; disappear

svantaggio m disadvantage; detriment; – **gioso** disadvantage

svaporare vent; evapor-

svariare vary [ate

svecchiare renew; reform

sveglia f alarm clock; – **re** wake; – **si** awake; – **toio, glierino** m alarm clock

svelare discover; reveal

sveltezza f nimbleness; – **to** nimble; slim

svenare kill [unfortunate

svenevole disagreeable;

svenire faint; – **mento** m swoon; eclipse

sventare fan; air; winnow; fail

sventura f misfortune; – **to** unfortunate; miserable

svergogna f dishonour; insult; – **to** impudent

svernare winter

svignare scamper

svigorire dibilitate

svilire abase; undervalue

svillaneggiare insult; outrage [plain

sviluppare discover; ex-

svincolare untie

svisare scratch

svista f error; oversight

svitare unscrew

sviticchiare take away; snatch
svivagnato stupid
sviziare amend
svocicchiare discredit
svogliare disgust
svolare fly
svolazzare flutter; vault
svolere alter one's mind
svolgere unfold
svoltare tolare turn aside; dissuade; – ta f turn; bending; –tura f fold; plait
svolvere unfold; dissuade

T

tabacco m tobacco; caio, caro, chino m tobacconist; – care take snuff; – chiera f snuff-box; presa di – pinch of snuff
taballo m kettle-drum
tabano slanderous
tabarro m overcoat
tabe rottenness; – fatto, bido putrefied
tabella f rattle

taccia f notch; gap;
taccagneria f stinginess
taccato spotted; speckled
tacchino. m peacock
taccia f defect; stain; –re accuse; blame
tacco m clog
taccola f magpie; sport
taccolaia f prattle
taccolino m babbler
tacconare mend
taccuino m pocket-book; almanack
tacere hold one's tongue
tacito tacit; –tamente tacitly
taciturnità f taciturnity;

– no silent; taciturn
tafanario m bottom
tafano m horse-fly
tafferia f wooden board
tafferugia, tafferuglio m riot; tumult
taffettà f taffetas
taglia f killing; tax
tagliaborse m cut-purse
tagliamento m cut; slaughter
tagliando m paring
tagliapietra m stone-cutter [cheat
tagliare cut; tax; carve;
talché so that
talco m talc
tale such; like; un – such a one; – lmente so; so much [agreeable
talentare please; be
talento m talent; ability; mal – grudge
talismano m talisman
tallero m thaler (coin)
tallire seed
tallone m heel
talora, volta sometimes
talpa f mole
taluno some; any; somebody
tamanto so great
tamburello. retto rino m tambourine; kettle-drum; –rino m kettle-drummer; – ro m trunk; drum; – rone m big drum
tambussare beat; bang
Tamigi m (geog.) Thames
tampoco not even; neither
tana f hole; den; socket
tanaglia f pincers; –re torture
tantino very small; a little

tanto so; so much; so many; as many; non – notwithstanding; per – however; a – per – at this rate; – per uno so much apiece; so long

tantosto immediately

tappette m carpet; cover

tappezzare hang with tapestry; deck; – zeria f hangings; tapestry; – ziere m upholsterer

tara n defect; waste

tarabuso m bittern

tarantella f tarantella; tarantula

tarantello f & m overplus

tarantola f tarantula

tarare abate

tarchiato strong-limbed

tarlare rot; get worm-eaten; – to rotten

tarma f worm; wood-louse

taroccare grow angry

tarsia f marquetry; miser

tartagliare stammer; – mento m stammering; – glione m stammerer

tasca f purse; pocket; –chino m purse

tassa f tax; duty; –re rate; assess; – tivo taxable; –tore m assessor

tassellare restore; repair

tassello m cape (cloak)

tassetto m hand-anvil

tasso m yew; badger

tastare, teggiare touch; try; sound

tastiera f key-board

tattamella f chat; tittle-tattle; –re chat

tattica f tactics; – co m tactician

tatto m touch; feeling;

taverna f tavern; pot-house; –naio, niere m tavern-keeper; drunkard

tavola ·f table; index

tavolare board; floor

tavolata f tableful

tavolato m wood-partition; floor; shed

tavoletta m small table

tavoliere m chess-board; card-table

tavolozza f pallet

tazza f cup; cupful

te thee

te m tea

teatro m theatre

technico technical; –nologia f technology; – gico technological

teco with thee

teda f wild fir; larch-tree

tedio m tediousness; disgust; – diare annoy; disgust; – so tedious; disgusting

tegame m earthen saucepan

tegghia pie-dish; linendrier

tegnente tenacious; sticky; – za f tenacity; stickiness [tile-maker

tegola f tile; – laio m

teismo m theism

tela f linen; picture; snare; – io m loom; painter's frame; – laiuolo m weaver; – leria f linen drapery

telegrafia f telegraphy; – fo m telegraph; – gramma m telegram

telescopio m telescope

teletta f fine linen

tema m theme; subject;

f fear; alarm

tempera *f* hardening; (paint) distemper; disposition; **a –** in watercolours

temperamento *m* temperament

temperante temperate; **– ranza** *f* temperance

temperare harden; agree; moderate; **– tivo** *a* sedative; **–** to temperate

temperatoio, rino *m* penknife [ture; hardening

temperatura *f* temperatemperie** *f* temper

tempesta *f* tempest; **– tare** be stormy; storm; trouble; **– toso** stormy; tempestuous

tempestivo seasonable

tempia *f* temple (of the head)

tempio *m* temple; church

tempissimo (per) very early

tendenza *f* tendency; **– dere** stretch; set (snares); tend; aim at

tendetta, dina *f* small tent; awning

tendine, done *m* tendon

tenebrare be dark; darken; **– bre** *f pl* darkness; **– broso** dark; gloomy

tenente lieutenant

tenere *m* handle; power

tenere hold; keep

tenerezza *f* tenderness

tenero tender

tenta *f* probe; try; **– tivo** *m* attempt; trial experiment

tentare try; urge; probe; **– zione** *f* temptation

tentellare resound

tentennare *,* vacillate

tenue tenuous; thin; **– amente** thinly; **– ità** *f* tenuity

tenuta *f* possession

tenuto kept; reputed

tenzonare fight; contest; **– ne, zione** *f* contest

teologale divine

teologia *f* theology; **– gico** theological; **– ologo** *m* theologian

teorema *m* theorem

teoria *f* theory

tepefare, pificare warm

tepido lukewarm; tepid

terapeutico therapeutic

terchio rough; coarse

tergemino triple

tergere cleanse; purge

teriaca *f* treacle

termale thermal

terme *f pl* hot baths

terminare terminate; **– zione** *m & f* termination; **– ne** *m* end; limit; term

termometro thermometer

terno *m* terne

terra *f* earth; land; ground; **– racqueo** terraqueous; **– ferma** *f* firm land; continent

terreno worldly; *m* ground; land; **pian –** ground floor

terretta *f* borough; village

terribile terrible

terriccio *m* mould

terriere *m* citizen

terrigno of the earth

territorio *m* territory; terse; **– riale** territorial

terrore *m* terror; **– rismo** *m* terrorism; **– rista** *m* terrorist

tersezza *f* neatness

terzo third; **– zo, zeria**

m & f third part
terzuolo sparrow-hawk
tesa *f* brim of a hat
teschio *m* skull
tesi *f* thesis
teso bent
tesoro *m* treasure; –
reria *f* treasury; – **riere**
m treasurer
tessera *f* sign; token
tessere weave
testa *f* head; chief; –
tardo, tereccio head-
strong
testare make one's will;
– **mento** will; testa-
ment; – **tore** *m* testator
teste *m* witness; – **tificare**
bear witness
testè lately; just now
testicolo *m* testicle
testuggine *m* tortoise;
turtle; vaul   [dark
tetricità *f* darkness; – **tro**
tetta *f* teat; – **te** suck
tetto *f* roof; house;
– **toia** *f* pent-house
ti thee
tiara *f* tiara; mitre
tibia *m* shin-bone
ticchio *m* whim
tiepidare grow lukewarm;
– **do** tepid; timid
tifo *m* typhus
tifolo *m* cry; squeak
tifone *m* typhoon
tiglio *m* filament; lime-
tree
tigna *f* scurf; scab;
– **gnoso** scurvy
tignamica *f* avarice
tignere dye
tignone *m* back-hair
timone *m* pole; helm;
– **niere** *m* helmsman
timore *m* fear; alarm;

– **rato, soro** timorous;
fearful
timpanista *m* kettle-
drummer
timpano *m* tympanum
tino *m* tub; tun; vat;
– **nozza** *f* basin
tinta *f* dying; tint
tintillo, tinnio *m* jingling
tintinnare ring; tinkle
tinto *m* tint; shade
tintore *m* dyer
tipo *m* type; model;
– **pico** typical
tipografia *f* typography;
– **fico** typographical;
– **fo** *m* printer
tira *f* debate; dispute
tiralinea *m* ruler
tiranno *m* tyrant
tiraneggiare tyrannize
over; – **nesco, nico** *a*
tyrannical; – **nia, nide**
f tyranny
tirante *m* boot-strap
tirare draw; attract;
extend; shoot; – **si**
escape
tirone *m* apprentice;
novice   [consumptive
tisichezza *f* phthis; – **co**
titano *m* titan; – **nico**
titillare titillate   [titanic
titolo *m* title; pretext;
– **lare** titular; entitle;
– **to** entitled
titubare waver; stagger
tizzo, tizzone *m* brand;
firebrand
to' oh!   [brocade
tocca *f* gold or silver
toccare touch; move;
– **ta** *m* feeling; prelude
tocca a me it is my turn
toeletta *f* toilet; dressing
toga *f* toga   [table
togliere take; take away

240

tolda *f* deck   [table
toletta *f* toilet; dressing
tollerare tolerate; – bile
  tolerable; – ranza *f*
  toleration
tolletta *f* theft
tolta *f* theft
tolto taken
tonare thunder; roar
tondare round; make
  round; – tura *f* pruning;
  shavings
tondeggiare be round
tondere shear (sheep
  etc.); – duto shorn;
  – ditura *f* shearing;
  parings
tondezza *f* roundness;
  rotundity; – do round;
  simple; – do, dino *m*
  sphere; plate; saucer

tonello *m* cask
tonfo *m* fall; noise of a
  fall; – lare fall; make
  a noise in falling
tonica *f* tunic; refuge
tonico tonic
tonnara tunny-net
tonneggiare tow; – gio
  m tow; towing
topografia *f* topography;
  – fico topographical; –
  fo *m* topographer
toppa *f* lock; door-lock
toppè *m* toupee
toppo *m* stump; stock
torace *m* thorax
torba *f* turf
torba, torbida *f* muddy
  water; – bidare trouble;
  make muddy; – bido
  thick; troubled
torcere twist; turn

torchio *m* press

torcia *f* torch; taper

torcigliare wrap up
torcimanno *m* interpreter

torcolare press; – liere
  m pressman
tordo *m* thrush
tormentare torment; in-
  fest; – to *m* torment;
  grief; – tore *m* tor-
  menter
tornaletto *m* basement'
tornare come back;
  remember; mend
tornasole *m* sunflower
torneo *m* tournament;
  compass; – nitore *m*
  turner; – nio *m* turning-
  wheel   [big; strong
toro *m* bull; bed; – so
torpedine *f* torpedo;'
  laziness
torpere grow torpid;
  – pido torpid
torpiglia *f* torpedo

torta *f* tart; twisting;
  – telleta, lina *f* small
  tart; – tello *m* pancake
tortola, ra *f* dove
tortore *m* tormenter
tortuosità *f* tortuosity;
  – so tortuous
torvità *f* haughtiness;
  – vo haughty
torzione *f* extortion
torzone *m* lay friar
tosa *f* young girl; lass
tosare shear; shave;
tosco *m* poison   [prune
tosone *m* golden fleece
  (order of); fleece
tossa, tosse *f* cough;
  – simento *m* coughing;
  – sire cough
tossicare poison; – co *m*
  poison; venom
tosto quick; saucy;
  – tamente quickly; soon
totale total; whole;
  – lizzare sum up
tovaglia *f* table-cloth

tovaglietta, gliuola, gliolo *f & m* napkin; towel

tozzetto *m* small bît

tozzo short; big; heavy; bit; piece

tozzolare beg

tra between; with

trabacca *f* hut; stall; tent

trabaccolo *m* ship

trabalderia *f* theft

traballare stagger; vacillate; – lio *m* swing

trabocchello, chetto *m* snare; deceit

tracannare sip; drink hard; – tore *m* drunkard

tracheggiare defer

traccia *f* track; treaty; – mento *m* plotting; – ciare trace; track

trachea *f* wind-pipe

trachiare most clear

tracocente very hot

tracollare be sleepy; tumble; nod

traconfortare console

tracotaggine, tanza *f* arrogance; –te arrogant

tradigione, mento *f & m* treason; – re betray; – tore, trice *m & f* traitor; traitress

tradimenticato forgotten

tradizione *f* tradition

tradurre translate; extend; – dotto translated; – ducibile translatable; – citore, duttore *m* translator; – zione *f* translation

trafitta, tura *f* wound; puncture

trafoglio *m* trefoil

traforare pierce

traforeria *f* deceit; trick

traforo *m* point-lace; hole [with

trafugare rob; run away

tragrande huge

traguardare level; foresee; – do *m* level

trainare pull; haul; – no *m* cart-load; train; sledge

tralasciare cease; omit

tralazione *f* translation; transport

tralignare degenerate; decay; – mento *m* adulteration; degeneration

tralineare get out of line

tralucere be transparent; shine; – cente transparent; shiny

trama *m* plot; woof; weft; – re conspire

tramaglio *m* drag-net

tramandare transmit

tramazzare overthrow; – zo *m* riot

trambasciare grieve

tramessa, messione *f* interposition; mediation

tramesso *m* side-dish

tramestare revolve; mingle [transmit

tramettere interpose;

tramezza *f* partition; lane

tramezzare interpose; insert; – mento *m* interposition; mediation; – tore *m* mediator

tramischianza *f* shuffle

tramite *m* path; way

tramoggia *f* hopper; feeder (machine)

tramontana *f* north-wind

tramontare set (sun, etc); go down; – to *m* set

tramortire faint; swoon

trampoli *m pl* stilts

tramutare transmute; transplant; – zione *f*

transmutation; change
trana cheer up! all right
tranare draw; struggle
tranellare deceive; cheat;
– leria, lo *f* & *m* deceit;
snare

transatare transact; –
satto, sazione *m* & *f*
transaction; comprom-
ise   [lantic
transatlantico transat-
transfiguramento, zione
m & *f* transfiguration

transfondere decant;
carry   [expire
transire pass; fade;
transitivo, torio transi-
ive; transitory; –to
m transit; death
transizione *f* transition
translucido pellucid
transuntare extract; –
zione *f* extract
transustanziare transub-
stantiate; – sione *f*
transubstantiation

trapanare trepan; – toio,
no *m* trepan; – zione *f*
trasalire, saltare jump
trasamare love fondly
trasandare pass beyond;
slight
trasattarsi apply; fit
trascegliere choose; –
glimento *m* choice
trascendentale, dente
transcendent; –dere sur-
pass; excel
trascinare draw
  trepaning
trapassare pass beyond;
cross over; transgress
trapelare distil; filter
trapensare mediate
trapprendere undertake;
trapuntare stitch; quilt;
– to stitched; stitch

traricchire grow wealthy
trarre draw; pull; reap
trarupare precipitate
trascolare distil
trascolorare change colour
trascorrere pass quickly;
escape; omit; repeat;
– rente, revole transitory
trascorsivo cursory
trascorso *m* error; oversight   [copy
trascrivere transcribe;
trascurare neglect; aban-
don; – raggine, ranza,
ratezza *f* negligence
trasecolare te astonished;
astonish
trasferire transfer; con-
vey; – si go; repair;
–ribile transferable
trasfigurare transfigure;
te transfigured; – zione
f transfiguration
trasfondere transfuse;
communicate; –fusione
f transfusion
trasformare transform;
– zione *f* transformation
trasgredire · transgress;
trespass; – dimento,
gressione *m* & *f* trans-
gression; – ditore *m*
transgressor
trasmettere transmit; –
missione *f* transmission
trasmigrare transmigrate
– zione *f* transmigration
trasmutare transmute;
transform; – mento,
zione *m* & *f* transmutation

trasordinario extraordin-
ary; –riamente extra-
ordinarily   [excess
trasordine *m* disorder;
traspallarsi rush upon
trasparenza *f* transpar-

ency; – **rire** get transparent   [transfer
traspiantare transplant;
traspirare perspire;
zione *f* perspiration
trasporre transfer
trasportare transport;
– **to** *m* transport; carriage   [treat
trassinare touch; ill-
trasvolare fly swiftly; rise
trasvolgere overturn
tratta *f* pull; space; throw; draft
trattatore *m* negotiator; interpreter
trattenere entertain; amuse; – **nimento** *m* amusement
tratto shot; pull; stroke; space; trot; **ad un** at once; **ad ogni** – every moment; **di primo** – at first; **tratto tratto** from time to time
trattoso kind; tractable
trattura *f* pulling
travagliare work; afflict; – **glio** trouble; labour
travalente most skilful
travasare decant; transfuse
trave *f* beam; high tree
travecchiezza *f* ancient
traversino *m* bolster
traverso oblique; **a** – across; through
travestire disguise; – **mento** *m* disguise
traviare mislead
travisare deceive; disguise; –**so** *m* mask;
travolare fly beyond
travolgere, volgere overturn

trazione *f* attraction
tre three
trebbia *f* flail; – **re** thrash (corn); – **mento, tura** *m & f* thrashing of (corn)
trecca. treccola *f* hawker; – **cheria** *f* greengrocer
treccia *f* tress; curl
trecciera *f* knot of ribands
treccolare chat
treccone *m* retailer; fruiterer; huckster
trecento three hundred; –**tesimo** three hundredth
tredici thirteen; –**cesimo** thirteenth

tremare shiver; tremble; – **mante, mebondo** timorous; – **rella** *m* panic
trementina *f* turpentine
tremola *f* torpedo (fish)
tremolare shiver; tremble; – **lio** *m* shivering; – **lante lo** tremulous; shivering
tremula *f* aspen
tremuoto *m* earthquake
treno *m* train; sledge; – **diretto** fast train
trenta thirty; – **tesimo** thirtieth
trepidare tremble; fear; – **dazione** *f* trepidation
treppiede *m* trivet
tresca *f* brawl; scrape
trespolo *m* trestle; prop
triaca *f* treacle
triangolo *m* triangle; – **lare** triangular
tribbiare smash; grind
tricolore tricoloured
tricorno with three horns
tricuspide *m* with three
tridente *m* trident [points
trifoglio *m* trefoil
triforcato. cuto with

triforme with three forms

trigesimo thirteenth

trigono *m* triangle; – **metria** *f* trigonometry

trilatero trilateral

trillare hum; trill

trillione *m* trillion

trilogia *f* trilogy

trilustre fifteen years old

trimestre *m* quarter; –**trale** quarterly

trina *f* fringe; lace

trincare tipple

trincea, ciera *f* trench; entrenchment

trincerare entrench; – **mento** *m* entrenchment

trinciare carve; cut up

trincone *m* drunkard

triplicare triplicate; – **ce plo** triple; treble

tripode *m* tripod

tripudiare dance; – **tore** *m* dancer; reveller

triregno *m* tiara

trisavolo *m* great great grand-father

tristanzuolo thin

tristarsi be sad; grieve

tristezza, tristizia *f* sadness; melancholy

tristo sad; wicked

tritare, tolare, turare grind; examine

tritatoio, tritapalgie chaff-cutter

tritello *m* coarse flour

tritico *m* corn

tritone *m* triton

triumviro *m* triumvir; – **rato** *m* triumvirate

trivella *f* probe; borer – **re** bore: bruise;

trombone *m* trombone; trombone-player

troncare cut off, mutilate; – **co** *m* trunk;

bust; – **cone** *m* stump; large trunk   [tedly

troncatamente interrup-

trono *m* throne; thunder

tropico *m* tropic; – **cale** tropical

troppo too much excess; much

trota *f* trout

trottare trot; go quick; –**tore** *m* trotter; –**to** *m* trot

trottola *f* top

trovare find; observe; – **tore** *m* inventor; minstrel; –**trovato** found; invention; discovery

trovatello *m* foundling

truce ferocious

trucidare massacre; – **tore** *m* murderer

truffa, feria *f* lie; deceit

truffare cheat; dupe; – **tore** *m* deceiver; cheat

trullare fart; – **lo** *m* fart

truogo, truogolo *m* trough

truppa *f* troop

tu thou

tuba *f* trumpet; horn

tubare coo; – **bante** cooing

tubercolo *m* tubercle; – **loso** tuberculous

tubero *m* truffle; medlar-tree

tubo *m* tube; pipe; socket; –**bulare** tubular

tuffare dip; plunge; – **tore** *m* diver; – **fo, folo** *m* immersion

tuffete suddenly

tugurio *m* hut; cottage

tulipano *m* tulip

tumefare tumefy; – **more** *m* tumour

tumulo *m* tumulus; tomb

tumulto *m* tumult; up-

roar; – **tuante, tuoso** tumultuous
tunica *f* tunic
tuo, tua thy; il – thine own; i **tuoi** thy family
turba *f* crowd; mob
turbante *m* turban
turbare trouble; disturb; –**si** get angry; darken; – **mento** trouble; dis-
turbina *f* turbine [order
turbinarsi whirl round
turbine, turbino, bo *m* whirlwind; storm; – **noso** stormy
turbo thick; disturbed
turchino blue; dark blue; – **niccio** bluish
turcimanno *m* interpreter
turco *m* Turk
turfa *f* crowd
turgenza, gidezza *f* swelling; – **gere** swell; – **gido** swollen; bombastic
turibolo *m* censer
turma *f* troop; crowd
turno *m* turning-wheel; turn
turpe base; indecent; – **mente** shamefully; – **pezza, pitudine** *f* vileness: shame
tutore, trice *m & f* guar-
tuttafiata, via, volta however; as often as; nevertheless; always
tutto, ta all; every; whole; **tutto tutto** entirely
tuttochè almost; though
tuttodi always
tuttora still; always

U

ubbia *f* bad omen; – **bioso** superstitious
ubbidire obey; – **diente** obedient; – **dienza** *f* obedience; submission
ubbriacare, ubriacare fuddle; – **co** drunk; tipsy; – **chezza** *f* intoxication [fertile
uberifero full-breasted;
ubero *m* breast; teat
ubertà *f* plenty; – **toso** plentiful
ubicazione *f* situation
ucchiello *m* button-hole
uccidere kill; cut off; – **sione** *f* murder; – **cisore** *m* murderer
udire hear; listen to; – **bile** audible; –**dienza** *f* audience; – **zione** *f* hearing; – **tore** *m* auditor
ufficiale *m* official; officer
ufo (a) at other people's expense
uggia *f* shade; omen; avere in – to hate; essere in – be hated
uggiolare howl
ugnere anoint; – **gnimento** *m* anointing
ugnome *m* claw
ugola *f* uvula
uguagliare equal; match; –**glianza, lità** *f* equality; – **le** equal; –**lmente** *ad* equality
ulcera *m* ulcer; – **re** ulcerate; – **mento, zione**
ultimare finish; – **mato**

finished; ultimatum;
– **zione** *f* conclusion;
– **mo** last; –**mente** at last
ululare howl; – **lato, lulo**
m howling
umanarsi take human
flesh; – **nità** *f* humanity;
– **no** human
umbè therefore
umbelico. bilico *m* navel
umettare wet; moisten
umidezza, dità *f* mois-
ture; – **dire** moisten
umido. detto moist; damp
umile humble; – **liare**
humble; quiet; – **zione**
humiliation; – **mil-
mente** humbly; – **miltà**
f humility
umore *m* humour; mois-
ture; – **rista** *m* humorist
unicità *f* particularity;
– **co** only; sole
unicorno *m* unicorn; –
nuto one-horned
unificare unify
uniformare conform; –
me uniform; – **mità**
f uniformity
unigenito *m* only son
unire unite; – **nione** *f*
union
unisonanza *f* concordance
unisono *m* unison; con-
unissimo only [cord
unità *f* unity; – **to**
united; –**tamente** jointly
universale universal;
–**lizzare** generalize; –
sità *f* university; gen-
erality; – **so** *m* universal;
universe
uno, na one
unqua, quanco. quema'
never
uomo *m* man; husband
(*pl* **uomini**)
uopo *m* usefulness; need

uracano, gano *m* hurricane
urano *m* Uranus
urbanità *f* urbanity; – **no**
polite
urente burning
uretra *f* urethra
urgente urgent; – **za** *f*
urgency; – **gere** urge
urlare howl; –**mento, lio
lo** *m* howling
urna *f* urn
urta (aver in) *f* hate
urtare knock; hit
usare use; frequent; –
sanza *f* use; habit;
– **to, sitato** usual; habi-
tual; – **uso** usual; use
usciere *m* porter; usher;
– **scio** *m* door
uscire go out
uscita *f* way out
usuale usual; – **lità** *f*
habit; – **lmente** usually
usura *f* usury; – **raio,
riere** *m* usurer; – **reggiare** practise usury
usurpare usurp; –**mento,
zione** *m* usurpation;
– **tore** *m* usurper
utensile *m* utensil
utero *m* uterus; womb
utile useful; profitable;
m advantage; – **lità** *f*
utility; profit; –**littare,
lizzare** utilize
utre *m* leather-bottle
uva *f* grapes; – **spina** *f*
gooseberry; – **secca**
raisin

V

vacante vacant [tion
vacanza *f* vacancy; vaca-
vacca *f* cow; – **ro** *m* cow-
herd;
vaccina *f* cow-pox; – **re**

vaccinate; – **tore** *m*
vaccinator; – **zione** *f*
vaccination
vacillare vacillate; –
mento, zione *m & f*
vacillation
vacuare evacuate; –
zione *f* evacuation;
vacuità *f* vacuity; – **cuo**
vado *m* ford. [vacuous
vagabondare wander; –**do**
vagabond; vagrant
vagamente gracefully
vagare ramble
vagheggiare court; – **tore**
m sweet-heart
vaglia *f* merit; courage
vagliare sift; despise;
– **tore** *m* sifter; lover
vago vague
vagolare wander

valere *m* value; courage;
be worth; –**za, zia** *f*
courage; virtue

valeriana *f* valerian
valetudine *f* health
valicare ford
validare ratify; confirm;
– **dità** *f* validity; – **do**
valid; strong
valigia *f* portmanteau;
valise
vallare surround; fortify
vallata, le, lea *f* valley;
trench; dale; – **letto** *m*
dale; – **lo** *m* valley;
– **ligiano** *m* inhabitant
of a valley

valorare confirm; fortify;
– **re** *m* courage; price;
– **roso** valorous
valuta *f* value; price;
– **re** appraise
valva *f* shell   [waltzer
valzare waltz; – **zer** *m*

vampa *f* flame; ardour
vampiro *m* vampire
vanagloria *f* vainglory;
– **riarsi** boast; – **so**
vainglorious
vanare dream; rave
vandalismo vandalism
vaneggiare rave; – **mento,**
gio *m* raving; furor;
vanezza *f* vanity; inanity
vanga *f* spade; mattock;
– **re** dig; – **ta** *f* spade-
ful; – **tore** *m* digger;
vaniglia *f* vanilla
vanire vanish; disappear
vanità *f* vanity; – **toso**
vainglorious; – **no** vain
vanni *m pl* wings
vantaggiare favour; – **gio**
m advantage; fortune;
– **gioso** advantageous;
– **samente** advantage-
ously
vantare praise; extol;
– **si** boast; – **to** celebrated; – **tore** *m* braggart
vaporarsi steam; – **zione**
f evaporation
vapore *m* vapour; steam;
– **vole** volatile; – **riera**
f steam-boat; steamer;
– **rosità** *f* vapour
varare launch (ship);
board
variabile variable; – **lità**
f variableness
variare, rieggare vary;
differ; – **mento, rietà**
m & f variety; change;
– **riante** variable; –
riazione *f* variation

vascolare, loso vascular
vascolo *m* small vase
vaso *m* vase; – **sellame** *m*

dishes and plates; plates
vasello *m* vase; ship
vaso *m* vase; vein;
vessel; – **da fiori** flower-
pot
vasto vast; immense
vate *m* poet
Vaticano *m* Vatican
ve you; there
vecchia *f* old woman;
– **chiaia, chiezza** *f* old
age; – **chiardo, da** *m*
& *f* old man, woman
vece *f* time; place; **in** –
instead   [derstand
vedere see; know; un-
vedetta *f* sentry
vedova *f* widow; – **vanza**
f widowhood; – **vo**
lonely; *m* widower
veemente vehement; –**za**
f vehemence
vegetare vegetate; –
zione *f* vegetation
vegghia vigil; evening –
party; – **ghiare** wake;
watch
veggia *f* cask; vessel
veglia *f* sentry; evening-
party; – **re** watch
vegliardo *m* old man
vegnente future; next
veicolo *m* vehicle
vela *f* sail; boat
velare veil; – **si** take the
veil; –**me, mento** *m*
veil; –**tamente** secretly

veleggiare set sail; sail;
– **mento; leggio** *m* sail-
ing; –**tore** *m* sailor
velenare poison; – **noso**
poisonous; – **no** poison
veleno *m* poison; venom
veleria *f* sails
veletta *f* sentry; top-
man; –**tare** stand sentry
veliere pull out; separate

vellicare prick; stimulate
vello *m* fleece; wool;
– **so** hairy; woolly
velluto *m* velvet; – **tato**
like velvet
velo *m* veil; crape; skin
veloce swift; quick;
– **mente** swiftly; – **cità**
f velocity; swiftness;
vendere sell
vendita *f* sale; – **tore** *m*
seller; vender; – **all'asta**
sale by action; **acon-
tanti** ready money sale
vendetta *f* revenge

vendicare avenge; vindicate; –**tivo** vindic-
tive; – **tore** *m* avenger
venerare venerate; – **bile**
venerable; –**.ranza, zi-
one** *f* veneration
Venere *v* Venus; – **reo**
venereal   [– **le** venial
venia *f* pardon; mercy;
venire come; arrive;
venti twenty; – **tesimo,
– simo** twentieth
ventiera *f* ventilator
ventilare ventilate; examine; – **zione** *f* ventila-
tion   [– **ticello** *m* breeze
vento *m* wind; vanity
ventola *f* fan; eyeshade
ventolare fan; winnow
ventosa *f* cupping-glass;
– **re** cup
ventoso windy
ventraia *f* belly; tripe
ventrata *f* litter
ventre *m* stomach; bosom

ventuno twenty-one
ventura *f* luck; chance;
– **riere** *m* adventurer
venturo future; – **to**
lucky
venustà *f* beauty
venuta *f* arrival; **ben** –

vepre *f* briar [welcome
ver towards; against
verbo *m* word; verb;
– a – word for word;
– so verbose
verdastro, dognolo greenish; – de green; young
verdeggiare be verdant;
– detto greenish; verdict
verdetto greenish; sourish; verdict
verdume, ra *m* & *f*
verdure; greenness
verecondia *f* bashfulness;
decency; – do modest
verga *f* rod; want;
stripe; – to striped
vergella *f* rod; switch
vergheggiare flog; switch
vergine, netta *f* virgin;
maid; Virgin Mary;
– nale, neo virginal;
– nità *f* virginity
vergolare put commas
veridicità *f* veracity
verificare verify; prove;
– zione *f* verification;
– tore *m* examiner
veriloquio *m* report;
relation
verisimiglianza *f* likelihood; – milmente likely
vermigliare paint vermilion; – glio scarlet
vernaccio *m* hard winter
vernacolo vernacular
vernale vernal
vernare winter; be very
cold; winter; – nereccio
wintery; – no *m* winter
vernicare, ciare varnish;
– ce varnish
vero true; certain
versare pour; pay; overthrow [*f* versatility
versatile versatile; – lità

versato poured out;
skilled
versatore *m* versifier;
– setto *m* small verse
versione *f* version
versipelle astute; crafty
verso *m* verse; air;
way; towards; concerning
versorio *m* compass
versuto astute; cunning
vertebra *f* vertebra
vertente (anno) the present year
vertenza *f* controversy
verticale vertical
vertice *m* top; zenith
vertigine *f* vertigo; –
noso giddy
veruno none; no; nobody
verzicola *f* flux
versiere *m* orchard;
kitchen-garden
verzotto *m* cabbage
vescia *f* puff-ball; chatter
vesciaia *f* chatter-box
vescica *f* bladder; blister
vesta, te *f* coat; robe;
– tiario *m* vestry
vestale *f* vestal
vestibolo, bulo *m* vestibule; porch
vestigio *m* step; trace
vestimento *m* garment;
– re clothe; dress
veterano *m* veteran
veterinaria *f* veterinary
art; –rio veterinary
vetero old
veto *m* veto
vetraia, trata *f* glasshouse; glass-window;
– traio *m* glazier
vetrice *f* osier; – ciaio
m osier-bed
vetrina *f* show-window

vetriolo, triuolo *m* vitriol
vetro *m* glass; — so
glassy; vitreous
vetta *f* top; ridge
vette *f* lever
vettina *f* pipe; duct;
canal
vettone *m* shoot; sprig
vettovaglia *f & m* vic-
tuals; — re victual
vettura *f* car, carriage;
freight — le *m* carrier;
— reggiare carry; —rino
m carrier; cabman
vetustà *f* age; —to old;
ancient

vezzeggiare flatter; caress
vezzo *m* amusement;
sport; caress; — so
charming
vi there; you
via *f* way; road; street;
away
viadotto *m* viaduct
viaggiare travel; journey;
— giatore viandante *m*
traveller; —gio *m* travel;
journey
viale *m* avenue

vicenda *f* return; event;
vicissitude; a — reci-
procally; — devole reci-
procal; mutual; — lezza
f vicissitude
vicenome *m* pronoun
viceprefetto *m* vice-prefect
vicinanza, nità *f* neigh-
bourhood
vicinato *m* vicinity
vicino neighbouring;
neighbour; near
vicissitudine *f* vicissitude
vico, lo *m* lane
vidente *m* seer; prophet
vidimare authenticate
vie much; by far
viera *f* ferrule

vietare forbid; — tivo *a*
vieto old [prohibitive
vievia directly

vigere subsist; last
vigesimo twentieth
vigilante, te vigilant;
— lanza *f* vigilance;
— lare watch
vigilia *f* vigil; eye

vigliacco cowardly; vile
vigliare choose; elect
viglietto *m* note; billet
vigna *f* vine; vineyard;
— gnazzo, gneto *m* vine-
yard
vignetta *f* headpiece
vigore ria *m & f* vigour;
strength; — rare streng-
then; —so vigorous
villania *f* injury; filth;
roughness; —no peasant;
rough [try
villareccio lereccio coun-
villata *f* borough
villeggiare enjoy one's
self in the country;
— tura *f* country life
villese, lico *m* farmer;
peasant
villoso hairy; woolly
viltà *f* vileness; — lume
m trifles
vincastro *m* rod; switch
vincere conquer; — cente
victorious; —ta *f* vic-
tory; conquest; — citore
m conqueror
vincido soft; flabby
vinciglio *m* band; tie
vincolare chain; bind by
contract; —lo *m* band;
tie
vinello *m* small wine
vino *m* wine; — lento
intoxicated; — lenza *f*
intoxication
vinto vanquished

viola *f* violet; viol
violare violate; – **zione** *f* violation
violentare force: constrain; -**tore** *m* transgressor
violente, to violent; impetuous; – **mente** violently; –**za** *f* violence
violetta *f* violet
violino *m* fiddle; violin;
virgineo virginal; –**nità** *f* virginity; maidenhead
virgola *f* comma; – **re** put commas [shoot
virile virile; – **lità** *f* virility; – **lmente** manly – **ro** *m* adult; man
virtù, de, te *f* virtue; power [virtually
virtuale virtual; –**lmente**
virtuoso virtuous; able; *m* virtuoso [*f* virulence
virulento virulent; – **za**
visaggio *m* visage; face
viscera *f* viscera; bowels
visciola *f* morello (black cherry)
visconte *m* viscount; – **tessa** *f* viscountess
visibile visible; – **lità** *f* visibility; – **lmente** visibly
visiera *f* vizor; mask
vivace lively; sprightly; – **cità** *f* liveliness
vivagno *m* shore
vivaio *m* fishbond; nursery
vivanda *f* food; victuals
vivandiera, re *f & m* sutler; caterer
vivere live; – **vente** living
vivezza *f* vivacity; – **vido** vivacious
viviparo viviparous

vivo living; lively
vivuolo *m* clove-tree
vivuto lived
viziare vitiate: – **mento** *m* adulteration
vizzo flabby; withered
vocabolario *m* vocabulary – **lo** *m* word; term
vocale vocal; oral; *m* vowel
vocalizzare vocalize
vocalmente vocally
vocare call; name; – **zione** *f* vocation
voce *f* voice; word; vote; **a viva** – by word of mouth; **sotto** – in a low voice
vogare row; – **tore** *m* rower
voglia *f* will; desire; – **glievole, so** desirous
voi you
volare fly; – **bile. lante** flying; –**ta** *f* flight
volatile volatile
volcano *m* volcano
.voleggiare flutter
volere will; consent; – **lente** willing; – **lentieri** willingly
volgare vulgar; common; – **rizzare** vulgarize; – **rità** *f* vulgarity; –
volontà *f* will; wish; – **rio** voluntary; –**riamente terosamente** voluntarily; –**tieri** willingly
volpe *f* fox; – **paia** *f* fox's hole; –**peggiare** be astute; –**picino** *m* fox's cub; – **pone** *m* cunning (old) fox
volta *f* vault; turning; time; **alla** – towards; **alcune volte, alle volte**

voltaica (pila) voltaic pile
voltare turn; change
volteggiare flutter; fly about; –tore m tumbler; sharp-shooter
volto, ta turned; m vault; face
voltoio m cup
voltolare turn; rove; roll
volubile voluble; –lità f volubility
volume m volume; book; mass; –noso voluminous
voluttà f delight; voluptuousness; –tuoso voluptuous: sensual
vomere mire vomit
vorare devour
vortice m whirlpool; vortex; – coso giddy
vosco with you
vostro your; yours
votaborse expensive

votacesso m night-man
votare empty; cleanse; vote; dedicate; –tezza f vacuum; emptiness
votivo m votive
voto empty; inane; m vow; suffrage
vulcano m volcano; – nico volcanic
vulnerare wound; hurt; – rio vulnerary; – to wounded
vulturno m north-east
vulva f womb; uterus
vuotare empty; – to empty; vacancy

W X Y

The W, X and Y letters do not exist in the Italian language

The letter S is used for X, and the letter I for Y.

Z

zambracca f prostitute; – re prostitute one's self
zampa f paw; talon; –re claw; –ta f scratch
zampettare begin to walk
zampetto m sausage
zampillare spout out
zampilletto m drunkard; feeding-bottle
zampillo m purveyor; water-spout
zampogna f blow-pipe
zana f basket; cradle; cheat; –iuolo m basket-maker; –ta f basketful
zanca f leg; claw; –to
zanco left-handed [coiled
zanna f tusk; fang; – re smooth
zappa f sap; mattock; spade; –re sap; dig; hoe; –tore m sapper; – ne m mattock; pick-axe
zara f risk; danger;
zecca f mint; –re stamp coin
zecchino m sequin
zeffiro, zefiro m zephyr
zelo m zeal; ardour; – lante, loso zealous; – tore m zealot
zenit m zenith
zenzero m ginger
zeppa f cradle; wedge
zeppare fill up
zerbineria f conceit; – no. notto m fop; dandy
zero m zero; cypher;

253

zibibbo *m* raisin
zigrino *m* shagreen
zis zag *m* zigzag
zimbellare call birds;
– mento. tura *m* & *f*
bird-call; – tore *m* bird-
caller; – lo *m* decoy-
bird; lure
zimino *m* fish; sauce
zinale *m* apron
zinco *m* zinc
zingano, ro *m* gipsy
zinna *f* nipple; breast
zinnale *m* apron
zinnare sip; – tore *m*
tippler; – sino *m*
zio *m* uncle [draught
zitella *f* young girl; – lo
m young boy
zittire make a noise
– to *n* & *int* silence
zizzania *f* dissension;
discord
zocco, lo *m* sandal;
slippers; wooden-shoe;
– laio *m* sandal-maker;
– lare wear sandals
zodiaco *m* zodiac
zolfa *f* gamut
zolfo *m* sulphur; brim-

stone; – lanaria, tara
fiera *f* sulphur-pit;
– naio *m* match-seller;
– nello, ferino *m* match
zoologia *f* zoology; – co
zoological; – gista, go
m zoologist
zoppaggine. picatura,
mento *f* & *m* lameness;
– peggiare, picare go
lame; – picante lame;
– picone, ni lame; –
po lame; defective
zoticaggine. chezza *f*
roughness; – co harsh
zuccaro. chero *m* sugar;
– cherare sugar; swee-
ten; – riera *f* sugar-
basin; – rino *m* sweet-
meat
zuccotto *m* helmet
zuffa *f* riot; strife
zufolare play the flute;
whistle; – mento, lio *m*
whistling; – lo. lone *m*
flute; whistle
zuppo full; satureted
zurlare play; sport;
– lo. ro *m* merriment;
play